Ninja® Foodi™ XL Pro Air Oven
COMPLETE COOKBOOK

Quiche, Two Ways, Lemon-Blueberry Crunch Coffee Cake, Heirloom Tomato Pie, Cheesy Spinach and Artichoke Pinwheels, *pages 30, 49, 209, and 73 (clockwise, from top left)*

NINJA® Foodi™

XL PRO AIR OVEN

COMPLETE COOKBOOK

100 RECIPES
TO FEED YOUR FAMILY FAST

NINJA
TEST
KITCHEN
APPROVED

Photography by Hélène Dujardin

ROCKRIDGE
PRESS

For general information on our other products and services or to obtain technical support, please contact our Customer Care Department within the United States at (866) 744-2665, or outside the United States at (510) 253-0500.

Rockridge Press publishes its books in a variety of electronic and print formats. Some content that appears in print may not be available in electronic books, and vice versa.

TRADEMARKS: Rockridge Press and the Rockridge Press logo are trademarks or registered trademarks of Callisto Media Inc. and/or its affiliates, in the United States and other countries, and may not be used without written permission. All other trademarks are the property of their respective owners. Rockridge Press is not associated with any product or vendor mentioned in this book.

Interior and Cover Designer: Antonio Valverde
Art Producer: Hannah Dickerson
Editor: Pam Kingsley
Production Editor: Andrew Yackira
Photography © Hélène Dujardin, 2020; food styling by Anna Hampton, assisted by Michelle Diminich. Icons courtesy of SharkNinja Operating LLC. Author photos courtesy of Julien Levesque.

ISBN: Print 978-1-64739-988-7 | eBook 978-1-64739-989-4
R0

CONTENTS

Introduction vi

1 **Welcome to Your Ninja® Foodi™ XL Pro Air Oven!** 1

2 **Getting Started** 13

3 **Breakfast** 25

4 **Snacks and Appetizers** 53

5 **Poultry** 89

6 **Beef, Pork, and Lamb** 113

7 **Seafood** 135

8 **Vegetarian Sides and Mains** 159

9 **Entertaining** 179

10 **Desserts** 225

Ninja® Foodi™ XL Pro Air Oven Charts 249

Measurement Conversions 255

Index 256

INTRODUCTION

EVERYONE IS SO BUSY THESE DAYS THAT IT CAN BE DIFFICULT for home cooks to feed their families freshly prepared, nutritious meals a couple of times a week, let alone daily. We have school, work, commuting, sports, school activities, committees, and other responsibilities that make us wish there were a few extra hours in the day. No one wants to come home from a nine-hour workday to tackle cooking a full dinner, with a main dish, sides, bread, and dessert. Too often, families depend on takeout, trips to the fast-food drive-through window, frozen dinners, or quick restaurant meals that are expensive and not very healthy. And those grab-and-go meals don't help build family harmony. We all know there's no replacement for eating together around the dining room table, enjoying fresh, homemade food.

We need an appliance that will let us cook delicious, nutritious meals quickly with a minimum of fuss and muss. We need an oven that can cook more than one dish at a time, in less time, so the food always turns out perfectly: crisp on the outside, tender and juicy on the inside, with fabulous flavor. And we need an easy-to-clean appliance with clear instructions, large capacity, and lots of different functions. The Ninja® Foodi™ XL Pro Air Oven is the answer.

This new appliance is an air fryer in oven form. Its capacity is much larger than that of other air fryers. You don't need to cook food in batches because you can use different levels in the oven without having to swap or rotate pans or even flip your food most of the time. A window in the front lets you check on the food as it cooks. And unlike some convection ovens, the XL Pro Air Oven has True Surround Convection™ with a heating element in the back, top, and bottom, along with a powerful fan that ensures there are no cold spots so the food cooks perfectly. And don't worry, in this oven you can still air-fry foods to crisp perfection with very little oil.

That means you can cook a five-pound chuck roast with several servings of vegetables on a separate pan at the same time, roast a

whole chicken along with five large potatoes or a sheet pan full of mixed vegetables, or crisp up two pounds of French fries without having to turn or shake them or cook in batches. Everything will be ready at the same time, and in a fraction of the time it would take to cook in a regular oven. The XL Pro Air Oven was designed with the home cook in mind to make cooking and baking faster and easier.

The XL Pro Air Oven also lets you easily make recipes that don't cook evenly in a traditional countertop toaster oven. Now you can bake an entire sheet pan of cookies or a 9-inch pan of brownies. The oven comes with the Air Fry Basket, the Ninja Roast Tray, two Ninja Sheet Pans, and two removable wire racks. It's easy to get food in and out of the oven—no need for aluminum foil slings or other contraptions. And with so many different functions, you can roast, bake, toast, dehydrate, broil, reheat, or make perfect pizza with the touch of a button.

This book contains 100 recipes that will make getting not just dinner but also breakfast, lunch, snacks, desserts, and breads on the table a snap. It even includes a chapter chock-full of recipes perfect for entertaining and holiday meals.

So, stop your mealtime worries. Use this cookbook and your Ninja® Foodi™ XL Pro Air Oven to feed your family fast and reap the compliments. You'll never look back!

Kung Pao Chicken Totchos, Air-Fried Fish Tacos, and Ratatouille, pages 85, 138, and 160 (clockwise, from left)

1

Welcome to Your Ninja® Foodi™ XL Pro Air Oven!

THE NINJA® FOODI™ XL PRO AIR OVEN IS A BREAKTHROUGH in kitchen technology. This appliance isn't like the air fryers you've seen before. It is a powerful convection oven with a rear-positioned fan that blows hot air around the food as it cooks. This speeds up the cooking process and makes everything taste better as the hot air caramelizes the surface of the food, creating delicious flavors and beautiful browning. Let's learn more about how this amazing appliance works.

SO MUCH MORE THAN AN AIR FRYER

The Ninja® Foodi™ XL Pro Air Oven cooks food like an air fryer, but it is so much more.

Greater Capacity: Roast a Chicken *and* Cook Your Veggies at the Same Time!

One of the best features of the XL Pro Air Oven is its greater capacity, including two cooking racks. Its unique WHOLE ROAST function lets you cook a roast or a whole chicken along with your vegetables for a complete meal that is ready all at once. And because of its True Surround Convection™ technology, you can be assured everything will cook evenly, with no cold spots like in regular ovens, whether you're baking potatoes, roasting carrots and broccoli, or cooking a pan of stuffing.

The oven's control panel lets you know where to place the racks in the four slots in the oven for best results for each function; this is called Smart Positioning. For WHOLE ROAST, the meat goes on Level 1 on the roast tray nested in the sheet pan and the vegetables are placed in an air fryer basket or sheet pan near the top. The vegetables will be crisp and tender, and the beef, pork, or chicken will be golden brown and juicy. And *you* barely have to do anything! Just sit back, relax, and wait for your perfectly cooked meal to be ready.

Have Dinner on the Table Fast

The time savings with the XL Pro Air Oven are considerable. First, it preheats in just 90 seconds. Compare that to the typical 15-minute preheat time in a conventional oven. And convection cooks up to 30 percent faster than a regular oven because of the circulating heat.

One of the best things about the circulating heat is that food is cooked evenly without having to flip it or rotate the pan. The heat is distributed to every corner of the oven. All of your food will be beautifully browned and flavorful every time.

It's Versatile

This oven is extremely versatile, with 10 distinct functions that cook food differently. The functions are WHOLE ROAST, AIR ROAST, AIR FRY, PIZZA, BAKE, DEHYDRATE, BROIL, TOAST, BAGEL, and REHEAT. The heating elements used and fan speeds are different for each function, ensuring perfectly cooked food every single time.

This amazing oven selects where the heat comes from and the racks you need to use for best results. For instance, WHOLE ROAST, AIR ROAST, and AIR FRY use heat from the back of the oven. The BROIL function uses heat from the top element. And the BAGEL function uses less heat on the top and more on the bottom for a perfectly toasted bagel that is hot all the way through.

HOW IT WORKS

The Ninja® Foodi™ XL Pro Air Oven is ingenious and simple to use. The oven does most of the work for you, including telling you where to put the easy-to-move racks for best results. It also optimizes the heat sources and fan speeds for whatever cooking function you select.

The oven sits on your counter and has a glass door that opens from the top, making it easy to add and remove the food. The control panel is incorporated into the handle on the front of the oven. There are three heating zones inside, with a powerful fan, and the oven chooses the heating elements and fan speed that will cook the food best according to each function.

It's important to note that because the oven preheats so quickly, you should turn it on only when you have all of the food ready to go. That 90-second preheat time can go by very quickly!

The Control Panel

The control panel is easy to use and intuitive. You just need to understand what each function does so you can choose the correct one for all the foods you want to cook. After telling you which racks to use, the oven will take over and cook your food to perfection. Although a default time and temperature will appear on the control panel after you choose the function, you can manually change either, if you like; the recipes in this book each indicate the optimal temperature and timing.

Whole Roast

This function lets you cook a large piece of protein (like a whole chicken, turkey breast, ham, leg of lamb, or pork tenderloin) along with a pan of vegetables or whole potatoes at the same time. The food will be crispy and brown on the outside and tender and juicy on the inside. The oven's large capacity lets you easily make a meal for 2, 4, 6, or even as many as 12 people. Two racks are typically used so you can cook more food at the same time.

Air Roast

This function lets you cook sheet pan meals including a protein, such as chicken breasts or meatballs, along with vegetables, yielding the same delicious results as WHOLE ROAST—beautiful, flavorful browning on the outside and moist and tender on the inside. This function is ideal for roasting lots of vegetables.

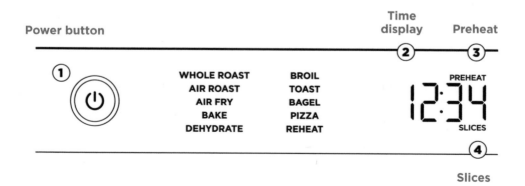

Power button — WHOLE ROAST, AIR ROAST, AIR FRY, BAKE, DEHYDRATE — BROIL, TOAST, BAGEL, PIZZA, REHEAT — Time display — Preheat — PREHEAT — 12:34 — SLICES — Slices

Air Fry

This function "fries" food to crispy golden brown perfection with little or no oil. Food is put into the air fryer basket that comes with the oven. And you don't have to shake the basket or rearrange the food in the XL Pro Air Oven for it to cook evenly. For foods that may drip (like glazed chicken wings), nest the roast tray in a sheet pan and place it on a rack below the air fryer basket. Cook French fries, chicken nuggets, and breaded foods with this function.

Broil

You can finish foods with a super crisp, dark golden brown exterior with this function. It's a great way to cook steaks, fish, and nachos and perfect for giving casseroles a delicious brown crust.

Pizza

You can cook fresh or frozen pizzas like a pro with the XL Pro Air Oven. The crust will be crisp and golden, the toppings hot and tender, and the cheese melted and starting to turn golden in spots.

Bake

You can bake everything from cookies and brownies to cakes and breads with this function. Prepare batter or dough as you normally would, then let the oven do the rest of the work. Your baked goods will be light golden brown and evenly cooked.

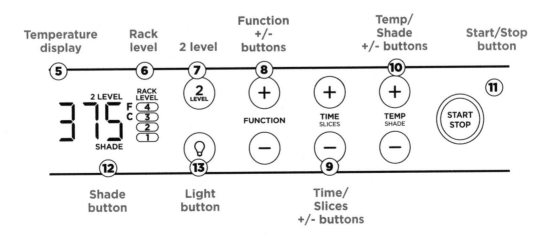

Toast

The Ninja® Foodi™ XL Pro Air Oven can toast up to 9 slices of bread perfectly at the same time. To use this function, choose the number of slices you want to toast and the shade of darkness. The oven does the rest. You can toast bread and English muffins or heat frozen waffles with this function.

Bagel

If you have ever had a bagel that is burned on one side and undertoasted on the other, you'll really appreciate this function. The heat comes from the top and bottom, but lower heat on top means that the bagel will be evenly crisp on both sides. This function also works well with thick slices of artisan breads, such as ciabatta or focaccia.

Dehydrate

Dehydrating food is a wonderful way to preserve it. You can also dehydrate fruits and vegetables for delicious and healthy snacks. Because of the low temperature used to do this (you want to dry the food, not cook it) and the much longer times needed to dehydrate, be sure to plan appropriately.

Reheat

If you have ever been disappointed with the quality of reheated food, the XL Pro Air Oven will solve that problem. Even, high heat from the top and bottom heats the food quickly so the outside stays crisp and the inside tender. No more soggy pizza crusts, burned leftovers, or cold spots!

Using the Ninja® Foodi™ XL Pro Air Oven

The control panel is where you choose how you want to cook the food, set the time and temperature, and specify the darkness of toast and bagels.

The first step is to choose the function, then press the 2 LEVEL button if you are cooking two pans at once. Select the temperature and time, then press START/STOP. The oven will immediately start preheating.

For Whole Roast:

- Press the power button to turn the oven on. Select WHOLE ROAST by pressing the + or − FUNCTION button. Press 2 LEVEL if that is what you are using. The oven will tell you which rack slots to use. You can choose your temperature, from 250ºF to 450ºF, and then the cooking time. The recipes in this book will include the time and temperature to select.

For Air Roast, Air Fry, Broil, Pizza, or Bake:

- Press the + or − FUNCTION button to select the function you want. Press 2 LEVEL if you are using two pans. The oven will suggest the temperature to use for the different functions, but you can manually override it.

For Toast or Bagel:

- Press the + or − FUNCTION button to select the function. Choose the number of slices you are putting in the oven (up to 9 slices) and how dark you want them to be.

For Dehydrate:

- Press the + or − FUNCTION button to select DEHYDRATE. Set your desired temperature and time.

For Reheat:

- Select REHEAT, then select 2 LEVEL if you are reheating two foods. If you set the temperature below 180ºF, this function can be used to keep food warm.

How to Convert Conventional Oven Recipes for the XL Pro Air Oven

Once you are an expert at using the Ninja® Foodi™ XL Pro Air Oven, you can expand your repertoire to include recipes written for a conventional oven. But be aware you'll need to adjust the cook times and temperatures or your food will be overcooked.

Because the XL Pro Air Oven uses fans to blow the air around the food, cooking time is significantly shorter than in a conventional oven. As a general rule, reduce the cooking time in the XL Pro Air Oven by about 30 percent. For instance, if a recipe for brownies indicates a baking time of 25 minutes in an ordinary oven, set the time on the XL Pro Air Oven to 17 minutes. Check the brownies at that time and bake for a minute or two more if necessary to reach desired doneness.

When following a recipe written for a conventional oven, also reduce the temperature by 25°F. For example, if a recipe is cooked at 350°F in a regular oven, bake it at 325°F in the XL Pro Air Oven.

For WHOLE ROAST, AIR FRY, or AIR ROAST:

To convert traditional-oven recipes, we recommend reducing cook time by 30 percent and lowering temperature by 25°F.

Always err on the side of a shorter cooking time, especially if you are still getting used to the oven. After all, it's easy to add more cooking time, but you can't save overcooked or burned food. Reduce the cooking or baking time by a few minutes every time you try a new recipe.

FREQUENTLY ASKED QUESTIONS

These are the most frequently asked questions we get about how to use the XL Pro Air Oven.

Q: Why is smoke coming from the oven?
White vapor is normal; in fact, it's usually steam, not smoke. If the oven isn't cleaned regularly, grease on the heating coils or on the inside of the oven may create white smoke. To reduce or eliminate that, keep the splatter shield clean. Also, always use the Ninja Roast Tray nested in a Ninja Sheet Pan when you are cooking greasy foods or using the AIR FRY, AIR ROAST, or WHOLE ROAST functions. If the smoking persists, run a TOAST cycle on Shade 7 with all of the accessories removed from the oven. This will burn off any accumulated grease.

But if you see black smoke coming out of the appliance, that means there's a problem. Unplug the appliance immediately, let it cool completely, then take it to a repair shop.

Q: Why is steam coming out of the oven door?
This is normal. Foods that have a high moisture content may release steam, which will seep through the oven door since it isn't an airtight seal. You may want to briefly open the oven door to release excess steam once or twice during cooking to promote crispness.

Q: Why do other Ninja Air Fryers say to not use cooking spray on the basket but this one does?
The air fryer basket with the XL Pro Air Oven is not made of nonstick material, so you can use cooking spray on it. The air fryer basket in most other air fryers has a nonstick coating. Cooking sprays used on those baskets can cause the finish to degrade or chip over time.

Q: **Sometimes my food doesn't get crisp using the AIR FRY function. What should I do?**

For the crispest results, make sure the food is not wet when you put it in the air fryer basket. Foods like chicken wings and French fries should be patted dry. Also make sure that you mist the food with a bit of cooking oil spray. Finally, make sure you are cooking the food at a high-enough temperature. Most air-fried foods should be cooked at 375ºF or 400ºF.

Q: **Can I use the Ninja Sheet Pan instead of the Air Fry Basket when using the AIR FRY function?**

Yes, you can, but since the hot air can't circulate all the way around the food in a sheet pan, the food may not turn out as crisp as it could. To help maximize crispiness in that case, turn the food over halfway through the cooking time.

Q: **Does food need to be rearranged in the XL Pro Air Oven?**

Since the oven is much larger than a typical air fryer, the food can be spread out more, so you don't need to shake the basket or rearrange the food. You can turn food over or rearrange it halfway through the cooking time if you want to, but it isn't necessary.

Q: **Can I open the oven door during cooking?**

Yes, you can. If you want to check on the food or add more food on another rack while the unit is on, opening the door will automatically pause the timer. The oven will resume cooking when you close the door, so if you are doing something more involved, you can press the START/STOP button to pause cooking.

Q: **How should I clean the sheet pan?**

The sheet pan usually cleans up without a problem using soap, water, and a soft brush. If food is stuck or burned onto the pan, soak it in water for an hour or two before cleaning. You can also line the sheet pan with aluminum foil or parchment paper before cooking to make cleanup much easier.

Q: **How often should I clean the Ninja® Foodi™ XL Pro Air Oven?**
The oven should be cleaned after every use. First unplug the oven
and let it cool completely. Wipe down the inside walls of the oven
and clean the crumb tray at the bottom of the appliance. Do not use
abrasive cleaners on any part of the oven.

2

Getting Started

NOW THAT YOU KNOW HOW THIS REMARKABLE OVEN works, it's time to get started cooking and baking. Although the XL Pro Air Oven comes with essential accessories, you may want to buy additional utensils and pans depending on what you like to bake and cook. In this chapter you'll get tips on how to cook a complete meal in the oven and how to use the different functions to their best advantage as well as the best staples to have on hand to make lots of delicious recipes. You'll learn how to cook foods even more efficiently and how to stagger the timing of dishes that use certain ingredients so everything is ready to go and on the table at the same time. Let's get started!

EQUIPPING YOUR KITCHEN

One of the best things about the Ninja® Foodi™ XL Pro Air Oven is that it comes with lots of accessories that make cooking a snap. Of course, you can use your own pans and dishes if you prefer, depending on what you like to cook and bake. Let's take a look at the items you'll be using.

Sheet Pans

The oven comes with two rimmed sheet pans that fit perfectly on the racks. You can buy baking sheets if you'd like (the oven accommodates a 9-by-13-inch baking sheet on each rack). And if you make pizzas, think about buying a 12-inch pizza pan. If you use your own baking sheets, they should be sturdy, preferably made from stainless steel; nonstick is fine.

Roast Tray

The oven comes with a roasting tray, which has slots to let fat drain into the sheet pan it is set into. If you'd prefer to use your own pan, the XL Pro Air Oven will accommodate a 9-by-13-inch roasting pan with 2-inch-tall sides.

Air Fry Basket

The air fryer basket that comes with the XL Pro Air Oven is long and has short sides, which is completely different from a typical air fryer basket. Don't try to use another brand of basket with the XL Pro Air Oven; it won't fit.

Casserole Dishes and Baking Pans

Ninja® Foodi™ offers for purchase a 9-by-13-inch casserole dish that fits into the oven perfectly, but you can use your own baking pan or casserole dish. If it fits, it will work. Additional pans that are called for in the recipes in this book include an 8-inch square baking pan, a 9-inch pie plate, a 9-inch round cake pan, a muffin tin, and others.

Creating Your Own Sheet Pan Combinations

One of the best ways to make an entire meal quickly is to use a sheet pan that will hold meats and veggies that cook at the same time. The sheet pans that come with the XL Pro Air Oven are perfectly sized to fit on the wire racks, and they hold a lot of food. You should be able to serve up to 10 people with this equipment.

The first thing you need to know is that food cut into small pieces or strips will cook much faster than whole meats and veggies. For instance, a sheet pan meal made of cubed chicken breast, cubed potatoes, and chopped onion and bell pepper will cook much more quickly than whole chicken breasts and potatoes cut into thick slices.

You also need to match foods that will cook in the same amount of time. You can make a meal of all vegetables, if you'd like. If you want to cook boneless chicken thighs, pair them with potato slices and onion wedges instead of quicker-cooking asparagus or snow peas; those vegetables would partner well with fish fillets, as would thinly sliced bell peppers and scallions.

A sheet pan of thinly sliced meat and veggies should cook for 12 to 16 minutes at 375°F. Whole cuts, such as boneless chicken thighs, and sturdier vegetables will take longer, usually 18 to 22 minutes. Always use an instant-read thermometer to make sure that meats are cooked to a safe final temperature. And don't be afraid to adjust the oven temperature or cooking time as needed as the food cooks.

Handy Utensils

Certain inexpensive utensils will help making cooking and baking easier. Think about buying a silicone spatula (make sure that it is rated heatproof to 500°F) for stirring food as it cooks. Also get a metal spatula to flip food or to remove it from baking pans, a carving fork, and/or spring-loaded tongs to help you rearrange and transfer food. For food safety purposes, a reliable instant-read thermometer is needed to ensure meats are cooked to safe temperatures. A large spoon and some good, sharp knives for preparing food are essential as well. And don't forget oven mitts to remove the hot pans after cooking! You can also buy small silicone mitts that fit over your fingers to protect your hands as you work.

ESSENTIALS TO HAVE ON HAND

The following foods are staples you should have on hand to cook many of the recipes in this book. You can vary them according to your taste—for instance, the types of cheese or herbs you prefer. Once you have a full pantry, refrigerator, and freezer, you will be set to cook many meals without having to make a special trip to the store.

In the Pantry

Pantry items are shelf-stable foods used to make many recipes and include spices and dried herbs, canned vegetables, and baking ingredients, like flour, sugar, and baking powder.

Flour: Our recipes use all-purpose flour, except where otherwise indicated. Store it in an airtight container in the pantry. Whole-wheat and other whole-grain flours should be stored in airtight containers in the freezer.

Sugar: Our recipes use granulated white sugar, powdered sugar, and brown sugar (light and dark). Store them in airtight containers.

Baking powder and baking soda: Have these on hand for baking cakes and cookies.

Salt and pepper: We tested our recipes using kosher salt. Freshly ground black pepper gives the best flavor, but pepper that has already been ground is a nice convenience. Use what works for you.

Spices and dried herbs: Buy the spices your family likes, and keep them stored in a cool, dark place to best preserve their flavor. You'll find the following and others in our recipes: cayenne pepper, chili powder, cinnamon, cumin, curry powder, garlic powder, onion powder, oregano, paprika, red pepper flakes, and thyme.

Canned tomatoes, soups, and broths: Diced and whole tomatoes, tomato paste, tomato sauce, and broths are used in many of our recipes. Condensed soups are a great shortcut to create tasty casseroles; you'll find them in several of our recipes.

Oil and vinegar: Both store well in the pantry. Oils are used to brown air-fried foods and ensure that roasted foods stay moist. Oils we use regularly include extra-virgin olive oil and canola oil. Also keep cooking oil spray on hand for coating pans. Vinegars are invaluable for making dressings and marinades—we like to have a selection of them in the pantry, including balsamic, rice vinegar, and red wine vinegar.

Canned beans and legumes: These items can be used to make sheet pan dinners and casseroles.

Nuts and seeds: These add tasty protein and great crunch to dishes. To extend their shelf life, store them in the refrigerator or freezer.

Cocoa powder and chocolate: For baking, these items are indispensable. Choose good-quality chocolate bars and chocolate chips and high-quality unsweetened cocoa powder.

Condiments: Worcestershire sauce, soy sauce, and hot sauce are easy ways to up the flavor quotient in lots of different dishes. They are fine to store at room temperature after being opened.

Potatoes, garlic, and onions: These foods should not be refrigerated. Store them away from light at cool room temperature and away from each other because each releases a gas that can make the others go bad more quickly.

In the Refrigerator

The refrigerator is used to store perishable foods, such as fruits and veggies, along with dairy, eggs, and longer-lasting staples, such as mayonnaise and mustard.

Eggs: Eggs should be stored in their carton and not in the door, where the temperature is higher. Most of the recipes in this book that call for eggs use large ones.

Milk and cream: Whether dairy or plant-based, milk and cream products should be stored in the refrigerator. They are great to have on hand for baking and creating creamy sauces. Keep an eye on expiration dates.

Butter: We use unsalted butter in our recipes.

Cheese: It's great to have a selection of longer-lasting cheeses on hand to enjoy for snacking but also for sauces or for melting. Depending on how you tend to use it (and whether you need to save time), buy either blocks or preshredded cheese, though preshredded cheeses are often coated with cornstarch and won't melt as smoothly as freshly grated cheese. Cheeses our recipes call for include cheddar, Brie, feta, Parmesan, provolone, Monterey Jack, and others.

Fresh vegetables: Store green beans, leafy greens, lettuce, carrots, ears of corn, bell peppers, asparagus, mushrooms, broccoli, eggplant, cauliflower, celery, and fresh herbs in the vegetable bins of the refrigerator. Fresh tomatoes should be stored at room temperature to maintain the best flavor.

Fresh fruits: Store lemons, limes, melons, apples, grapes, blueberries, strawberries, and blackberries in the refrigerator. These foods have only a 3- to 5-day shelf life.

Condiments: Once opened, store ketchup, mayonnaise, mustard, pickles, olives, pesto, jams and jellies, and toasted sesame oil in the refrigerator.

Fresh meats: Any kind of fresh meat or fish should be stored in the coldest part of the refrigerator and only for a few days; smoked or cured meats will keep longer.

In the Freezer

You can keep many foods in the freezer to help make meal planning easier. Frozen veggies, meats, and convenience foods will help you get dinner on the table fast.

Meats: Freeze ground beef, chicken, pork tenderloin, bacon, sausage, steaks, and roasts within three days of purchasing them. To prevent freezer burn, wrap them in freezer wrap, label with the contents and the date the food was frozen, and put them in a heavy-duty freezer bag.

Frozen seafood: Keep frozen shrimp, crab, salmon fillets and steaks, and fish fillets in the freezer.

Breads: Do you find your bread getting moldy before you have a chance to use it? Freeze it while it's still fresh.

Dough: Frozen dough is a great help in the kitchen. Buy and freeze pizza and/or dough, piecrust, and puff pastry.

Frozen fruits: Produce that is flash-frozen is often healthier than fresh because fresh produce loses some nutrients while in transit. We like to keep a selection of frozen strawberries, peaches, mixed fruit, mangos, and mixed berries on hand.

Complete Meal Cooking

The XL Pro Air Oven can make an entire meal at once because it can hold two racks full of food at the same time.

The only trick is to get the timing right for cooking all of the different foods. You can achieve this in one of two ways: Choose foods that cook at about the same time at the same temperature, or stagger the times you put the different foods into the oven.

For example, for a roast chicken dinner with vegetables, you can roast a whole chicken along with whole baked potatoes and carrots. All of the food would be put into the oven at the same time and would be done at the same time. If your side takes less time to cook than the protein, start the protein first, then add the veggies later so they finish at the same time.

Or for pizza night, you can cook two 11- or 12-inch pizzas at the same time, or stagger when you put them into the oven so one is crisp and the other has a softer crust.

Check out the Perfect Partner tip at the end of some of the recipes, which suggests side dishes for many of our protein main courses. Once you get a feel for staggering cooking times, it will become second nature.

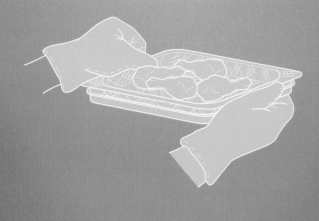

Frozen vegetables: Frozen vegetables cook beautifully in the XL Pro Air Oven directly from the freezer. Great choices are broccoli, green beans, peas, onion rings, chopped spinach, and corn.

Frozen potatoes: The air fryer is famous for transforming frozen French fries into perfectly cooked fries that are super crisp and delectable. Steak fries, tater tots, and waffle fries are also nice to have on hand.

ABOUT THE RECIPES

All of these recipes were developed to be easy to make and family friendly. You can change them as you'd like, substituting different herbs, spices, and cheeses according to your preferences. We do recommend you follow the recipe exactly as written the first time you make it; then feel free to experiment. Keep notes of the changes or substitutions you make so you know what to do the next time you plan to cook it.

Most of the recipes contain one or more of the following labels to help you with your menu planning:

- 5 Ingredients or Less (recipe has no more than five ingredients, not including water, oil, salt, and pepper)
- 30 Minutes or Less (the entire recipe, including prep, can be prepared in 30 or fewer minutes)
- Dairy-Free
- Gluten-Free
- Nut-Free
- Vegan
- Vegetarian

Each recipe tells you the number of people it will serve along with the prep time, the cooking function you need to select on the oven, and the cook time and temperature.

At the end of many recipes you will find helpful tips:

Substitution offers suggestions for stand-ins to make use of what you have on hand or alternative ingredients that will work just as well.

Prep Tip gives advice on how to make a particular part of the recipe simpler or offers a shortcut, like buying precut vegetables instead of peeling and chopping them yourself.

Variation suggests simple swaps for ingredients that will yield a different flavor profile.

Perfect Partner suggests sides that go particularly well with a main course recipe. These tips also tell you when the side dish should be put in the oven so it is done at the same time as the protein.

Freezer Friendly is for recipes that yield larger quantities of food that will freeze and reheat beautifully. This tip will tell you how to store the food and how long it will last in the freezer.

Make Ahead tips tell you if a recipe or part of a recipe can be prepped in advance and held in the refrigerator to make getting dinner on the table even easier. We'll be sure to let you know how far in advance the meal or component can be made.

Finally, each recipe also includes its nutritional content: calories per serving, fat, saturated fat, sodium, protein, carbohydrates, and sugar.

Mexican-Inspired Turkey Meat Loaf with Chili-Rubbed Street Corn, *page 110*

Quiche, Two Ways, *page 30*

3

Breakfast

Toad in a Hole with Crispy Bacon 26

Italian Eggs in Purgatory with Garlic Bread 28

Quiche, Two Ways 30

Sweet and Savory Breakfast Stratas 32

Mushroom and Swiss Bagel Pudding 35

Brown Sugar and Cinnamon French Toast Bake 37

Spiced Apple Sheet Pan Pancake 40

Chocolate, Nut Butter, and Oat Breakfast Bars 42

Cocoa Breakfast Popovers 44

Prosciutto, Chive, and Parmesan Scones 47

Lemon-Blueberry Crunch Coffee Cake 49

Toad in a Hole with Crispy Bacon

SERVES 6

This recipe is a twist on an all-time classic. Whether you call it Toad in a Hole or Eggs in a Basket, it is one of my favorite recipes to cook for breakfast. In fact, in college this was one of my favorite meals to make when we had friends and family visiting. Back then I used a stove, but I have found it is so much easier in the XL Pro Air Oven. Not to mention I added a few twists—like adding crispy bacon. When whipping up this recipe, you can toast up the center of the bread, too, as a little snack. —Kenzie Swanhart

---

30 MINUTES OR LESS, DAIRY-FREE, NUT-FREE

PREP TIME: 15 minutes
COOK TIME: 15 minutes

FUNCTION: Bake
TEMPERATURE: 400°F

ACCESSORIES: 2 Ninja Sheet Pans

PREP TIP: If you don't have a 3-inch biscuit cutter, you can use the top of a drinking glass to make the hole in the center of each bread slice.

12 bacon slices

6 slices bread

3 tablespoons unsalted butter, at room temperature

Cooking oil spray

6 large eggs

½ teaspoon dried thyme

Kosher salt and freshly ground black pepper, to taste

2 tablespoons chopped fresh chives (optional)

1. Divide the bacon between the sheet pans and arrange the slices in a single layer on each.

2. Install the wire racks on Levels 1 and 3. Select BAKE, select 2 LEVEL, set the temperature to 400ºF, and set the time to 15 minutes. Press START/STOP to begin preheating.

3. When the unit has preheated, place a sheet pan on each wire rack. Close the oven door to begin cooking.

4. Meanwhile, using a 3-inch biscuit cutter, make a hole in the center of each bread slice. Butter one side of each slice.

5. After 10 minutes of cooking, remove the sheet pans and transfer the bacon to a paper-towel-lined plate (the bacon will not be fully cooked; that's okay).

6. Leaving any rendered bacon fat on the pans, lightly coat the sheet pans with cooking spray.

7. Place the bread on the oiled sheet pans in a single layer, buttered-side down. Place 2 slices of bacon on each bread slice in an X shape, covering the hole in the bread. Crack an egg onto the center of each X, taking care not to break the yolk. Sprinkle with the thyme and season with salt and pepper.

8. Place the sheet pans in the oven and close the door to resume cooking. Bake until the egg whites have set, about 5 minutes.

9. When cooking is complete, serve immediately, garnished with the chives (if using).

Per serving: Calories: 289; Total Fat: 18g; Saturated Fat: 8g; Cholesterol: 219mg; Sodium: 578mg; Carbohydrates: 15g; Fiber: 1g; Protein: 15g

Italian Eggs in Purgatory with Garlic Bread

SERVES 3 TO 5

This is a fun version of baked eggs in tomato sauce. If you are a fan of shakshuka, you will love this dish! Be sure not to skimp on the bread. It's necessary to sop up all that tomatoey goodness. I like to use Scali bread—readily available in the Boston area—for this dish because my mother always had a loaf in the house. Whenever we had pasta, I would wipe my plate clean with that sesame-covered bread. If you can't locate Scali bread, Italian bread works great, too. —Craig White

NUT-FREE, VEGETARIAN

PREP TIME: 15 minutes
COOK TIME: 30 to 35 minutes

FUNCTION: Air Roast
TEMPERATURE: 400°F, 375°F

ACCESSORIES: 2 Ninja Sheet Pans, 10-inch pie pan

VARIATION: You can turn this into shakshuka very easily by making a few simple changes. Replace the Italian seasoning with ½ teaspoon ground cumin and ½ teaspoon paprika. You could also use feta cheese instead of ricotta and cilantro instead of basil.

- 1 (15-ounce) can tomato sauce
- 1 (10-ounce) can diced tomatoes with green chiles
- ⅓ cup grated Parmesan cheese, divided
- ½ teaspoon red pepper flakes
- 1 teaspoon Italian seasoning
- 5 slices Italian or Scali bread
- Extra-virgin olive oil, for drizzling
- 6 medium eggs
- ⅓ cup ricotta cheese
- 1 garlic clove
- Kosher salt and freshly ground black pepper, to taste
- Fresh basil leaves, torn, for garnish

1. Install the wire racks on Levels 1 and 3. Select AIR ROAST, select 2 LEVEL, set the temperature to 400ºF, and set the time to 30 minutes. Press START/STOP to begin preheating.

2. In the pie pan, mix together the tomato sauce, diced tomatoes with green chiles, half of the Parmesan, the red pepper flakes, and Italian seasoning until combined. Place the pie pan on a sheet pan.

3. When the unit has preheated, place the sheet pan with the tomato mixture on Level 3. Close the oven door to begin cooking. Roast for 15 minutes.

4. Meanwhile, place the bread on the other sheet pan and drizzle with the olive oil.

5. After the tomato mixture has roasted for 15 minutes, reduce the heat to 375°F. Remove the tomato mixture from the oven and stir. Make 6 wells in the mixture and crack an egg into each. Dollop the ricotta between the eggs. Insert the bread on Level 1 and close the oven door to begin cooking.

6. After 5 minutes, flip the bread and bake another 5 minutes. Remove the bread from the oven and rub it with the garlic clove while the bread is hot. Season with salt and pepper.

7. Return the pie pan to the oven and bake until the eggs are done to your liking—5 minutes for softer eggs, 10 minutes for well done.

8. Garnish the dish with the remaining Parmesan and basil.

Per serving: *Calories: 375; Total Fat: 18g; Saturated Fat: 6g; Cholesterol: 351mg; Sodium: 1089mg; Carbohydrates: 31g; Fiber: 5g; Protein: 23g*

Quiche, Two Ways

SERVES 16

One of the favorite things my stepmother, Denise, used to make when I was a kid was quiche. She loved cooking French food, and quiche was always a great go-to breakfast. The buttery, flaky crust with perfectly cooked eggs, cheese, and meat is to die for. This recipe is a nod to my stepmother and my favorite memories of her food. And with the Ninja® Foodi™ XL Pro Air Oven, you can cook two quiches to satisfy various diets. Meat eaters and vegetarians can coexist! —Meg Jordan

NUT-FREE

PREP TIME: 15 minutes, plus 10 minutes to cool
COOK TIME: 35 minutes

FUNCTION: Bake
TEMPERATURE: 350°F

ACCESSORIES: 2 (9-inch) pie pans

PREP TIP: Buy precut vegetables at the super-market to cut down on prep time.

Unsalted butter, for greasing

2 frozen puff pastry sheets, thawed

10 large eggs

½ cup heavy cream

2 teaspoons kosher salt

1 teaspoon freshly ground black pepper

6 slices deli ham, cut into 1-inch strips

1½ cups shredded cheddar cheese

5 asparagus spears, cut into ½-inch pieces

2 small yellow onions, diced

1. Grease the pie pans with butter. Press a puff pastry sheet into the bottom and up the sides of each pie pan.

2. Install the wire racks on Levels 1 and 3. Select BAKE, select 2 LEVEL, set the temperature to 350°F, and set the time to 10 minutes. Press START/STOP to begin preheating.

3. When the unit has preheated, place a pie pan on each wire rack. Close the oven door to begin cooking.

4. Meanwhile, in a medium bowl, whisk together the eggs, cream, salt, and pepper.

5. After 10 minutes, remove the pans from the oven and put them on trivets or a wooden cutting board. Allow to cool for about 10 minutes.

6. Arrange the ham and cheese in the crust of one pan and the asparagus and onions in the other. Pour the egg mixture over both, dividing equally. Select BAKE, set the temperature to 350ºF, and set the time to 20 minutes. Press START/STOP to begin preheating.

7. When the unit has preheated, return the pie pans to the wire racks and close the oven door to begin cooking.

8. Cooking is complete when a toothpick in the center of the quiches comes out clean.

9. Remove the quiches from the oven and let sit for 10 to 15 minutes. Then cut each quiche into 8 slices and serve.

Per serving: *Calories: 298; Total Fat: 22g; Saturated Fat: 8g; Cholesterol: 141mg; Sodium: 450mg; Carbohydrates: 15g; Fiber: 1g; Protein: 11g*

Sweet and Savory Breakfast Stratas

SERVES 20

With sweet and savory options, this recipe is a real crowd-pleaser. Not entertaining? Make one and enjoy leftovers all week long! These egg-and-bread-based breakfast casseroles are easily customizable, so feel free to play with ingredients and use whatever fruits and vegetables you have in your refrigerator. Simply assemble the night before and throw them in the oven in the morning. I like to make these stratas for big family gatherings and postwedding brunches. —Kelly Gray

PREP TIME: 20 minutes, plus 6 hours or overnight to chill
COOK TIME: 1 hour

FUNCTION: Bake
TEMPERATURE: 350°F

ACCESSORIES: 2 Ninja Casserole Dishes (9 by 13 inches)

VARIATION: Customize your strata by using whatever ingredients you have on hand. Don't have peppers and onions? Use spinach and asparagus. No raspberry preserves? Try strawberry.

Cooking oil spray

1 medium sweet onion, diced

1 red bell pepper, diced

8 ounces Canadian bacon, diced

1 tablespoon Cajun seasoning (or your favorite savory spice blend), divided

12 ounces day-old crusty bread, cut into 1-inch cubes (about 4 packed cups), divided

2 cups shredded cheddar cheese

16 large eggs, divided

4 cups whole milk, divided

1 cup heavy cream, divided

Kosher salt, to taste, plus ¼ teaspoon

Freshly ground black pepper, to taste

14 ounces day-old brioche bread, cut into 1-inch cubes (about 4 packed cups), divided

2 tablespoons vanilla extract, divided

Grated zest of 1 lemon

2 cups ricotta cheese, divided

1 (12-ounce) jar raspberry preserves, divided

⅓ cup sliced almonds

1. Lightly coat the casserole dishes with cooking spray.

2. In a large skillet over high heat, combine the onion, bell pepper, Canadian bacon, and ½ tablespoon of Cajun seasoning. Sauté until the onion is golden and fragrant and the bacon lightly browned, about 5 minutes.

3. **To assemble the savory strata:** Place half the crusty bread cubes in one of the prepared casserole dishes. Top with three-quarters of the cooked bacon-and-onion mixture and 1 cup of cheddar. Top with the remaining crusty bread cubes and the cooked bacon-and-onion mixture.

4. In a large bowl, whisk together 8 eggs, 2 cups of milk, ½ cup of cream, and the remaining ½ tablespoon of Cajun seasoning, and season with salt and pepper. Slowly pour the egg mixture into the casserole dish. Push the bread down into the liquid, adding more milk if necessary, so the bread is just barely submerged when pressed down.

5. **To assemble the sweet strata:** Place half the brioche cubes in the other casserole dish. In another large bowl (or wash and dry the used bowl), whisk together the remaining 8 eggs, remaining 2 cups of milk, remaining ½ cup of cream, the vanilla, lemon zest, and ¼ teaspoon of salt. Pour half the mixture over the brioche cubes in the dish.

6. Dollop 1½ cups of ricotta by the spoonful over the top, followed by three-quarters of the preserves. Use a spatula to spread the ricotta and preserves over the entire surface area of the layer of bread, then sprinkle the almonds on top.

7. Arrange the remaining brioche cubes on top, then pour the remaining egg mixture over them. Spoon the remaining ½ cup of ricotta over the strata, followed by the remaining preserves.

8. Cover both stratas with foil and refrigerate for at least 6 hours or overnight.

CONTINUED ▶

9. After the stratas have been chilled, install the wire racks on Levels 1 and 3. Select BAKE, select 2 LEVEL, set the temperature to 350ºF, and set the time to 60 minutes. Press START/STOP to begin preheating.

10. When the unit has preheated, place a covered casserole dish on each wire rack. Close the oven door to begin cooking.

11. When there are 20 minutes remaining, carefully remove the foil from both stratas, and top the savory strata with the remaining 1 cup of cheddar cheese. Continue cooking, uncovered.

12. Cooking is complete when the stratas are golden brown on top and a knife inserted into the center comes out clean. Let cool for 5 minutes before serving.

Per serving: *Calories: 406; Total Fat: 19g; Saturated Fat: 10g; Cholesterol: 200mg; Sodium: 477mg; Carbohydrates: 39g; Fiber: 2g; Protein: 18g*

Mushroom and Swiss Bagel Pudding

SERVES 8

I have always hated brunch because in restaurants, brunch prep is done on Saturday night at the tail end of the dinner rush. For me, that meant prepping and cooking two giant pans of bread pudding at 10:30 p.m. and waiting for them to finish cooking after we had completed cleaning the kitchen for the night. But this bagel pudding is so quick and easy, I might have to change my mind. —Sam Ferguson

5 INGREDIENTS OR LESS, NUT-FREE, VEGETARIAN

PREP TIME: 15 minutes
COOK TIME: 40 minutes

FUNCTION: Air Fry, Bake
TEMPERATURE: 390°F, 350°F

ACCESSORIES: Air Fry Basket, Ninja Casserole Dish (9 by 13 inches)

SUBSTITUTION: You can use any bagels and cheese you like with this recipe. Everything, sesame, poppy seed, and garlic bagels all work great as a substitute for plain bagels. Similarly, cheddar, mozzarella, or Parmesan cheese is a great substitute for the Swiss cheese.

2 (8-ounce) containers white button mushrooms, stemmed and halved

2 tablespoons canola oil

Kosher salt and freshly ground black pepper, to taste

6 large eggs

2 cups heavy cream

1 (6-ounce) bag shredded Swiss cheese

6 plain bagels, cut or torn into cubes

1. In a large bowl, combine the mushrooms and oil, and season with salt and pepper. Mix well to combine. Place the mushrooms in the air fryer basket.

2. Ensure no wire racks are in the oven. Select AIR FRY, set the temperature to 390°F, and set the time to 10 minutes. Press START/STOP to begin preheating.

3. When the unit has preheated, insert the air fryer basket on Level 3. Close the oven door to begin cooking.

4. In another large bowl (or wash and dry the used bowl), whisk together the eggs and cream, and season with salt and pepper. Add the cheese and mix again.

5. When the mushrooms have completed cooking, remove the basket from the oven. Let cool for about 5 minutes, then add the mushrooms to the egg mixture. Add the bagel pieces and, using your hands, mix well to combine. Pour the mixture into the casserole dish and press down gently to make the mixture sit flat.

CONTINUED ▶

Mushroom and Swiss Bagel Pudding continued

6. If necessary, remove the crumb tray from the oven and wash away any mushroom bits. Install the wire rack on Level 3. Select BAKE, set the temperature to 350°F, and set the time to 30 minutes. Press START/STOP to begin preheating.

7. When the unit has preheated, place the casserole on the wire rack. Close the oven door to begin cooking.

8. When cooking is complete, remove from the oven and let cool for 5 minutes before serving.

Per serving: *Calories: 579; Total Fat: 36g; Saturated Fat: 19g; Cholesterol: 241mg; Sodium: 436mg; Carbohydrates: 44g; Fiber: 2g; Protein: 21g*

Brown Sugar and Cinnamon French Toast Bake

SERVES 6 TO 10

I am not a breakfast person—during the week. I'm always on the go and just don't have time to sit down and have a big breakfast. But on the weekends, that all changes. In my house we brunch on Sundays. This dish is perfect for when you are feeding a large group or are entertaining and putting out a big spread. It's that sweet and indulgent item on the table that folks always freak out over. Offer strawberries and/or blueberries and whipped cream on the side. —Craig White

---

NUT-FREE, VEGETARIAN

PREP TIME: 20 minutes
COOK TIME: 45 to 55 minutes

FUNCTION: Bake
TEMPERATURE: 350°F

ACCESSORIES: 8-inch square baking pan

Cooking oil spray

For the French toast base

1 (8-ounce) package cream cheese, at room temperature

2 tablespoons powdered sugar

Grated zest and juice of 1 lemon

6 large eggs, beaten

1 cup whole milk

⅓ cup packed light brown sugar

2 teaspoons vanilla extract

½ teaspoon ground cinnamon

18 (1-ounce) Hawaiian sweet rolls, quartered

For the topping

½ cup all-purpose flour

⅓ cup packed light brown sugar

½ teaspoon ground cinnamon

4 tablespoons (½ stick) cold unsalted butter, cut into 3 pieces

---

1. Coat the baking pan with cooking spray and set aside.

2. **To make the French toast base:** Using a hand mixer or stand mixer, beat together the cream cheese, powdered sugar, and lemon zest and juice until creamy.

3. In a large bowl, mix together the eggs, milk, brown sugar, vanilla, and cinnamon until well combined. Fold the rolls into the egg mixture, swirl the cream cheese mixture in, then pour into the prepared pan.

CONTINUED ▶

Brown Sugar and Cinnamon French Toast Bake continued

MAKE AHEAD: This breakfast is even better if you assemble it the night before. The flavor and texture will only improve with an overnight soak. Follow steps 1 through 4. Cover the French toast base with plastic wrap, transfer the topping to an airtight container, and refrigerate both. When you wake up and have had your mimosa, pull the French toast base and topping out of the refrigerator and continue with steps 5 through 8.

4. To make the topping: In a small bowl, mix together the flour, brown sugar, and cinnamon. Using your fingers, work the cold butter into the dry ingredients. The topping should look like small pebbles. Sprinkle the topping evenly over the French toast base.

5. Install a wire rack on Level 3. Select BAKE, set the temperature to 350°F, and set the time to 45 minutes. Press START/STOP to begin preheating.

6. When the unit has preheated, place the sheet pan on the wire rack. Close the oven door to begin cooking.

7. Bake for 30 minutes for a softer texture or up to 55 minutes for a firmer, crispier texture.

Per serving: Calories: 773; Total Fat: 32g; Saturated Fat: 16g; Cholesterol: 295mg; Sodium: 721mg; Carbohydrates: 102g; Fiber: 4g; Protein: 19g

Spiced Apple Sheet Pan Pancake

SERVES 8 TO 12

Spiced apple sheet pan pancakes are great for a sweet yet simple weekend breakfast. And if you're like me, you will find any way possible to save time and energy in the morning—this recipe is just that. No need to make pancakes the hard way, one by one, when you can make a whole sheet pan's worth at once. With a few basic pantry items, you can provide a nice, hot breakfast for you and your family in no time. And trust me, you won't be caught making pancakes the traditional way ever again. —Caroline Schliep

30 MINUTES OR LESS, VEGETARIAN

PREP TIME: 10 minutes
COOK TIME: 15 minutes

FUNCTION: Bake
TEMPERATURE: 425°F

ACCESSORIES: Ninja Sheet Pan

SUBSTITUTION: Don't have apples on hand? Substitute another fresh fruit, like sliced bananas, pears, or even cranberries. Don't have pancake mix? You can make your own by combining 4 cups all-purpose flour, 3 tablespoons sugar, 3 tablespoons baking powder, 2 teaspoons baking soda, and 1 teaspoon salt.

Cooking oil spray

For the pancake

4 cups pancake mix

2 tablespoons apple pie spice

2 cups milk

4 large eggs

¼ cup applesauce

2 teaspoons vanilla extract

1 apple, cored, peeled, and thinly sliced

For the glaze

1 cup powdered sugar

1 teaspoon apple pie spice

2 tablespoons apple juice

¼ cup pecans, chopped

1. Coat the sheet pan with cooking spray and set aside.

2. **To make the pancake:** In a large bowl, whisk together the pancake mix, apple pie spice, milk, eggs, applesauce, and vanilla until well combined.

3. Install a wire rack on Level 3. Select BAKE, set the temperature to 425°F, and set the time to 15 minutes. Press START/STOP to begin preheating.

4. Pour the batter onto the prepared sheet pan and use a spatula to spread it into an even layer. Arrange the apple slices evenly on top of the batter.

5. When the unit has preheated, place the sheet pan on the wire rack. Close the oven door to begin cooking.

6. **To make the glaze:** In a small bowl, whisk together the powdered sugar, apple pie spice, and apple juice until smooth and pourable.

7. The pancake is finished cooking when a toothpick inserted in the center comes out clean. Remove the pan from the oven and cut the pancake into your desired dimensions. Drizzle it with the glaze and sprinkle with the pecans.

Per serving: *Calories: 369; Total Fat: 8g; Saturated Fat: 2g; Cholesterol: 99mg; Sodium: 901mg; Carbohydrates: 63g; Fiber: 4g; Protein: 11g*

VARIATION: To make pancakes for a crowd, simply double the recipe, using two sheet pans and adjusting time as needed!

Chocolate, Nut Butter, and Oat Breakfast Bars

MAKES 12 TO 14 BARS

Breakfast in my house is always a whirlwind with my kids. Having small children can always make for a wild time, and my kids each have their own preferences, likes, and dislikes. One thing they always agree on is this breakfast bar recipe. We call them "breakfast brownies," but they are loaded with complete carbs, whole grains, and good protein to keep their little engines going. This recipe is simple and straightforward and can be made in advance for a quick breakfast you can take with you. They are sure to be a crowd-pleaser no matter how picky the eater! —Chelven Randolph

30 MINUTES OR LESS, VEGETARIAN

PREP TIME: 10 minutes
COOK TIME: 20 minutes

FUNCTION: Bake
TEMPERATURE: 325°F

ACCESSORIES: Ninja Sheet Pan

SUBSTITUTION: This recipe works just as well with any type of nut or seed butter. From peanut butter to soy butter, you can substitute any nut or seed butter you have on hand and still get the same delicious results.

1 cup maple almond butter
¼ cup packed light brown sugar
¼ cup honey
2 large eggs
2 teaspoons vanilla extract

2 cups old-fashioned rolled oats
1 cup whole-wheat flour
1 teaspoon baking soda
1 cup semisweet chocolate chips

1. In a large bowl, mix together the almond butter, brown sugar, honey, eggs, and vanilla until fully combined.

2. In a separate large bowl, mix together the oats, flour, and baking soda. Fold the flour mixture into the egg mixture until fully combined. Add the chocolate chips and mix to combine.

3. Line the sheet pan with parchment paper. Spread the batter onto the pan and spread evenly with a spatula or knife.

4. Install a wire rack on Level 3. Select BAKE, set the temperature to 325°F, and set the time to 20 minutes. Press START/STOP to begin preheating.

5. When the unit has preheated, place the sheet pan on the wire rack. Close the oven door to begin cooking.

6. Cooking is complete when the top is set and golden brown in color. Remove the pan from the oven and let cool completely in the pan, then cut into bars before serving.

Per serving: *Calories: 350; Total Fat: 19g; Saturated Fat: 5g; Cholesterol: 32mg; Sodium: 168mg; Carbohydrates: 38g; Fiber: 6g; Protein: 10g*

Cocoa Breakfast Popovers

MAKES 12 POPOVERS

Popovers are our Saturday-morning tradition. When served, they are beautiful and dramatic, but the truth is we started cooking them to avoid the mess that pancakes make. No drips of batter or burning pans here! Making these popovers in a muffin or popover tin cuts down the cooking time and makes them easy to hand out to guests. And what's better than chocolate and cinnamon? I like to serve these with a side of tart jam, laid out on a long platter sprinkled with powdered sugar. —Kara Bleday

30 MINUTES OR LESS, NUT-FREE, VEGETARIAN

PREP TIME: 5 minutes
COOK TIME: 11 minutes

FUNCTION: Bake
TEMPERATURE: 425°F

ACCESSORIES: 12-cup muffin tin

VARIATION: The base for these popovers, which is the flour, eggs, and milk, makes this a versatile recipe that can take on almost any flavor you'd like. Sometimes we omit the cocoa packet and toss in a few chocolate chips. These usually sink to the bottom and create a nice chocolaty crust.

For the popovers

¾ cup all-purpose flour

¾ cup whole milk, warmed

3 large eggs

1 packet instant hot cocoa

1 tablespoon sugar

1 tablespoon ground cinnamon

½ teaspoon salt

1 teaspoon vanilla

2 tablespoons cold unsalted butter, cut into 12 small cubes

For the topping

2 tablespoons unsalted butter, at room temperature

2 tablespoons strawberry jam

1 packet instant hot cocoa

Powdered sugar, for sprinkling

1. **To make the popovers:** Put the flour, milk, eggs, hot cocoa, sugar, cinnamon, salt, and vanilla in a blender and pulse until the batter is smooth.

2. Place 1 cube of butter into each muffin tin well. Install a wire rack on Level 3, place the muffin tin on the rack, and close the oven door. Select BAKE, set the temperature to 425°F, and set the time to 11 minutes. Press START/STOP to begin preheating.

3. When the unit has preheated, carefully remove the hot muffin tin. Pour the batter evenly into the cups on top of the melted butter so the cups are about three-quarters full.

4. Return the muffin tin to the wire rack. Close the oven door to begin cooking.

5. Bake for 10 minutes, until the tops are brown. Do not open the oven door during cooking.

6. **To make the topping:** While the popovers are baking, combine the butter, jam, and hot cocoa in a small bowl. Set aside.

7. When 1 minute of cooking remains, remove the muffin tin from the oven and distribute the chocolate topping evenly among the popovers. Continue cooking for 1 minute, or until the topping is softened.

8. Serve warm sprinkled with powdered sugar.

Per serving: *Calories: 119; Total Fat: 6g; Saturated Fat: 3g; Cholesterol: 58mg; Sodium: 151mg; Carbohydrates: 13g; Fiber: 1g; Protein: 3g*

Prosciutto, Chive, and Parmesan Scones

SERVES 8 TO 12

I love coming up with different flavor combinations, especially when it comes to taking something that is usually sweet and making it savory. These scones are a great example of a recipe that can be easily customized with your favorite flavors and can be made vegetarian as well. —Melissa Celli

NUT-FREE

PREP TIME: 10 minutes
COOK TIME: 23 to 27 minutes

FUNCTION: Bake
TEMPERATURE: 400°F

ACCESSORIES: Ninja Sheet Pan

SUBSTITUTION: If you don't have pancake mix, you can substitute a mixture of 2½ cups all-purpose flour, 2 tablespoons granulated sugar, and 1 tablespoon baking powder. If you use this mixture instead, increase the milk to ½ cup plus 3 tablespoons.

6 thin slices prosciutto

1½ cups pancake and baking mix

8 tablespoons (1 stick) cold unsalted butter, cut into small pieces

¼ cup whole milk, plus more if needed

2 tablespoons freeze-dried or fresh chives

½ cup shredded Parmesan cheese

1 tablespoon unsalted butter, melted

1. Lay the prosciutto slices flat on the sheet pan.

2. Install a wire rack on Level 3. Select BAKE, set the temperature to 400°F, and set the time to 10 minutes. Press START/STOP to begin preheating.

3. When the unit has preheated, place the sheet pan on the wire rack. Close the oven door to begin cooking.

4. When the prosciutto is cooked and crispy, transfer it to paper towels to drain. Pour off any fat from the sheet pan and wipe it dry.

5. Pour the pancake mix into a large bowl. Add the cold butter and, using a pastry cutter or two knives, cut it into the mix until the butter is in small pieces no larger than peas.

CONTINUED ▶

Prosciutto, Chive, and Parmesan Scones continued

VARIATION: Feel free to create different combinations of flavors, such as white chocolate and cranberry, apricot and ginger, garlic and herb, or garden vegetable, to name a few.

6. Make a well in the center, pour in the milk, and add the chives. Gently stir together with a wooden spoon until well incorporated. The dough should be slightly sticky. If the mixture seems too dry, add an additional tablespoon of milk.

7. Roughly chop the cooked prosciutto into small pieces and add to the dough along with the Parmesan. Stir well to combine.

8. Shape the dough into a large circle about ½ inch thick and place it on the sheet pan. Using a sharp knife, cut the dough into 8 wedges. Brush the top of the dough with the melted butter.

9. Select BAKE, set the temperature to 400°F, and set the time to 20 minutes. Press START/STOP to begin preheating.

10. When the unit has preheated, place the sheet pan on the wire rack. Close the oven door to begin cooking.

11. Check the scones after 13 to 17 minutes. They are finished cooking when they are lightly golden brown and firm to the touch. Remove the pan from the oven. Let cool before dividing into individual scones.

Per serving: Calories: 253; Total Fat: 16g; Saturated Fat: 9g; Cholesterol: 48mg; Sodium: 711mg; Carbohydrates: 20g; Fiber: 0g; Protein: 8g

Lemon-Blueberry Crunch Coffee Cake

SERVES 10

This twist on the classic coffee cake is a new family favorite. Tangy, sweet, and crunchy breakfast cake is the best way to start your day. Think moist lemon-infused cake layered with veins of cinnamon sugar and blueberries and topped with streusel and nuts. —Kelly Gray

VEGETARIAN

PREP TIME: 20 minutes
COOK TIME: 1 hour

FUNCTION: Bake
TEMPERATURE: 350°F

ACCESSORIES: Ninja Casserole Dish (9 by 13 inches)

SUBSTITUTION: If fresh blueberries aren't in season, you can use frozen blueberries.

Cooking oil spray

8 tablespoons (1 stick) unsalted butter, at room temperature

1 cup packed dark brown sugar

1 cup all-purpose flour

¾ cup chopped pecans

1 teaspoon ground cinnamon

½ teaspoon kosher salt

1 (16-ounce) box yellow cake mix

1 (3.4-ounce) packet lemon instant pudding

3 large eggs

½ cup canola oil

1 cup water

2 cups fresh blueberries, divided

1. Coat the casserole dish with the cooking spray and set aside.

2. In a small bowl, mix the butter, brown sugar, flour, pecans, cinnamon, and salt until combined. Set the streusel aside.

3. In a large bowl, mix the cake mix, pudding, eggs, oil, and water until smooth. Pour half the batter into the prepared casserole dish.

4. Top with 1½ cups of blueberries. Pour the remaining batter over the blueberries, then top with the remaining ½ cup of blueberries and the streusel.

CONTINUED ▶

Lemon-Blueberry Crunch Coffee Cake continued

5. Install a wire rack on Level 2. Select BAKE, set the temperature to 350ºF, and set the time to 60 minutes. Press START/STOP to begin preheating.

6. When the unit has preheated, place the casserole dish on the wire rack. Close the oven door to begin cooking.

7. The cake is done when a toothpick inserted in the center comes out clean.

Per serving: Calories: 636; Total Fat: 33g; Saturated Fat: 8g; Cholesterol: 81mg; Sodium: 575mg; Carbohydrates: 82g; Fiber: 3g; Protein: 6g

Soft Pretzel Sticks with Beer Cheese Dip, *page 59*

4

Snacks and Appetizers

Tropical Fruit Leather 54

Bacon and Kale Ranch Dip 55

Jalapeño Corn Dip with Homemade Tortilla Chips 57

Soft Pretzel Sticks with Beer Cheese Dip 59

Cheesy Sausage Bread 62

Margherita Pizza 65

Spanakopita Star 67

Asparagus, Ham, and Cheese Puff Pastry Bundles 70

Cheesy Spinach and Artichoke Pinwheels 73

Philly Cheesesteak Egg Rolls 75

Potato Crisps with Creamy Pesto Dip 76

Loaded Air-Fried Potato Wedges 77

Jalapeño Poppers 79

French Onion Ring Soup Fritters 80

Crab and Avocado Rangoon 82

Kung Pao Chicken Totchos 85

Soy-Braised Chicken Wings 86

Chili-Lime Beef Jerky 87

Tropical Fruit Leather

MAKES 15 LEATHER STRIPS

These fruit strips tend to disappear quickly. Best of all, the recipe is easy enough for the smallest of hands. They take a bit of time to dehydrate, but I like to start them before school so there's a fun surprise waiting when the kids get home. It's best to use fresh, ripe fruit for these, but since that's not always available, you can also substitute frozen fruit. Make sure the fruit is thawed first, and keep in mind you may have to adjust the sweetness. —Kara Bleday

5 INGREDIENTS OR LESS, DAIRY-FREE, GLUTEN-FREE, NUT-FREE, VEGETARIAN

PREP TIME: 10 minutes
COOK TIME: 6 to 8 hours

FUNCTION: Dehydrate
TEMPERATURE: 150°F

ACCESSORIES: Ninja Sheet Pan

SUBSTITUTION: The XL Pro Air Oven is the perfect tool for any flavor of fruit leather. Try your favorite fruits for variety. If you're using strawberries, raspberries, or any other fruit with larger seeds, use a mesh strainer or cheesecloth to strain out the seeds after blending. This will result in smooth fruit leather.

2 cups cubed mango
2 cups cubed pineapple
About 2 tablespoons honey

1. Put the mango and pineapple in a blender. Blend until smooth. Add the honey a little bit at a time, to taste.

2. Line the sheet pan with parchment paper (do not use wax paper).

3. Using a spatula, spread the fruit mixture over the parchment paper in an even layer, making it as thin as possible.

4. Install the wire rack on Level 3. Select DEHYDRATE, set the temperature to 150°F, and set the time for 8 hours. Press START/STOP to begin preheating.

5. When the unit has preheated, place the sheet pan on the wire rack. Close the oven door to begin dehydrating.

6. Check the fruit leather after 6 hours. It is done when it is dry and firm all the way through. Gently touch the leather in the center, and if the pressure creates an indent, it's not finished. If more time is needed, dehydrate for up to 2 hours more.

7. Remove the pan from the oven and let cool completely before cutting.

Per serving: Calories: 33; Total Fat: 0g; Saturated Fat: 0g; Cholesterol: 0mg; Sodium: 1mg; Carbohydrates: 8g; Fiber: 1g; Protein: 0g

Bacon and Kale Ranch Dip

SERVES 6 TO 8

Dips are a go-to for me when it comes to entertaining family and friends. There is something magical about sharing food with people you love. I created this dip for a Thanksgiving dinner we held in the Ninja Test Kitchen. This hot and cheesy dip took home the gold for the best dish of the dinner. Make it for your family or friends and try to act surprised when everyone tells you how great it is. —Craig White

GLUTEN-FREE, NUT-FREE

PREP TIME: 15 minutes
COOK TIME: 1 hour

FUNCTION: Air Fry, Bake, Broil
TEMPERATURE: 400°F, 375°F, HI

ACCESSORIES: Air Fry Basket, Ninja Sheet Pan, 8-inch square baking pan

MAKE AHEAD: Having people over the next day? Make this dip the day before. Complete it through step 6, then cover and refrigerate. The next day, just pull it out of the refrigerator, complete the rest of the steps, and open a bag of chips to go with it!

8 thick-cut bacon slices

1 (10-ounce) package frozen chopped kale, thawed and squeezed dry

1 (8-ounce) package cream cheese, at room temperature

1 (1-ounce) packet ranch dressing mix

1 cup sour cream

⅓ cup sliced scallions, divided

¼ cup mayonnaise

1 cup shredded Swiss cheese blend, divided

½ teaspoon red pepper flakes

Kosher salt and freshly ground black pepper, to taste

1. Lay the bacon in the air fryer basket in a single layer.

2. Install a wire rack on Level 2. Select AIR FRY, set the temperature to 400°F, and set the time to 20 minutes. Press START/STOP to begin preheating.

3. When the unit has preheated, place the sheet pan on the wire rack to catch any drippings, and insert the air fryer basket on Level 3. Close the oven door to begin cooking.

4. Cook the bacon 15 to 20 minutes, flipping every 5 minutes, or until cooked to your liking. Transfer the bacon to a paper-towel-lined plate to drain, and remove the sheet pan. Once the bacon is cool, chop it.

CONTINUED ▶

5. In a large bowl, combine half of the bacon, the kale, cream cheese, ranch dressing mix, sour cream, half of the scallions, the mayonnaise, ½ cup of Swiss cheese blend, and the red pepper flakes until well mixed. Season with salt and pepper.

6. Spoon the mixture into the baking pan, spreading it evenly over the bottom.

7. Select BAKE, set the temperature to 375ºF, and set the time to 20 minutes. Raise the wire rack to the Level 3 position. Press START/STOP to begin preheating.

8. Once the unit has preheated, place the baking pan on the wire rack. Close the oven door to begin cooking.

9. When cooking is complete, the dip will be bubbling around the edges. Remove the pan from the oven and top the dip with the remaining ½ cup of Swiss cheese blend.

10. Select BROIL, set the temperature to HI, and set the time to 4 minutes. Press START/STOP to begin.

11. Place the sheet pan on the wire rack and close the oven door to begin cooking. Broil for 2 to 4 minutes, or until the top is golden brown.

12. Remove the dip from the oven and top it with the remaining scallions and the bacon. Serve warm.

Per serving: Calories: 527; Total Fat: 39g; Saturated Fat: 18g; Cholesterol: 93mg; Sodium: 561mg; Carbohydrates: 27g; Fiber: 10g; Protein: 24g

Jalapeño Corn Dip with Homemade Tortilla Chips

SERVES 8

For a simple, crowd-pleasing dip, give this one a try. The blend of sweet corn, spicy jalapeños, and creamy melted cheese pairs perfectly with hearty home-made tortilla chips! Make it for cookouts, potlucks, the big game, and even tailgating. This dip is sure to draw a crowd, so don't count on any leftovers.
—Kelly Gray

NUT-FREE, VEGETARIAN

PREP TIME: 20 minutes
COOK TIME: 20 minutes

FUNCTION: Air Fry
TEMPERATURE: 405°F

ACCESSORIES: Air Fry Basket, 9-inch square casserole dish

MAKE AHEAD: Have a busy day of preparation? Assemble the dip through step 2 the night before so it can be popped in the oven when you're ready to party!

---

2 tablespoons canola oil, divided

1 (12-ounce) bag frozen corn

1 medium red onion, diced

2 jalapeños, finely diced

1 red bell pepper, diced

1 (4.5-ounce) can green chiles, drained

2 cups shredded pepper Jack cheese, divided

1 cup grated Parmesan cheese

½ cup mayonnaise

Kosher salt, to taste

15 (6-inch) flour tortillas

1. In a large skillet over high heat, heat 1 tablespoon of oil. Once hot, add the corn, onion, jalapeños, and bell pepper and sauté for 5 minutes, then remove from heat.

2. Add the green chiles, 1 cup of pepper Jack, the Parmesan, and mayonnaise. Mix well. Transfer the mixture to a casse-role dish and top with the remaining pepper Jack cheese.

3. Install a wire rack on Level 1. Select AIR FRY, select 2 LEVEL, set the temperature to 405ºF, and set the time to 20 minutes. Press START/STOP to begin preheating.

4. When the unit has preheated, place the casserole dish on the wire rack. Close the oven door to begin cooking

CONTINUED ▶

Jalapeño Corn Dip with Homemade Tortilla Chips continued

5. Meanwhile, cut the tortillas into quarters and place in an even layer in the air fryer basket. Brush the tortillas with the remaining 1 tablespoon of canola oil and sprinkle with salt.

6. After 5 minutes, open the door and insert the air fryer basket on Level 3.

7. When cooking is complete, remove the bubbling dip and crispy chips from the oven. Serve warm.

Per serving: *Calories: 503; Total Fat: 30g; Saturated Fat: 10g; Cholesterol: 43mg; Sodium: 992mg; Carbohydrates: 44g; Fiber: 4g; Protein: 17g*

Soft Pretzel Sticks with Beer Cheese Dip

SERVES 8 TO 16

A good soft pretzel for me is one that comes from a street vendor in New York City. Soft pretzels made in the XL Pro Air Oven come pretty close to the ones I love. I enjoy them alongside a cheesy beer dip—not something a New York City vendor has on hand— that would be perfect for any tailgate party or just at home with the family. —Melissa Celli

NUT-FREE

PREP TIME: 10 minutes, plus 1 hour to rise
COOK TIME: 20 minutes

FUNCTION: Bake
TEMPERATURE: 450°F

ACCESSORIES: 2 Ninja Sheet Pans

SUBSTITUTION: If you don't have smoked paprika, sweet paprika is fine to use as well, or it can be omitted altogether.

VARIATION: These pretzel sticks are also great as a sweet treat! After brushing with melted butter, toss the sticks in a mixture of cinnamon and granulated sugar.

For the soft pretzels

1½ cups warm water

1 tablespoon sugar

1 packet (2¼ teaspoons) active dry yeast

4½ cups all-purpose flour, plus more for dusting

1 tablespoon kosher salt

3 tablespoons vegetable oil, divided

⅔ cup baking soda

2 large eggs, beaten with a splash of water

1 tablespoon unsalted butter, melted

Coarse salt, to taste

For the beer cheese dip

2 tablespoons unsalted butter

2 tablespoons all-purpose flour

1 cup lager-style beer

½ cup whole milk

1½ teaspoons Dijon mustard

1 teaspoon Worcestershire sauce

½ teaspoon smoked paprika

1 cup shredded cheddar cheese

1 cup shredded pepper Jack cheese

Kosher salt and freshly ground black pepper, to taste

¼ cup sliced scallions

1. **To make the soft pretzels:** In a large bowl, mix the water and sugar until combined. Stir in the yeast and set aside to rest for 5 minutes, until the yeast starts to foam.

2. Add the flour, salt, and 2 tablespoons of oil. Mix thoroughly until a dough forms.

CONTINUED ▶

3. Remove the dough from the bowl and use the remaining 1 tablespoon of oil to grease the inside of the bowl. Place the dough back in the bowl and cover with plastic wrap. Leave in a warm place for 1 hour. The dough should double in size.

4. Once the dough has risen, fill a large pot of water about half full and heat over high heat. Whisk in the baking soda and bring to a rolling boil.

5. While the water comes to a boil, dust a clean work surface with some flour. Turn the dough out onto the surface and cut it into 16 pieces. Roll each piece into medium-thin ropes and shape them into sticks.

6. Once the water is boiling, add the pretzel sticks, 3 or 4 at a time, and boil on one side for 30 seconds. Flip over each stick and boil for 30 seconds more. Transfer them to a sheet pan. Repeat with the remaining pretzel sticks, distributing them evenly between the two sheet pans.

7. Brush the tops of the pretzel sticks with the egg wash.

8. Install the wire racks on Levels 1 and 3. Select BAKE, select 2 LEVEL, set the temperature to 450°F, and set the time to 15 minutes. Press START/STOP to begin preheating.

9. When the unit has preheated, place a sheet pan on each wire rack. Close the oven door to begin cooking.

10. Bake the pretzels for 10 to 15 minutes, until golden brown.

11. Remove the pans from the oven. Brush the pretzel sticks with the melted butter and sprinkle with coarse salt.

12. To make the beer cheese dip: Melt the butter in a large saucepan or sauté pan over medium-high heat. Once melted, add the flour and whisk until completely combined. Add the beer, milk, mustard, Worcestershire sauce, and paprika, and whisk until smooth. Continue cooking until the mixture has thickened and has nearly reached a simmer.

13. Add the cheeses and whisk until smooth. Season with salt and pepper. Reduce the heat to low and cook for 2 minutes. Remove the pan from the heat. Transfer the dip to a heatproof bowl, top with the scallions, and serve alongside the soft pretzels.

Per serving: *Calories: 511; Total Fat: 21g; Saturated Fat: 9g; Cholesterol: 87mg; Sodium: 544mg; Carbohydrates: 60g; Fiber: 2g; Protein: 17g*

Cheesy Sausage Bread

SERVES 8 TO 12

When I was younger, we had this great Italian bakery down the street from our house that made the best sausage bread. It was one of those items we got only for special occasions, like family parties or holidays. It didn't matter if it was warm or cold; it was always delicious. This cheesy sausage bread always brings up those wonderful memories. —Melissa Celli

NUT-FREE

PREP TIME: 15 minutes
COOK TIME: 35 minutes

FUNCTION: Air Fry, Bake
TEMPERATURE: 350°F

ACCESSORIES: 2 Ninja Sheet Pans

VARIATION: This is a very versatile recipe. You can use diced pepperoni or another type of protein in place of the sausage, and veggies, like peppers and onions, can be added, as well.

1 (1-pound) premium pork sausage roll

1 medium onion, chopped

1 tablespoon minced garlic

2 tablespoons dried sage

Kosher salt and freshly ground black pepper, to taste

All-purpose flour, for dusting

1 (1-pound) package store-bought pizza dough, at room temperature

4 cups shredded mozzarella cheese, divided

1 large egg, beaten

Marinara sauce, for dipping

1. In a large bowl, using your hands or a whisk, break the sausage into very small chunks. Add the onion and garlic and mix well. Spread the mixture evenly on a sheet pan.

2. Install a wire rack on Level 3. Select AIR FRY, set the temperature to 350°F, and set the time to 15 minutes. Press START/STOP to begin preheating.

3. When the unit has preheated, place the sheet pan on the wire rack. Close the oven door to begin cooking.

4. When cooking is complete, drain off any oil. Transfer the sausage to a medium bowl. Add the sage, season with salt and pepper, and toss to combine.

5. Dust a clean work surface and rolling pin with flour. Place the pizza dough on the surface and roll it out into a rectangle no longer than the length of the sheet pan. Try not to let it get any thin spots or holes.

6. Sprinkle 2 cups of mozzarella evenly over the dough, leaving a 1-inch border. Using a slotted spoon, evenly spread the sausage mixture over the cheese. Sprinkle the remaining 2 cups of mozzarella over the sausage.

7. Starting at one of the longer sides, roll up the dough like a log, but tuck in the ends like a burrito just before you get to the end of the roll. Place the log seam-side down on the other sheet pan and brush with the beaten egg.

8. Select BAKE, set the temperature to 350°F, and set the time to 35 minutes. Press START/STOP to begin preheating.

9. When the unit has preheated, place the sheet pan on the wire rack and close the oven door to begin cooking.

10. Bake until golden brown, adding up to 5 more minutes at the end if needed.

11. Let the bread rest for 10 minutes. Slice and serve with marinara sauce.

Per serving: *Calories: 486; Total Fat: 29g; Saturated Fat: 12g; Cholesterol: 107mg; Sodium: 908mg; Carbohydrates: 30g; Fiber: 2g; Protein: 27g*

Margherita Pizza

MAKES 12 TO 16 SLICES

Who doesn't enjoy pizza? It is the one dish that even if it is not great, people will still eat it. Good pizza, though, will not have a chance to get cold before it's devoured. For anyone intimidated to try making homemade pizza, this recipe will challenge that notion and maybe even keep you from ordering out. This is a classic margherita (basically a cheese pizza), but the options are endless. Once you get the technique down, try adding your favorite toppings and tailoring it to your own tastes. —Chelven Randolph

5 INGREDIENTS OR LESS, NUT-FREE, VEGETARIAN

PREP TIME: 20 minutes
COOK TIME: 15 minutes

FUNCTION: Pizza
TEMPERATURE: 450°F

ACCESSORIES: Ninja Sheet Pan

PREP TIP: The colder the dough is, the harder it is to stretch. Allow enough time for dough to come to room temperature to make stretching easier. And if you are in a pinch, try covering the dough with a clean, warm kitchen towel out of the dryer to speed up the process.

28 ounces store-bought pizza dough, at room temperature

All-purpose flour, for dusting

1 cup marinara sauce, divided

2 (5-ounce) balls fresh mozzarella cheese, cut into ½-inch slices, divided

1 bunch fresh basil, torn

1. Divide the pizza dough into two balls. Lightly flour a large, clean work surface and place one of the dough balls on it and dust the top with flour. Press around the dough by pinching with your fingers to form the edges of the crust. Starting from the center of the dough, use a flour-dusted rolling pin or your hands to push the dough outward to stretch it into a rectangle shape. Flip the dough over and repeat. Lightly flour the dough as needed to retain its stretched shape.

2. Lightly flour the sheet pan. Transfer the dough to the pan and continue stretching it out by hand to cover the pan, about 11 by 13 inches. Do not worry about it fitting perfectly.

3. Install the wire rack on Level 2. Select PIZZA, set the temperature to 450°F, and set the time to 10 minutes. Press START/STOP to begin preheating.

CONTINUED ▶

4. When the unit has preheated, place the sheet pan on the wire rack. Close the door to begin cooking.

5. After 10 minutes, remove the pan with the partially cooked dough and allow it to cool enough to handle.

6. Remove the crust from the pan and place it on a large cutting board or clean work surface. Spread ½ cup of marinara sauce over the crust. Cover with half of the sliced mozzarella cheese.

7. Select PIZZA again, set the temperature to 450°F, and set the time to 15 minutes. Press START/STOP to begin preheating.

8. When the unit has preheated, using a spatula or pizza peel, slide the pizza directly onto the wire rack. Close the oven door to begin cooking.

9. After 10 minutes, check the pizza for doneness. If you prefer a crispier crust, cook for up to 5 more minutes.

10. While the pizza is cooking, repeat steps 1 and 2 for the second pizza, or place the dough in a resealable bag and refrigerate it, the remaining marinara, and remaining mozzarella for later use.

11. Carefully remove the pizza from the oven and let cool for 5 minutes. If cooking the second pizza right away, proceed from step 3. Evenly arrange the basil on the pizza before slicing and serving.

Per serving: Calories: 511; Total Fat: 15g; Saturated Fat: 7g; Cholesterol: 37mg; Sodium: 1032mg; Carbohydrates: 72g; Fiber: 4g; Protein: 23g

Spanakopita Star

Sophisticated yet simple, this recipe is quite literally a twist on the classic Mediterranean favorite spanakopita. Everyone will think you spent hours on this beautiful appetizer that takes only 15 minutes to assemble. It'll go into the oven looking like a spinach explosion and come out a photo-worthy work of edible art that can be enjoyed year-round. —Kelly Gray

NUT-FREE, VEGETARIAN

PREP TIME: 20 minutes, plus 20 minutes to chill
COOK TIME: 20 minutes

FUNCTION: Bake
TEMPERATURE: 375°F

ACCESSORIES: Ninja Sheet Pan

MAKE AHEAD: Assemble ahead of time through step 9 and chill overnight. When you're ready to cook, pick up with step 10 and it will be ready to pop into the XL Pro Air Oven.

2 (10-ounce) packages frozen spinach, thawed
½ tablespoon canola oil
1 medium yellow onion, diced
2 garlic cloves, minced
6 ounces feta cheese, crumbled
Grated zest of 1 lemon
Kosher salt and freshly ground black pepper, to taste
2 frozen puff pastry sheets, thawed in refrigerator for 6 hours
1 cup all-purpose flour
1 large egg, beaten

1. Place the thawed spinach in a clean dish towel and squeeze over the sink to remove as much moisture as possible. Chop and place in a medium bowl.

2. In a medium skillet over medium-high heat, heat the oil. Once it is hot, add the onion and garlic and sauté until fragrant and translucent, about 5 minutes.

3. Add the onion mixture, feta, and lemon zest to the spinach. Season with salt and pepper. Mix until thoroughly combined.

4. Have a round object about 11 inches in diameter, like a lid to a stockpot or a mixing bowl, on hand. Place 1 sheet of puff pastry on parchment paper. Dust some of the flour on both sides of the dough. Using a flour-dusted rolling pin, roll out the dough on all sides until it will fit on a sheet pan with a 1- to 2-inch border around the edges.

CONTINUED ▶

5. Place the round object in the center of the dough and press down. Remove the object and cut out the excess dough around the circle, using the imprint as your guide.

6. Place the dough circle in the refrigerator on the parchment while you repeat steps 4 and 5 with the second sheet of puff pastry.

7. Using a pastry brush, brush some of the egg over the second dough circle. Spread the spinach mixture in an even layer over the dough, leaving a 1-inch border. Place the chilled dough circle on top and press the edges of the two circles together to seal.

8. Press a small cup (about 2 inches in diameter) in the center of the dough to make an indent. Chill in the refrigerator for about 10 minutes.

9. Using a chef's knife, cut the dough into quarters starting from the edge of the small circular indent in the center. Then cut those 4 quarters in half the same way, creating 8 sections. Finally, cut those 8 sections in half, for a total of 16 sections.

10. Using the parchment paper to help lift it, transfer the pastry to the sheet pan, trimming the edges of paper to fit if necessary. Twist each of the 16 sections three times by gently pulling to elongate each section and twisting it clockwise. Return to the refrigerator to chill for 10 more minutes.

11. Brush the remaining egg over the top of the pastry and, if desired, sprinkle the top with salt and pepper.

12. Install a wire rack on Level 2. Select BAKE, set the temperature to 375°F, and set the time to 30 minutes. Press START/STOP to begin preheating.

13. When the unit has preheated, place the sheet pan on the wire rack. Close the oven door to begin cooking.

14. The spanakopita is done when it has risen and the top is crispy and brown. Cook for up to 5 minutes more if needed.

Per serving: *Calories: 432; Total Fat: 29g; Saturated Fat: 9g; Cholesterol: 42mg; Sodium: 426mg; Carbohydrates: 33g; Fiber: 3g; Protein: 11g*

Asparagus, Ham, and Cheese Puff Pastry Bundles

SERVES 12

Tangy Swiss cheese, tender asparagus, salty ham, and flaky puff pastry meld together flawlessly for this heavenly combination. Whether you need to bring an hors d'oeuvre to your next dinner party or are looking for the perfect pair to your main course, these delicious bundles never disappoint. And I'll let you in on a little secret: Whenever you make them, reserve one in the refrigerator overnight and reheat in the morning for an extra-special breakfast treat. —Caroline Schliep

NUT-FREE

PREP TIME: 15 minutes
COOK TIME: 15 to 20 minutes

FUNCTION: Bake
TEMPERATURE: 425°F

ACCESSORIES: 2 Ninja Sheet Pans

SUBSTITUTION: Don't like Swiss cheese? You can substitute any other sliced or shredded cheese of your choice, like sharp cheddar, pepper Jack, or Parmesan.

Cooking oil spray

All-purpose flour, for dusting

2 frozen puff pastry sheets, thawed in refrigerator

1 bunch asparagus, woody ends trimmed

1 tablespoon extra-virgin olive oil

½ teaspoon kosher salt

½ teaspoon freshly ground black pepper

6 slices deli ham, halved

6 slices Swiss cheese, halved

1 large egg, beaten

1. Coat the sheet pans with cooking spray and set aside.

2. On a lightly floured work surface, use a flour-dusted rolling pin to roll out each puff pastry sheet to about double its original size. Using a sharp knife, cut each sheet into 6 squares.

3. In a large bowl, toss the asparagus in the olive oil and season with salt and pepper.

4. On top of each puff pastry square, place a half slice of ham and a half slice of cheese. Divide the asparagus spears evenly among the squares and lay them diagonally over the cheese. Lift two opposite corners of each pastry square and wrap them around the asparagus. Press to seal.

5. Brush the bundles with the egg. Sprinkle with more salt and pepper if desired. Place them evenly spaced on the prepared sheet pans.

6. Install the wire racks on Levels 1 and 3. Select BAKE, select 2 LEVEL, set the temperature to 425°F, and set the time to 20 minutes. Press START/STOP to begin preheating.

7. When the unit has preheated, place a sheet pan on each wire rack. Close the oven door to begin cooking.

8. Bake for 15 to 20 minutes, or until the puff pastry is golden brown.

Per serving: *Calories: 323; Total Fat: 22g; Saturated Fat: 7g; Cholesterol: 36mg; Sodium: 327mg; Carbohydrates: 21g; Fiber: 1g; Protein: 10g*

Cheesy Spinach and Artichoke Pinwheels

MAKES **16 PINWHEELS**

I love to entertain, whether it is game night with friends or big celebrations with family. I have a handful of go-to snack and appetizer recipes that are quick and simple crowd-pleasers. Pinwheels are easy to pull together and are a great option because they use premade crescent rolls. In fact, these pinwheels can be customized based on the occasion. I've included a few of my favorite fillings, but have fun and make this recipe your own! —Kenzie Swanhart

NUT-FREE, VEGETARIAN

PREP TIME: 20 minutes
COOK TIME: 15 minutes

FUNCTION: Air Roast
TEMPERATURE: 375°F

ACCESSORIES: Ninja Sheet Pan

VARIATION: This recipe is easy to customize with your favorite dips and flavor profiles. Try substituting a buffalo chicken dip for the artichoke-and-spinach mixture. Or go the sweet route by using your favorite jam or jelly.

1 (14-ounce) can artichoke hearts, drained and chopped

2 cups baby spinach, chopped

½ cup sour cream

1 (8-ounce) package cream cheese

⅓ cup mayonnaise

1 garlic clove

¼ teaspoon onion powder

Kosher salt and freshly ground black pepper, to taste

1 cup shredded mozzarella cheese

¼ cup grated Parmesan cheese

2 (8-ounce) tubes crescent rolls

Cooking oil spray

1 large egg, beaten

1. In a large bowl, combine the artichoke hearts, spinach, sour cream, cream cheese, mayonnaise, garlic, and onion powder. Season with salt and pepper. Add the mozzarella and Parmesan cheeses and stir to combine.

2. Unroll 1 tube of crescent rolls and press the perforations to seal, creating a rectangle about 13 by 18 inches. Repeat with second tube of crescent rolls.

3. Divide the spinach-artichoke mixture between the two rectangles, spreading it into an even layer across the surface of each.

CONTINUED ▶

4. Starting at the shortest side, roll up each rectangle to create a log, and press the visible edges to seal. Cut each log crosswise into 8 pieces.

5. Lightly coat the two sheet pans with cooking spray. Arrange the pinwheels cut-side down on the two pans. Brush the tops of the pinwheels with the egg.

6. Install the wire racks on Levels 1 and 3. Select AIR ROAST, select 2 LEVEL, set the temperature to 375ºF, and set the time to 15 minutes. Press START/STOP to begin preheating.

7. When the unit has preheated, place the sheet pans on the wire racks. Close the oven door to begin cooking.

8. When cooking is complete, let the pinwheels cool slightly before serving.

Per serving: Calories: 223; Total Fat: 15g; Saturated Fat: 7g; Cholesterol: 40mg; Sodium: 481mg; Carbohydrates: 16g; Fiber: 3g; Protein: 6g

Philly Cheesesteak Egg Rolls

MAKES 12 EGG ROLLS

When food trucks first became a big trend, my friends and I would come up with fun food truck ideas. One of our favorites was for an egg roll food truck that would offer a variety of different fillings, even dessert egg rolls. With that inspiration I developed this recipe. These egg rolls are ideal for the XL Pro Air Oven because the Air Fry function crisps them without deep-frying! —Kenzie Swanhart

30 MINUTES OR LESS, NUT-FREE

PREP TIME: 15 minutes
COOK TIME: 15 minutes

FUNCTION: Air Fry
TEMPERATURE: 400°F

ACCESSORIES: Air Fry Basket

VARIATION: Switch things up and transform this recipe into cheeseburger egg rolls. Simply omit the green bell pepper and add 2 tablespoons ketchup and 1 tablespoon yellow mustard in step 3 before folding the egg roll wrapper.

1 pound finely ground beef
1 green bell pepper, chopped
1 white onion, chopped
1 tablespoon Worcestershire sauce
Kosher salt and freshly ground black pepper, to taste
12 square egg roll wrappers
6 slices American cheese, halved
Cooking oil spray

1. In a large bowl, combine the ground beef, bell pepper, onion, and Worcestershire sauce. Season with salt and pepper.

2. Lay out an egg roll wrapper and place a half slice of cheese in the center. Spoon 2 to 3 tablespoons of filling over the cheese slice. Fold in the sides of the wrapper and roll it up around the filling, using water to seal the edge. Coat the egg roll on all sides with cooking spray. Repeat with the remaining wrappers, cheese, and filling.

3. Evenly arrange the egg rolls in the air fryer basket.

4. Select AIR FRY, set the temperature to 400°F, and set the time to 15 minutes. Press START/STOP to begin preheating.

5. When the unit has preheated, insert the air fryer basket on Level 3. Close the oven door to begin cooking.

6. When cooking is complete, let the egg rolls cool before serving.

Per serving: Calories: 159; Total Fat: 5g; Saturated Fat: 3g; Cholesterol: 29mg; Sodium: 399mg; Carbohydrates: 17g; Fiber: 1g; Protein: 11g

Potato Crisps with Creamy Pesto Dip

SERVES 4 TO 6

This dip is inspired by one of my sister-in-law's most famous dishes. The whole family swears by the combination of fresh basil and tangy cream cheese and loves how the flavors are just as appropriate on Thanksgiving as they are on the Fourth of July. Served here with potato crisps, the dip is great with fresh vegetables and crostini. —Kara Bleday

5 INGREDIENTS OR LESS, GLUTEN-FREE, NUT-FREE, VEGETARIAN

PREP TIME: 10 minutes, plus 30 minutes to soak
COOK TIME: 30 minutes

FUNCTION: Air Fry
TEMPERATURE: 425°F

ACCESSORIES: Air Fry Basket, small oven-safe bowl

VARIATION: This dip has many faces! My favorite variation is to swap out half of the cream cheese for goat cheese and top with fresh chopped cherry tomatoes after cooking. Toasted pine nuts are also always a great garnish for this dip.

1 pound russet potatoes, peeled

12 ounces cream cheese, at room temperature

1 (9-ounce) jar pesto

¼ cup grated Parmesan cheese

¼ cup vegetable oil

Kosher salt, to taste

1. Using a mandoline or a sharp knife, cut the potatoes into ⅛-inch-thick slices. Place the slices in a large bowl and cover them with cool water. Let soak for 30 minutes.

2. Spread the cream cheese in the bottom of a small oven-safe bowl. Cover with the pesto and sprinkle with the Parmesan.

3. Remove the potatoes from the water and dry them well on a clean kitchen towel. Coat the slices with the oil and arrange them in the air fryer basket in a single, even layer.

4. Install a wire rack on Level 2. Select AIR FRY, select 2 LEVEL, set the temperature to 425°F, and set the time to 30 minutes. Press START/STOP to begin preheating

5. When the oven has preheated, insert the air fryer basket on Level 4, and place the bowl on the wire rack. Close the oven door to begin cooking.

6. When cooking is complete, season the crisps with salt. Serve warm with the dip.

Per serving: Calories: 891; Total Fat: 82g; Saturated Fat: 25g; Cholesterol: 110mg; Sodium: 1043mg; Carbohydrates: 28g; Fiber: 2g; Protein: 16g

Loaded Air-Fried Potato Wedges

SERVES 8 TO 12

Appetizer? Meal? Side dish? These loaded potato wedges can be whatever you imagine them to be. Air-fried to perfection, yet still fluffy and tender on the inside, these potatoes speak for themselves. Layered with gooey cheese, topped with crispy bacon and fresh chives, and finished with a drizzle of sour cream, these potato wedges will surely have all of your game-day guests hurrying for seconds. —Caroline Schliep

GLUTEN-FREE, NUT-FREE

PREP TIME: 10 minutes
COOK TIME: 25 minutes

FUNCTION: Air Fry, Broil
TEMPERATURE: 400°F, HI

ACCESSORIES: Air Fry Basket, Ninja Roast Tray, Ninja Sheet Pan

VARIATION: Want to make these loaded potato wedges Greek style? Toss the cooked potatoes with diced red onion, tomatoes, olives, crumbled feta cheese, and fresh dill. Serve with tzatziki sauce.

2 pounds russet potatoes, cut into wedges

2 tablespoons extra-virgin olive oil

1 tablespoon garlic powder

1 tablespoon onion powder

1 tablespoon paprika

2 teaspoons kosher salt

2 teaspoons freshly ground black pepper

8 bacon slices

2 cups shredded cheddar cheese

½ cup sour cream

1 bunch fresh chives or scallions, thinly sliced

1. Place the potato wedges in a large bowl. Drizzle them with the olive oil and sprinkle with the garlic powder, onion powder, paprika, salt, and pepper. Toss to evenly coat.

2. Arrange the wedges in the air fryer basket evenly in a single layer and set aside.

3. Lay the bacon in an even layer on the roast tray set into a sheet pan.

4. Install a wire rack on Level 2. Select AIR FRY, select 2 LEVEL, set the temperature to 400°F, and set the time to 20 minutes. Press START/STOP to begin preheating.

5. When the unit has preheated, place the roast tray and sheet pan on the wire rack and insert the air fryer basket on Level 4. Close the oven door to begin cooking

6. After 10 minutes, remove the bacon from the oven. Let the bacon cool, then crumble it.

CONTINUED ▶

7. After another 10 minutes, check the potatoes. They should be fork-tender and golden brown. Remove the basket from the oven and evenly top the potato wedges with the cheese.

8. Select BROIL, set the temperature to HI, and set the time to 5 minutes. Press START/STOP to begin.

9. Place the basket on the sheet pan, and place both on the wire rack. Close the oven door to begin cooking.

10. When cooking is complete, remove the basket from the oven. Transfer the potatoes to a platter and top them with the sour cream, bacon, and chives before serving.

Per serving: *Calories: 327; Total Fat: 20g; Saturated Fat: 9g; Cholesterol: 48mg; Sodium: 973mg; Carbohydrates: 24g; Fiber: 2g; Protein: 14g*

Jalapeño Poppers

SERVES 6 TO 8

I love going to parties, especially those with passed appetizers like this one. There are many variations of poppers—some breaded or wrapped in bacon—but this version provides the cheesy and salty goodness that make jalapeño poppers so irresistible. These are great to prep ahead and freeze for later, but as they are ready in 15 minutes, they are also a low-stress party option. —Meg Jordan

NUT-FREE

PREP TIME: 20 minutes
COOK TIME: 15 minutes

FUNCTION: Air Fry
TEMPERATURE: 425°F

ACCESSORIES: Air Fry Basket, Ninja Sheet Pan

FREEZER FRIENDLY: Any leftover poppers are perfect to "pop" into the freezer for your next party. Place them in an airtight container to freeze. Refrigerate overnight to thaw. To reheat, select AIR FRY and set the temperature to 390°F. Press START/STOP to begin preheating. When the unit has preheated, place the poppers in the air basket and insert it on Level 3. Check the poppers frequently; they are ready when heated through.

12 ounces cream cheese, at room temperature

½ cup grated Parmesan cheese

2 teaspoons garlic powder

2 teaspoons smoked paprika

1 teaspoon kosher salt

1 teaspoon freshly ground black pepper

¼ cup bacon bits

12 jalapeño peppers, halved lengthwise and seeded

1. In a medium bowl, mix together the cream cheese, Parmesan cheese, garlic power, paprika, salt, black pepper, and bacon bits until well combined.

2. Stuff the jalapeño halves with the cream cheese mixture. Place the stuffed jalapeños in the air fryer basket in a single layer.

3. Install a wire rack on Level 1. Select AIR FRY, set the temperature to 425ºF, and set the time to 15 minutes. Press START/STOP to begin preheating.

4. When the unit has preheated, insert the air fryer basket on Level 3 and place the sheet pan on the wire rack to catch any drippings. Close the oven door to begin cooking.

5. Check the poppers after 10 minutes. They are ready when the cheese is bubbling and starting to brown. When cooking is complete, remove the basket from the oven.

Per serving: Calories: 270; Total Fat: 24g; Saturated Fat: 13g; Cholesterol: 75mg; Sodium: 650mg; Carbohydrates: 7g; Fiber: 1g; Protein: 8g

French Onion Ring Soup Fritters

SERVES 10 TO 12

I have a bad rap with the Ninja Test Kitchen team for using too much frozen "fried" food in the recipes that I develop. Well, team, I'm not sorry that I'm not sorry; frozen fried foods are fun and delicious! These fritters are the perfect example: easy to prepare, quick to cook, and creative enough to not feel like plain old onion rings. —Sam Ferguson

NUT-FREE

PREP TIME: 45 minutes
COOK TIME: 20 minutes

FUNCTION: Air Fry
TEMPERATURE: 360°F

ACCESSORIES: Air Fry Basket, Ninja Roast Tray, Ninja Sheet Pan

FREEZER FRIENDLY:
Make these fritters ahead and freeze them for later. Follow the recipe through step 3. Arrange the balls on a sheet pan or a baking sheet, cover with plastic wrap, then freeze overnight. Transfer the frozen fitters to a resealable bag. To cook, place the frozen fritters in the air fryer basket and proceed from step 4.

4 large eggs

2 tablespoons soy sauce

3 tablespoons Worcestershire sauce, divided

2 (1-pound) bags frozen onion rings, roughly chopped

1 (6-ounce) bag shredded Parmesan cheese

Kosher salt, to taste

1 (1-ounce) packet onion soup mix, divided

1 cup mayonnaise

1. In a small bowl, whisk the eggs with the soy sauce and 2 tablespoons of Worcestershire sauce.

2. In a large bowl, combine the chopped onion rings, Parmesan, salt, and half of the onion soup mix. Pour the egg mixture evenly over the top, then use your clean hands to toss and mix together. Allow the mixture to sit at room temperature for 30 minutes to allow the frozen onion rings to soften.

3. Using your hands or a 2-ounce ice cream scoop, form the batter into 2-ounce balls.

4. Place the fritters 2 inches apart in the air fryer basket. They should all fit.

5. Install a wire rack on Level 1. Place a sheet pan with the roast tray set into it on the wire rack. This will catch some of the drippings from the fritters and prevent the oven from smoking. Select AIR FRY, set the temperature to 360°F, and set the time to 20 minutes. Press START/STOP to begin preheating.

6. When the unit has preheated, insert the air fryer basket on Level 3. Close the oven door to begin cooking.

7. While the fritters are cooking, combine the remaining onion soup mix with the mayonnaise and remaining 1 tablespoon of Worcestershire sauce in a small bowl. Mix well.

8. When cooking is complete, serve the fritters with the mayo dipping sauce.

Per serving: *Calories: 461; Total Fat: 33g; Saturated Fat: 8g; Cholesterol: 90mg; Sodium: 1066mg; Carbohydrates: 33g; Fiber: 2g; Protein: 8g*

Crab and Avocado Rangoon

SERVES 6 TO 8

I was first introduced to crab rangoon by my mom when I was about 10 years old, and I thought they were all created equal. I quickly learned that was not the case. Some restaurants use different wonton wrappers, and others fold them differently. There are even variations in their filling. So, when I first learned of crab and avocado rangoon, I immediately turned my nose up at them. To appease my partner, I tried them, and I have been hooked ever since. The combination of cream cheese, avocado, and imitation crabmeat is like that of peanut butter, jelly, and fluff—they just go together! —Chelven Randolph

30 MINUTES OR LESS, NUT-FREE

PREP TIME: 15 minutes
COOK TIME: 10 minutes

FUNCTION: Air Fry
TEMPERATURE: 375°F

ACCESSORIES: Air Fry Basket

8 ounces imitation crabmeat

2 ripe Hass avocados, mashed well

1 (8-ounce) container whipped cream cheese

½ cup chopped scallions, green parts only

30 square wonton wrappers

Canola oil cooking spray

Sweet chili sauce, for serving

1. In a large bowl, combine the crabmeat, avocados, cream cheese, and scallions. Mix until well combined.

2. On a large, clean workspace, and working in batches if necessary, lay out the wonton wrappers. Fill a small bowl with water.

3. Spoon 1 to 2 tablespoons of the cream cheese mixture on center of a wrapper. Dip a finger in the water and trace the edges of the wonton wrapper. Carefully bring the edges of the wrapper together to form a triangle and pinch firmly to secure. Repeat with the remaining wrappers and filling.

4. Arrange the wontons in a single layer in the air fryer basket. Liberally spray both sides of each wonton with the canola oil.

5. Select AIR FRY, set the temperature to 375ºF, and set the time to 10 minutes. Press START/STOP to begin preheating.

6. Once the unit has preheated, insert the air fryer basket on Level 3. Close the oven door to begin cooking.

7. When cooking is complete, remove the basket from the oven and let the wontons cool slightly before serving. Serve with sweet chili sauce.

Per serving: *Calories: 375; Total Fat: 21g; Saturated Fat: 8g; Cholesterol: 43mg; Sodium: 538mg; Carbohydrates: 38g; Fiber: 7g; Protein: 11g*

MAKE AHEAD: These are easy to make ahead of time and freeze for later. To do so, follow steps 1 through 3. Lightly spray a sheet pan or baking sheet with cooking spray. Arrange the wontons on the pan, being sure they do not touch, and freeze for 2 to 4 hours. Once they are completely frozen, transfer them to a resealable freezer bag until you are ready to use them. When ready to cook, follow steps 4 through 7, but add 5 minutes to the cook time (for 15 minutes total cook time).

Kung Pao Chicken Totchos

SERVES 6 TO 8

Kung pao chicken is my favorite takeout dish. This version is even more Americanized, adding tater tots to the tasty mix. —Sam Ferguson

GLUTEN-FREE

PREP TIME: 10 minutes
COOK TIME: 35 minutes

FUNCTION: Air Fry
TEMPERATURE: 360°F

ACCESSORIES: Air Fry Basket

VARIATION: Instead of tots, use frozen French fries, mozzarella sticks, or jalapeño poppers.

2 red bell peppers, seeded and cut into 2-inch pieces

1 teaspoon canola oil

1 (2-pound) bag frozen tater tots

4 grilled chicken breasts (1 pound total), cut into 1-inch pieces

1 cup gluten-free kung pao sauce

1 cup roasted peanuts, chopped, divided

1 (8-ounce) can water chestnuts, drained and roughly chopped

1 (6-ounce) bag shredded mozzarella cheese

3 scallions, white and green parts, thinly sliced

1. In a small bowl, toss the peppers with the canola oil. Place the peppers and tater tots in the air fryer basket.

2. Ensure no wire racks are installed in the oven. Select AIR FRY, set the temperature to 360°F, and set the time to 35 minutes. Press START/STOP to begin preheating.

3. When the unit has preheated, insert the air fryer basket on Level 3. Close the oven door to begin cooking.

4. Put the chicken, kung pao sauce, ½ cup of peanuts, and the water chestnuts in a large bowl, and mix to combine.

5. When there are 10 minutes remining, remove the basket from the oven. Scoop the chicken mixture over the tots and peppers evenly. Sprinkle the cheese over the top.

6. Place the basket back in the oven on Level 3, then close the oven door to resume cooking.

7. When cooking is complete, remove the basket from the oven. Garnish with the remaining peanuts and the scallions.

Per serving: Calories: 745; Total Fat: 40g; Saturated Fat: 10g; Cholesterol: 71mg; Sodium: 1621mg; Carbohydrates: 65g; Fiber: 9g; Protein: 32g

Soy-Braised Chicken Wings

SERVES 6

This recipe is so easy! All you have to do is 5 minutes of ingredient prep, combine a few pantry ingredients, then put a dish into your XL Pro Air Oven. This is one of those recipes that I like to use when I don't feel like trying to be a chef and cooking something complicated or extraordinary. Dinner party, weekend TV watching, or Tuesday night "get food on the table"—this recipe works for any occasion. —Sam Ferguson

DAIRY-FREE, NUT-FREE

PREP TIME: 10 minutes, plus 30 minutes to 6 hours to marinate
COOK TIME: 1 hour 30 minutes

FUNCTION: Air Roast
TEMPERATURE: 300°F

ACCESSORIES: Ninja Casserole Dish (9 by 13 inches)

SUBSTITUTION: Frozen wings are a great substitute for the fresh chicken wings called for in this recipe. Just make sure that they marinate in the refrigerator for 8 hours so they're mostly thawed before being cooked.

3 cups soy sauce
2 tablespoons minced fresh ginger
6 garlic cloves, minced
2 tablespoons dark brown sugar
¼ cup rice wine
1 tablespoon Chinese five-spice powder
3 scallions, white and green parts, chopped
2 tablespoons sesame oil
3 pounds chicken wings

1. In a large bowl, whisk together the soy sauce, ginger, garlic, brown sugar, rice wine, five-spice powder, scallions, and sesame oil.

2. Place the chicken wings in the casserole dish. Pour the marinade evenly over the wings. Cover the dish with plastic wrap and refrigerate for at least 30 minutes but ideally for 6 hours.

3. Install the wire rack on Level 3. Select AIR ROAST, set the temperature to 300°F, and set the time to 1 hour, 30 minutes. Press START/STOP to begin preheating.

4. When the unit has preheated, unwrap the dish and place it on the wire rack. Close the oven door to begin cooking.

5. When cooking is complete, serve the chicken wings in the casserole dish.

Per serving: Calories: 529; Total Fat: 38g; Saturated Fat: 10g; Cholesterol: 173mg; Sodium: 663mg; Carbohydrates: 4g; Fiber: 0g; Protein: 42g

Chili-Lime Beef Jerky

SERVES 4 TO 6

I love dehydrating in my Ninja Foodi™ XL Pro Air Oven at home as I can control exactly what ingredients are going into my jerky, and I can also adjust the texture based on time. —Meg Jordan

DAIRY-FREE, NUT-FREE

PREP TIME: 10 minutes, plus 8 hours to marinate
COOK TIME: 5 to 6 hours

FUNCTION: Dehydrate
TEMPERATURE: 155°F

ACCESSORIES: Ninja Sheet Pan, Air Fry Basket

VARIATION: Spicy jerky not your thing? Omit the chili garlic paste and use chopped garlic instead. You'll get great flavor without the heat.

¼ cup soy sauce

2 tablespoons Worcestershire sauce

Juice of 2 limes

2 tablespoons dark brown sugar

2 tablespoons chili garlic paste

1½ pounds beef eye of round, cut into ¼-inch-thick slices

1. In a small bowl, whisk together the soy sauce, Worcestershire sauce, lime juice, brown sugar, and chili garlic paste.

2. Place the sliced meat in a large resealable plastic bag and pour in the marinade. Seal the bag and massage it to coat the meat evenly. Marinate in the refrigerator for a minimum of 8 hours.

3. Once marinated, remove the meat and discard the excess marinade. Lay the meat slices flat in the air fryer basket in a single layer, without any slices touching each other.

4. Install a wire rack on Level 2 and place a sheet pan on it to catch any drippings. Select DEHYDRATE, set the temperature to 155°F, and set the time to 6 hours. Press START/STOP to begin preheating.

5. When the unit has preheated, insert the air fryer basket on Level 4. Close the oven door to begin dehydrating.

6. After 5 hours, check the jerky for desired doneness. Jerky will be softer with less dehydrating time.

7. Cool the jerky completely. Store in an airtight container.

Per serving: *Calories: 309; Total Fat: 15g; Saturated Fat: 6g; Cholesterol: 119mg; Sodium: 342mg; Carbohydrates: 3g; Fiber: 0g; Protein: 37g*

Korean-Style Fried Chicken, *page 92*

5

Poultry

Orange and Rosemary Chicken with Sweet Potatoes 90

Korean-Style Fried Chicken 92

Creamy Spinach Chicken Cordon Bleu 94

"Fried" Chicken Po' Boys with Remoulade Coleslaw 97

Sheet Pan Chicken Fajitas 99

Honey Mustard Chicken with Pretzel Crust and Crispy Potato Wedges 102

Baked Chicken Tacos 104

French-Inspired Chicken Stew 106

Green Chicken Enchiladas 107

Cheesy Chicken Casserole 109

Mexican-Inspired Turkey Meat Loaf with Chili-Rubbed Street Corn 110

Orange and Rosemary Chicken with Sweet Potatoes

SERVES 6 TO 8

I called my dad Executive Chef growing up as he cooked large family meals for us every weekend. Rack of lamb, burgers, ribs, and his ultimate go-to: roasted chicken and vegetables. Although the chicken was utterly delicious, his method of cooking in a conventional oven wasn't a quick task. With the XL Pro Air Oven's Whole Roast function, you can cook large cuts of meat, like a whole chicken, along with sides in less than an hour! I may not be an executive chef like my dad, but this recipe gets me closer. —Meg Jordan

GLUTEN-FREE, NUT-FREE

PREP TIME: 10 minutes, plus 1 hour to marinate
COOK TIME: 55 minutes

FUNCTION: Whole Roast
TEMPERATURE: 375°F

ACCESSORIES: Air Fry Basket, Ninja Roast Tray, Ninja Sheet Pan

- **8 tablespoons (1 stick) unsalted butter, at room temperature**
- **Grated zest and juice of 1 orange**
- **2 tablespoons fresh rosemary, chopped**
- **2 teaspoons kosher salt, divided**
- **2 teaspoons freshly ground black pepper, divided**
- **1 (5-pound) whole chicken, patted dry**
- **3 large sweet potatoes, cut into 1-inch-thick wedges**
- **1 tablespoon canola oil**

1. In a medium bowl, combine the butter, orange zest and juice, rosemary, 1 teaspoon of salt, and 1 teaspoon of pepper and mix well.

2. Place the chicken on a cutting board. Rub the outside of the chicken with the butter mixture. Let the chicken marinate in the refrigerator for 1 hour.

3. Put the sweet potatoes in a large bowl and toss with the canola oil and remaining 1 teaspoon of salt and remaining 1 teaspoon of pepper. Place the sweet potatoes in the air fryer basket in a single layer.

4. Place the chicken on the roast tray nested into a sheet pan.

5. Install the wire rack on Level 1. Select WHOLE ROAST, select 2 LEVEL, set the temperature to 375ºF, and set the time to 55 minutes. Press START/STOP to begin preheating.

6. When the unit has preheated, place the sheet pan with the roast pan on the wire rack. Insert the air fryer basket on Level 4. Close the oven door to begin cooking.

7. Cooking is complete when an instant-read thermometer inserted into the chicken reads 165ºF. Remove the chicken and potatoes from the oven. Let the chicken rest at least 10 minutes before carving and serving.

Per serving: *Calories: 531; Total Fat: 39g; Saturated Fat: 15g; Cholesterol: 160mg; Sodium: 440mg; Carbohydrates: 10g; Fiber: 2g; Protein: 33g*

Korean-Style Fried Chicken

With my Southern background, I consider myself a fried chicken connoisseur of sorts. From buttermilk marinated to cornflake battered, the variations are endless these days. One type that I have always sought out is Korean-style fried chicken, or KFC! Traditional KFC is a multistep process that requires deep-frying cornstarch-battered chicken pieces twice to achieve the ultimate crispy skin and then tossing them in a delightfully balanced sweet-and-spicy sauce that is akin to barbecue sauce. I've adapted the method to make it a bit healthier by air-frying instead of deep-frying. This recipe works just as well for wings on game day, too! —Chelven Randolph

---

DAIRY-FREE, NUT-FREE

PREP TIME: 20 minutes, plus 20 minutes to cool
COOK TIME: 35 minutes

FUNCTION: Air Fry
TEMPERATURE: 375°F

ACCESSORIES: Air Fry Basket, Ninja Roast Tray, Ninja Sheet Pan

---

PREP TIP: Not familiar or comfortable with cutting up a whole chicken? Ask your butcher to do it for you.

PERFECT PARTNER: Serve alongside Coconut Curried Tofu and Vegetables (page 167) for an Asian-inspired feast.

---

1 (5-pound) whole chicken, cut into serving pieces (drumsticks, thighs, breasts)

2 tablespoons rice vinegar

2 tablespoons kosher salt

1 tablespoon freshly ground black pepper

1 tablespoon ground ginger

1 cup cornstarch

¼ cup honey

3 tablespoons ketchup

2 tablespoons Korean chili paste (*gochujang*)

2 tablespoons soy sauce

Canola oil cooking spray

1. In a large bowl, toss the chicken pieces with the rice vinegar, salt, pepper, and ginger. Working in batches, liberally coat all the pieces in the cornstarch, shaking off any excess. Set aside.

2. In a separate bowl, whisk together the honey, ketchup, chili paste, and soy sauce until smooth. Set aside.

3. Install a wire rack on Level 2. Select AIR FRY, set the temperature to 350°F, and set the time to 15 minutes. Press START/STOP to begin preheating.

4. Arrange the chicken in the air fryer basket. Liberally spray both sides of each piece with canola oil.

5. When the unit has preheated, nest the roast tray in the sheet pan and place on the wire rack to catch any drippings. Insert the air fryer basket on Level 3. Close the oven door to begin cooking.

6. After 15 minutes, remove the basket, sheet pan, and roast tray, and let the chicken cool for 20 to 30 minutes. Once cool, spray the chicken again with canola oil.

7. Select AIR FRY, set the temperature to 375°F, and set the time to 20 minutes. Press START/STOP to begin preheating.

8. When the unit has preheated, return the sheet pan and roast tray to the wire rack and insert the air fryer basket on Level 3. Close the oven door to begin cooking.

9. Cooking is complete when an instant-read thermometer inserted into the chicken reads 165°F. Remove the chicken and immediately toss the pieces in the reserved sauce, or serve the sauce on the side. Serve immediately.

Per serving: *Calories: 676; Total Fat: 32g; Saturated Fat: 9g; Cholesterol: 206mg; Sodium: 588mg; Carbohydrates: 53g; Fiber: 1g; Protein: 45g*

Creamy Spinach Chicken Cordon Bleu

SERVES 8

Chicken cordon bleu was one of the first recipes I ever made for my family as a project for my high school cooking class. I had to set a proper table and serve my family a complete meal with protein, vegetable, and starch. I've always loved the chicken cordon bleu flavor combination of creamy cheese, salty ham, and crispy chicken. Here, I omit the bread crumbs and add a creamy spinach sauce to add another level of flavor. —Melissa Celli

GLUTEN-FREE, NUT-FREE

PREP TIME: 10 minutes
COOK TIME: 30 minutes

FUNCTION: Air Roast
TEMPERATURE: 375°F

ACCESSORIES: 2 Ninja Sheet Pans

VARIATION: If you are really missing the crunch of breaded chicken, after rolling up the chicken breasts, dip each piece in flour, then beaten egg, and then panko bread crumbs before cooking.

8 (6- to 8-ounce) boneless, skinless chicken breasts, pounded thin (about ½ inch thick)

Kosher salt and freshly ground black pepper, to taste

1 teaspoon garlic powder

1 teaspoon onion powder

1 teaspoon paprika

16 slices Swiss cheese

16 slices deli honey ham

Oil, for drizzling

1 (8-ounce) package cream cheese, at room temperature

1 (10-ounce) package frozen spinach, thawed and well drained

½ medium white onion, finely chopped

1 teaspoon Dijon mustard

¼ teaspoon ground nutmeg

½ cup whole milk

1. Sprinkle the pounded chicken breasts on both sides with salt and pepper, the garlic powder, onion powder, and paprika.

2. Layer 1 slice of Swiss cheese, 2 slices of ham, then 1 more slice of Swiss cheese on top of each chicken breast. Roll up each piece of chicken and secure it with a toothpick.

3. Place the chicken on one sheet pan and top with a drizzle of oil.

4. Install the wire racks on Levels 1 and 3. Select AIR ROAST, select 2 LEVEL, set the temperature to 375°F, and set the time to 30 minutes. Press START/STOP to begin preheating.

5. When the unit has preheated, place the sheet pan with the chicken on the wire rack on Level 3. Close the oven door to begin cooking.

6. In a medium bowl, mix together the cream cheese, spinach, onion, mustard, and nutmeg. Spread the mixture evenly on the other sheet pan. After 20 minutes have passed, place the sheet pan with spinach mixture on the wire rack on Level 1, and cook along with the chicken for the remaining 10 minutes.

7. Remove the spinach mixture from the oven, transfer it in a bowl, and whisk in the milk to thin and create a sauce. Set aside.

8. Cooking is complete when an instant-read thermometer inserted in the chicken reads 165°F. Remove the pan from the oven and top the chicken with the spinach sauce.

Per serving: *Calories: 478; Total Fat: 25g; Saturated Fat: 12g; Cholesterol: 199mg; Sodium: 560mg; Carbohydrates: 7g; Fiber: 2g; Protein: 54g*

"Fried" Chicken Po' Boys with Remoulade Coleslaw

Celebrate Mardi Gras any time of year in the comfort of your own home with these delicious chicken po' boys. Shake things up for lunch, dinner, or game day with crispy Cajun-spiced chicken and tangy remoulade slaw on a lightly toasted baguette. I recommend topping with sliced dill pickles, thinly sliced beefsteak tomatoes, and shredded iceberg lettuce. This recipe is sure to be a new favorite. Don't forget the napkins! —Kelly Gray

NUT-FREE

PREP TIME: 20 minutes, plus 6 hours or overnight to marinate
COOK TIME: 30 minutes

FUNCTION: Air Fry
TEMPERATURE: 360°F

ACCESSORIES: Air Fry Basket, Ninja Sheet Pan

VARIATION: If you're craving seafood or don't have time to marinate, replace the chicken with 1 pound peeled and deveined shrimp. Skip the marinade and instead dip the shrimp in the buttermilk mixture before dredging in the flour. Increase the oven temperature to 375°F, reduce the cooking time to 25 minutes, and add the baguettes at 22 minutes.

5 (8-ounce) boneless, skinless chicken breasts, cut lengthwise into 1-inch-wide strips

2½ cups buttermilk

8 tablespoons hot sauce, divided

5 tablespoons Cajun seasoning, divided

2 cups all-purpose flour

Kosher salt and freshly ground black pepper, to taste

Coleslaw mix

½ cup mayonnaise

¼ cup apple cider vinegar

¼ cup Dijon mustard

2 tablespoons dill pickle brine

3 (12-inch) baguettes

1. **To make the chicken:** Put the chicken strips, buttermilk, 6 tablespoons of hot sauce, and 1 tablespoon of Cajun seasoning into a resealable freezer bag. Mix until fully incorporated and the chicken is coated. Seal and refrigerate for at least 6 hours or overnight.

2. Remove the chicken from the marinade and strain over the sink to drain any excess liquid.

3. In a medium bowl, whisk together the flour, remaining 4 tablespoons of Cajun seasoning, salt, and pepper. Dredge the chicken strips in the seasoned flour, gently shaking off any excess. Place the strips in the air fryer basket.

CONTINUED ▶

4. Install a wire rack on Level 1. Select AIR FRY, select 2 LEVEL, set the temperature to 360°F, and set the time to 30 minutes. Press START/STOP to begin preheating.

5. When the unit has preheated, insert the air fryer basket on Level 3. Close the oven door to begin cooking.

6. To make the remoulade coleslaw: While the chicken is cooking, combine the coleslaw mix, mayonnaise, vinegar, mustard, pickle brine, remaining 2 tablespoons of hot sauce, salt, and pepper in a medium bowl and set aside.

7. When there are 5 minutes remaining, place the baguettes on the sheet pan. Place the sheet pan on the wire rack on Level 1, and cook along with the chicken for the remaining 5 minutes.

8. Cooking is complete when an instant-read thermometer inserted in the chicken reads 165°F and the exterior is crispy.

9. Carefully remove the bread and chicken from the oven. Let the bread cool for a few minutes. Cut the baguettes into top and bottom halves. Top the bottom halves with the chicken, slaw, and any desired toppings, then cover with the top baguette halves. Cut each sandwich crosswise to serve.

Per serving: *Calories: 706; Total Fat: 20g; Saturated Fat: 4g; Cholesterol: 116mg; Sodium: 987mg; Carbohydrates: 71g; Fiber: 4g; Protein: 57g*

Sheet Pan Chicken Fajitas

SERVES 4 TO 6

Looking for a simple weeknight dinner for the family? These sheet pan chicken fajitas are an amazing option. Tender chicken paired with loads of fresh peppers and onions are perfect for when you're in a Tex-Mex kind of mood. With little prep needed, the Ninja® Foodi™ XL Pro Air Oven does all the heavy lifting, giving you time to whip up your favorite sides, like fresh guacamole, refried beans, or even Spanish rice. —Caroline Schliep

30 MINUTES OR LESS, DAIRY-FREE, NUT-FREE

PREP TIME: 10 minutes
COOK TIME: 20 minutes

FUNCTION: Air Roast
TEMPERATURE: 400°F

ACCESSORIES: Ninja Sheet Pan

PREP TIP: For even easier prep, you can simply replace the seasonings with a pre-mixed fajita seasoning packet, found where taco seasoning packets are located in your grocery store.

Cooking oil spray

1½ pounds boneless, skinless chicken breasts, cut into ½-inch-thick strips

1 green bell pepper, seeded and sliced

1 red bell pepper, seeded and sliced

1 medium red onion, halved lengthwise, then sliced crosswise

3 garlic cloves, minced

Juice of 2 limes

3 tablespoons canola oil

2 teaspoons chili powder

1½ teaspoons ground cumin

1 teaspoon paprika

1 teaspoon garlic powder

½ teaspoon kosher salt

½ teaspoon freshly ground black pepper

Tortillas, for serving

1. Lightly coat a sheet pan with cooking spray and set aside.

2. Place the chicken, bell peppers, and onion in a large bowl. Add the garlic, lime juice, and oil and toss to coat evenly.

3. Sprinkle the chili powder, cumin, paprika, garlic powder, salt, and pepper over the chicken mixture and toss again to coat evenly. Spread the fajita mixture in an even layer on the sheet pan.

4. Install a wire rack on Level 3. Select AIR ROAST, set the temperature to 400°F, and set the time for 20 minutes. Press START/STOP to begin preheating.

CONTINUED ▶

5. When the unit has preheated, place the sheet pan on the wire rack. Close the oven door to begin cooking.

6. After 10 minutes, remove the pan and toss the fajitas using tongs. Return the pan to the oven to finish cooking.

7. Cooking is complete when an instant-read thermometer inserted into the chicken reads 165°F. Serve warm with tortillas and desired toppings.

Per serving: *Calories: 324; Total Fat: 14g; Saturated Fat: 2g; Cholesterol: 99mg; Sodium: 450mg; Carbohydrates: 8g; Fiber: 2g; Protein: 41g*

Honey Mustard Chicken with Pretzel Crust and Crispy Potato Wedges

SERVES 4

This recipe was inspired by my husband. Although he inspires a lot of my recipes and taste tests all of them, this one is particularly fun because it combines two of his favorite things: pretzels and honey mustard. The chicken is first coated in a honey mustard mixture, which adds a punch of flavor, and is then coated in crushed pretzels for a crunchy texture. For a complete meal, we pair the chicken with crispy potato wedges. And in our house, this meal is always served with a side of ranch dressing. —Kenzie Swanhart

NUT-FREE

PREP TIME: 15 minutes, plus 30 minutes to soak
COOK TIME: 20 minutes

FUNCTION: Air Fry
TEMPERATURE: 400°F

ACCESSORIES: Air Fry Basket, Ninja Sheet Pan

FREEZER FRIENDLY:
This dish can be stored in freezer-safe containers for up to 1 month. To reheat, select AIR FRY and set the temperature to 400°F. Once the unit is preheated, place the chicken and potatoes on a sheet pan and place in the oven for about 10 minutes.

- 2 russet potatoes, cut into 2-inch-thick wedges
- 2 cups ice cubes
- ¼ cup Dijon mustard
- ¼ cup plain yogurt or sour cream
- 2 tablespoons honey
- 1½ pounds boneless, skinless chicken breasts
- 2 cups finely crushed salted pretzels
- 1 teaspoon onion powder
- 1¼ teaspoons garlic powder, divided
- 1 teaspoon smoked paprika, divided
- ½ teaspoon freshly ground black pepper, divided
- 2 tablespoons extra-virgin olive oil
- 1 teaspoon kosher salt

1. Place the potato wedges in a large bowl and cover them with cold water and ice cubes. Let them soak for at least 30 minutes, then drain and pat dry with paper towels.

2. In a large bowl, whisk together the mustard, yogurt, and honey. Add the chicken to the mixture and toss to evenly coat. Let sit for 30 minutes.

3. Meanwhile, in a medium bowl, combine the crushed pretzels, onion powder, 1 teaspoon of garlic powder, ½ teaspoon of paprika, and ¼ teaspoon of black pepper.

4. Line a sheet pan with parchment paper. Remove each piece of chicken from the honey mustard and dredge it through the pretzel mixture, pressing gently to ensure the crumbs adhere, then place it on the prepared sheet pan.

5. In the bowl used to soak the potatoes, whisk together the olive oil, remaining ½ teaspoon of paprika, remaining ¼ teaspoon of garlic powder, the salt, and the remaining ¼ teaspoon of black pepper. Add the potato wedges and toss to coat. Arrange the potatoes evenly in the air fryer basket.

6. Install a wire rack on Level 1. Select AIR FRY, select 2 LEVEL, set the temperature to 400°F, and set the time to 28 minutes. Press START/STOP to begin preheating.

7. When the unit has preheated, place the sheet pan on the wire rack and insert the air fryer basket on Level 4. Close the oven door to begin cooking.

8. Cooking is complete when an instant-read thermometer inserted into the chicken reads 165°F and the potato wedges are cooked to your desired crispiness. Serve hot.

Per serving: *Calories: 603; Total Fat: 21g; Saturated Fat: 4g; Cholesterol: 104mg; Sodium: 910mg; Carbohydrates: 61g; Fiber: 4g; Protein: 45g*

Baked Chicken Tacos

SERVES 4 TO 6

When my family lived in San Diego, tacos were a staple at our dinner table. We loved the flavorful and lean chicken we could get at our neighborhood taqueria. To replicate the experience of sharing our feast by the beach, I place all of the tacos together in a baking dish and make them easy to grab one-handed. Sprinkled with cheese and warm from the oven, these are best served with fresh taco toppings, such as fresh cilantro or avocado, for everyone to enjoy. —Kara Bleday

GLUTEN-FREE, NUT-FREE

PREP TIME: 10 minutes
COOK TIME: 30 minutes

FUNCTION: Air Roast, Broil
TEMPERATURE: 400°F, HI

ACCESSORIES: Ninja Casserole Dish (9 by 13 inches), Ninja Sheet Pan

FREEZER FRIENDLY: This freezes really well. Once the chicken is cooked, portion it into resealable bags and freeze for up to 4 weeks. Thaw the frozen chicken in the refrigerator overnight. To reheat, place the chicken on foil in a baking pan and reheat on BAKE at 350°F for 10 to 15 minutes. Proceed with the recipe from step 6.

- 1 tablespoon extra-virgin olive oil
- 1 small onion, sliced
- 2 garlic cloves, minced
- 1 tablespoon kosher salt
- 1 teaspoon ground cumin
- ½ teaspoon ground cinnamon
- 3 or 4 boneless, skinless chicken breasts (about 2½ pounds total), cut into thin strips
- 1 (14.5-ounce) can fire-roasted diced tomatoes
- 2 tablespoons chopped mild green chiles
- 2 tablespoons tomato paste
- ½ teaspoon smoked paprika
- 2 tablespoons freshly squeezed lime juice
- 10 flat-bottomed corn taco shells
- 1 lime, cut into wedges
- 1 cup sour cream
- 1½ cups shredded Mexican-blend cheese

1. Put the olive oil, onion, garlic, salt, cumin, cinnamon, and chicken strips on a sheet pan. Gently toss to combine.

2. Install a wire rack on Level 3. Select AIR ROAST, set the temperature to 400°F, and set the time to 28 minutes. Press START/STOP to begin preheating.

3. When the unit has preheated, place the sheet pan on the wire rack. Close the oven door to begin cooking.

4. While the chicken is cooking, combine the tomatoes with their juices, chiles, tomato paste, paprika, and lime juice in a small bowl. Set aside.

5. When there are 15 minutes remaining, remove the pan from the oven and drain any excess liquid. Gently pour the tomato mixture over the chicken and return the sheet pan to the oven. Close the oven door to resume cooking.

6. Meanwhile, line up the taco shells in the casserole dish.

7. When cooking is complete, remove the sheet pan from the oven. Using tongs, place a bit of chicken in each taco shell. Squeeze a bit of lime juice from the lime wedges over each taco, spoon a bit of sour cream in each, then sprinkle with the cheese.

8. Select BROIL, set the temperature to HI, and set the time to 2 minutes. Press START/STOP to begin.

9. Place the sheet pan on the wire rack and close the door to begin cooking. Broil until the cheese is melted, adding more time if necessary.

10. Serve with your favorite taco toppings.

Per serving: Calories: 665; Total Fat: 32g; Saturated Fat: 15g; Cholesterol: 231mg; Sodium: 1022mg; Carbohydrates: 20g; Fiber: 3g; Protein: 76g

French-Inspired Chicken Stew

SERVES 6

This recipe is inspired by cassoulet, a French dish. The stew is cooked low and slow until all of the ingredients have melded together to create wonderful depths of flavor. A great partner for this stew is a loaf of crusty French bread; use it to scoop up the rest of the stew that your spoon can't get. —Sam Ferguson

DAIRY-FREE, GLUTEN-FREE, NUT-FREE

PREP TIME: 15 minutes
COOK TIME: 1 hour

FUNCTION: Air Roast
TEMPERATURE: 325°F

ACCESSORIES: Ninja Casserole Dish (9 by 13 inches)

SUBSTITUTION: This recipe is super easy to scale up: Double all the ingredients and divide it between two casserole dishes. The cook time is the same; just use Levels 1 and 3 for cooking.

Meat from
  1 rotisserie chicken, roughly shredded
1 (12-ounce) package precooked chicken sausages, sliced
3 medium carrots, diced
1 (16-ounce) bag frozen pearl onions
1 (15-ounce) can cannellini beans, drained and rinsed
3 garlic cloves, minced
2 cups chicken stock
Kosher salt and freshly ground black pepper, to taste

1. In a large bowl, combine the chicken, sausages, carrots, pearl onions, beans, garlic, stock, salt, and pepper. Pour the mixture into a casserole dish.

2. Install a wire rack on Level 3. Select AIR ROAST, set the temperature to 325°F, and set the time to 60 minutes. Press START/STOP to begin preheating.

3. When the unit has preheated, place the casserole dish on the wire rack. Close the oven door to begin cooking.

4. When cooking is complete, let the stew cool for 10 minutes before serving.

Per serving: *Calories: 591; Total Fat: 27g; Saturated Fat: 8g; Cholesterol: 228mg; Sodium: 1062mg; Carbohydrates: 24g; Fiber: 6g; Protein: 63g*

Green Chicken Enchiladas

This recipe brings me back to my childhood. Enchiladas were one of my favorite family meals. Just like my mom's version, this recipe calls for cooked chicken, so it is the perfect dish to use up leftovers. Don't have leftover chicken? Pick up a rotisserie chicken, shred the meat, and you're ready to make this dish! I also use store-bought green chile enchilada sauce, but you can easily swap in a red enchilada sauce or your own homemade version. —Kenzie Swanhart

NUT-FREE

PREP TIME: 15 minutes
COOK TIME: 25 minutes

FUNCTION: Air Roast
TEMPERATURE: 350°F

ACCESSORIES: Ninja Casserole Dish (9 by 13 inches)

FREEZER FRIENDLY:
Make a double batch to enjoy some now and to freeze the rest for another night. To freeze, let the enchiladas cool, then cover with foil and place in a freezer bag. Thaw in the refrigerator overnight. Reheat on AIR ROAST at 350°F for 15 to 20 minutes, until hot and bubbly.

2 to 3 cups shredded cooked chicken

2 cups shredded Monterey Jack cheese, divided

1 (4.5-ounce) can chopped green chiles

Kosher salt and freshly ground black pepper, to taste

1 cup sour cream

8 (10-inch) flour tortillas

1 (8-ounce) jar green chile enchilada sauce

1. In a medium bowl, combine the chicken, 1 cup of cheese, the green chiles, salt, and pepper.

2. Spoon ⅓ cup of the chicken mixture and 2 tablespoons of sour cream down the middle of each tortilla. Roll up the tortillas and place them seam-side down in a casserole dish. Pour the enchilada sauce over the tortillas and top with remaining 1 cup of cheese.

3. Install a wire rack on Level 3. Select AIR ROAST, set the temperature to 350°F, and set the time to 25 minutes. Press START/STOP to begin preheating.

CONTINUED ▶

Green Chicken Enchiladas continued

PREP TIP: This recipe calls for 2 to 3 cups shredded cooked chicken, so I often reach for leftovers or pick up a rotisserie chicken to keep things simple. However, you can start with raw chicken instead. Cook two boneless, skinless chicken breasts on AIR FRY at 375°F for 20 to 30 minutes, until the internal temperature is 165°F.

4. When the unit has preheated, place the casserole dish on the wire rack. Close the oven door to begin cooking.

5. When cooking is complete, let the enchiladas cool for 10 minutes before serving.

Per serving: Calories: 720; Total Fat: 37g; Saturated Fat: 19g; Cholesterol: 133mg; Sodium: 1099mg; Carbohydrates: 53g; Fiber: 3g; Protein: 42g

Cheesy Chicken Casserole

SERVES 6 TO 8

This recipe is dedicated to all the casseroles our grandmothers used to make. There's nothing like the mixture of "cream of something" soup, cheese, and chicken to remind me of being a kid and eating some form of this dish. To really take things up a notch, the bread crumbs can be swapped out for tater tots as a topping. Even the pickiest kids will love this dish! —Meg Jordan

NUT-FREE

PREP TIME: 15 minutes
COOK TIME: 35 minutes

FUNCTION: Bake
TEMPERATURE: 375°F

ACCESSORIES: Ninja Casserole Dish (9 by 13 inches)

2 (10.5-ounce) cans cream of chicken soup

2 cups chicken stock

2 cups chopped cooked chicken breast

1 cup grated Parmesan cheese

1 cup shredded Gouda cheese

Kosher salt and freshly ground black pepper, to taste

½ cup panko bread crumbs

4 tablespoons (½ stick) unsalted butter, melted

1. In a large bowl, combine the soup, stock, chicken breast, Parmesan, Gouda, salt, and pepper. Transfer the mixture to a casserole dish.

2. Install a wire rack on Level 3. Select BAKE, set the temperature to 375ºF, and set the time to 35 minutes. Press START/STOP to begin preheating.

3. When the unit has preheated, place the casserole dish on the wire rack. Close the oven door to begin cooking.

4. In a small bowl, mix together the panko bread crumbs and melted butter. After the chicken has cooked for 30 minutes, spoon the panko bread crumbs over the top of the casserole. Continue cooking for the remaining 5 minutes.

5. When cooking is complete, let the casserole cool for 10 minutes before serving.

Per serving: Calories: 381; Total Fat: 26g; Saturated Fat: 13g; Cholesterol: 99mg; Sodium: 970mg; Carbohydrates: 10g; Fiber: 0g; Protein: 26g

Mexican-Inspired Turkey Meat Loaf with Chili-Rubbed Street Corn

SERVES 6 TO 8

As a child, meat loaf was one of the dishes in my mother's culinary repertoire that I truly loved. It makes sense when you think about it—it's just a giant baked burger. Hers was glazed with ketchup; what's not to love? This recipe comes together quickly as it utilizes pantry items and requires no extra prep or pans. Just open the cans! This recipe will have your kids yelling, "Ma! The meat loaf!" just like Will Ferrell in Wedding Crashers. —Craig White

GLUTEN-FREE, NUT-FREE

PREP TIME: 15 minutes
COOK TIME: 45 minutes

FUNCTION: Air Roast
TEMPERATURE: 350°F

ACCESSORIES: 2 Ninja Sheet Pans

SUBSTITUTION: If you have a hard time finding cotija cheese at the market, substitute feta cheese. You are looking for a salty, crumbly cheese. If you aren't a fan of those types of cheese, grate some Parmesan over the corn instead. Just make sure you use some kind of cheese!

For the meat loaf

Cooking oil spray

2 pounds ground turkey

⅓ cup salsa

1 cup quick-cooking oats

2 large eggs

1 (4-ounce) can chopped green chiles

⅓ cup chopped fresh cilantro, divided

1 (1-ounce) packet taco seasoning

1 (15-ounce) can red enchilada sauce, divided

⅓ cup ketchup

Kosher salt and freshly ground black pepper, to taste

For the corn

6 ears corn, shucked

3 tablespoons butter, at room temperature

2 teaspoons chili powder

Salt and freshly ground black pepper to taste

¼ cup plain Greek yogurt

¼ cup crumbled cotija cheese

Lime wedges, for serving

1. **To make the meat loaf:** Line a sheet pan with parchment paper and spray the parchment with cooking spray.

2. In a large bowl, combine the turkey, salsa, oats, eggs, green chiles, half of the cilantro, the taco seasoning, and half of the enchilada sauce. Mix until well combined.

3. Transfer the meat mixture to the prepared pan and form it into cylinder about 5 inches wide.

4. In a small bowl, whisk together the remaining half of the enchilada sauce and the ketchup, and season with salt and pepper to taste. Evenly glaze the top of the meat loaf, reserving half for a second glaze.

5. Install the wire racks on Levels 1 and 3. Select AIR ROAST, select 2 LEVEL, set the temperature to 350°F, and set the time to 45 minutes. Press START/STOP to begin preheating.

6. Once the unit has preheated, place the sheet pan on Level 3. Close the oven to begin cooking.

7. **To make the corn:** On a separate sheet pan, place a piece of foil that is long enough to wrap the 6 ears of corn.

8. Rub the corn evenly with the butter. Season the ears all over with the chili powder, salt, and pepper. Wrap all the corn in the foil, creating a foil package.

9. When there are 30 minutes remaining, place the sheet pan with the corn on the lower wire rack. Glaze the meat loaf again with the remaining glaze and continue cooking for the remaining 30 minutes.

10. Cooking is complete when an instant-read thermometer inserted in the center reads 165°F. Let the meat loaf rest for 5 to 10 minutes before slicing.

11. Remove the corn from the oven and open the foil packet. Slather the corn with the yogurt and sprinkle with the cheese. Serve alongside the meat loaf with the lime wedges and remaining cilantro on the side.

Per serving: Calories: 563; Total Fat: 26g; Saturated Fat: 9g; Cholesterol: 195mg; Sodium: 954mg; Carbohydrates: 45g; Fiber: 7g; Protein: 41g

Garlic-Crusted Flank Steak with Roasted Vegetables, *page 115*

6

Beef, Pork, and Lamb

Carne Asada Street Tacos 114

Garlic-Crusted Flank Steak with Roasted Vegetables 115

Barbecue Meat Loaf and Crispy Ranch Potatoes 117

Honey-Garlic Glazed Pork Tenderloin with Roasted Vegetables 119

Pork Wellington with Garlic Green Beans 122

Cuban-Style Pork Roast with "Fried" Sweet Plantains 124

Mojito Mojo Pulled Pork Sandwiches 126

Chorizo-Stuffed Poblano Peppers 129

Mustard-and-Herb-Crusted Rack of Lamb with Warm Potato Salad 131

Carne Asada Street Tacos

SERVES **4 TO 6**

When my husband and I go to our local taco joint, we always order the carne asada street tacos. Although traditional carne asada is grilled, this version uses the BROIL function on the XL Pro Air Oven. The quick and easy marinade makes every bite juicy and flavorful. —Kenzie Swanhart

---

DAIRY-FREE, NUT-FREE

PREP TIME: 15 minutes, plus 1 hour to marinate
COOK TIME: 15 minutes

FUNCTION: Broil
TEMPERATURE: HI

ACCESSORIES: Ninja Sheet Pan

VARIATION: Put your own twist on these by switching up the toppings. I like pico de gallo, salsa verde, guacamole, and cabbage slaw.

2 tablespoons soy sauce
Juice of 2 limes
2 tablespoons avocado oil, divided
4 garlic cloves, minced
2 teaspoons chili powder
1 teaspoon ground cumin
½ teaspoon salt
¼ teaspoon freshly ground black pepper
1½ pounds skirt steak or flank steak
12 corn tortillas
1 small red onion, diced
1 jalapeño, sliced
½ cup chopped fresh cilantro

1. In a medium bowl, whisk together the soy sauce, lime juice, avocado oil, garlic, chili powder, cumin, salt, and pepper. Pour the marinade into a large resealable bag. Add the steak, seal the bag, and marinate in the refrigerator for 1 hour.

2. Remove the steak from the marinade (discarding any liquid) and place it in the center of the sheet pan.

3. Install a wire rack on Level 4. Select BROIL, set the temperature to HI, and set the time to 15 minutes. Press START/STOP to begin. Place the sheet pan on the wire rack and close the door to begin cooking.

4. When cooking is complete, transfer the steak to a cutting board and let it rest for 10 minutes before slicing.

5. Divide the sliced steak among the tortillas, then topping with the onion, jalapeño, and cilantro.

Per serving: *Calories: 533; Total Fat: 24g; Saturated Fat: 7g; Cholesterol: 116mg; Sodium: 897mg; Carbohydrates: 39g; Fiber: 6g; Protein: 42g*

Garlic-Crusted Flank Steak with Roasted Vegetables

SERVES 4 TO 6

I love how the tart and savory topping in this recipe complements almost any protein it's served on. Here it's paired with a lean and tender flank steak—one of the easiest cuts to cook and one of the most flavorful. The garlic crust will become golden brown on top, and I recommend letting the meat sit for 5 to 10 minutes before slicing against the grain. This will help the crust set and preserve its texture. —Kara Bleday

NUT-FREE

PREP TIME: 10 minutes
COOK TIME: 15 minutes

FUNCTION: Air Roast
TEMPERATURE: 425°F

ACCESSORIES: Air Fry Basket, Ninja Sheet Pan

VARIATION: A great way to make this dish vegetarian is to substitute portabella mushroom caps for the flank steak. Simply brush them with a damp paper towel to clean the tops, and use a spoon to scoop out the gills. Rub with olive oil and place a few tablespoons of the cheese mixture inside the caps. Put them on the sheet pan and cook on AIR ROAST at 425°F for 10 to 15 minutes, or until golden brown on top.

¼ cup mayonnaise

3 tablespoons grated Parmesan cheese

2 garlic cloves, crushed

1 tablespoon freshly squeezed lemon juice

2 tablespoons panko bread crumbs

2 pounds flank steak

12 ounces Brussels sprouts, halved

2 red bell peppers, seeded and cut into 1-inch pieces

½ red onion, cut into 1-inch pieces

3 tablespoons vegetable oil

Kosher salt and freshly ground black pepper, to taste

1. In a small bowl, combine the mayonnaise, Parmesan cheese, garlic, lemon juice, and panko bread crumbs. Spread the mixture evenly over the top of the steak. Place the steak on the sheet pan.

2. In a large bowl, toss the Brussels sprouts, bell peppers, and onion with the oil. Season with salt and pepper. Place the vegetables in a single layer in the air fryer basket.

3. Install a wire rack on Level 1. Select AIR ROAST, select 2 LEVEL, set the temperature to 425°F, and set the time to 15 minutes. Press START/STOP to begin preheating.

CONTINUED ▶

4. When the unit has preheated, place the sheet pan on the wire rack, and insert the air fryer basket on Level 3. Close the oven door to begin cooking.

5. When cooking is complete, remove the meat and vegetables from the oven. Let the meat rest for at least 5 minutes before slicing.

Per serving: Calories: 644; Total Fat: 41g; Saturated Fat: 12g; Cholesterol: 163mg; Sodium: 314mg; Carbohydrates: 15g; Fiber: 5g; Protein: 53g

Barbecue Meat Loaf and Crispy Ranch Potatoes

SERVES 6

Meat loaf is one of those comfort foods that is versatile enough to make your own. I love a country-style meat loaf with barbecue sauce instead of ketchup. I make it a complete meal by pairing it with crispy potatoes coated in ranch dressing. And of course, there is definitely bacon. —Melissa Celli

NUT-FREE

PREP TIME: 5 minutes
COOK TIME: 55 minutes

FUNCTION: Air Roast
TEMPERATURE: 400°F

ACCESSORIES: Air Fry Basket, Ninja Sheet Pan

PREP TIP: The potatoes can be cut in advance and held in a bowl of water in the refrigerator for up to 1 day. Drain the water when ready to use and pat the potatoes dry with a paper towel.

For the meat loaf

1½ pounds ground beef

2 tablespoons minced garlic

1 medium white onion, finely chopped

½ cup panko bread crumbs

1 large egg

1 cup prepared barbecue sauce, divided

2 tablespoons yellow mustard

2 tablespoons barbecue seasoning

Kosher salt and freshly ground black pepper, to taste

5 bacon slices, halved crosswise

For the potatoes

4 russet potatoes, peeled and cut into 1-inch cubes

2 tablespoons canola oil

1 teaspoon kosher salt

1 (1-ounce) packet ranch dressing mix

Cooking oil spray

¼ cup grated Parmesan cheese

1 tablespoon chopped fresh parsley

1. **To make the meat loaf:** In a large bowl, mix together the ground beef, garlic, onion, panko bread crumbs, egg, ½ cup of barbecue sauce, mustard, and barbecue seasoning until well combined. Season with salt and pepper to taste.

2. Place the mixture on the sheet pan and form it into a rounded football-like shape. Lay the bacon slices over the top, covering the meat loaf from end to end.

CONTINUED ▶

3. **To make the potatoes:** In a separate large bowl, toss the potatoes with the canola oil, salt, and ranch dressing mix. Spray the air fryer basket with cooking oil and place the potatoes in the basket.

4. Install a wire rack on Level 1. Select AIR ROAST, select 2 LEVEL, set the temperature to 400°F, and set the time to 55 minutes. Press START/STOP to begin preheating.

5. When the unit has preheated, place the sheet pan on the wire rack, and insert the air fryer basket on Level 3. Close the oven door to begin cooking.

6. When 10 minutes remain, remove the meat loaf and brush the remaining ½ cup of barbecue sauce over the meat loaf. Remove the air fryer basket and toss the potatoes with the Parmesan. Return the meat loaf and potatoes to the oven and continue cooking.

7. When cooking is complete, an instant-read thermometer inserted into the meat loaf should read at least 155°F.

8. Toss the potatoes with the parsley, and let the meat loaf rest for about 5 minutes before slicing and serving.

Per serving: Calories: 531; Total Fat: 22g; Saturated Fat: 7g; Cholesterol: 116mg; Sodium: 992mg; Carbohydrates: 51g; Fiber: 3g; Protein: 32g

Honey-Garlic Glazed Pork Tenderloin with Roasted Vegetables

SERVES 8 TO 12

Perfectly cooked pork is doused in a delightful balsamic glaze and served with a combination of roasted potatoes, green beans, and onions. This is a delicious yet effortless meal that feels a little fancy. It will be sure to impress your family, and if cooking larger cuts of meats feels daunting, this will put you at ease. If you love roasted vegetables just as much as I do, this is a recipe to keep in your back pocket. —Caroline Schliep

DAIRY-FREE, GLUTEN-FREE, NUT-FREE

PREP TIME: 15 minutes
COOK TIME: 25 minutes

FUNCTION: Air Roast
TEMPERATURE: 425°F

ACCESSORIES: Ninja Roast Tray, 2 Ninja Sheet Pans

FREEZER FRIENDLY:
This is a perfect recipe to make for a family of 4; just freeze the leftovers for when you are busy and don't have any time to cook. Reheat on a sheet pan at 425°F for 10 to 20 minutes.

6 tablespoons balsamic vinegar

¼ cup honey

2½ tablespoons extra-virgin olive oil

2 teaspoons minced garlic

4 teaspoons minced rosemary

2 pork tenderloins (2 to 2½ pounds total)

Kosher salt and freshly ground black pepper, to taste

1 pound green beans, trimmed

1 pound baby red potatoes, halved

1 large red onion, thinly sliced

1. In a small bowl, whisk together the balsamic vinegar, honey, olive oil, garlic, and rosemary. Set aside.

2. Pat the pork tenderloins dry with paper towels. Season with salt and pepper and place them on the roast tray set into a sheet pan. Brush or spoon the balsamic mixture over the tenderloins, reserving about ¼ cup.

3. In a large bowl, combine the green beans, potatoes, and onion and season with salt and pepper. Add the reserved balsamic mixture to the bowl and toss to evenly coat the vegetables. Arrange the vegetables on the other sheet pan in an even layer.

CONTINUED ▶

Honey-Garlic Glazed Pork Tenderloin with Roasted Vegetables continued

VARIATION: The variations on this recipe are endless. You can easily swap the balsamic glaze for any store-bought or homemade marinade or sauce, such as teriyaki, honey mustard, barbecue, lemon herb, or jerk. And you could even change the veggies, too; try Brussels sprouts, diced butternut squash, broccoli, asparagus, or whatever vegetable tickles your fancy.

4. Install the wire racks on Levels 1 and 4. Select AIR ROAST, select 2 LEVEL, set the temperature to 425°F, and set the time to 25 minutes. Press START/STOP to begin preheating.

5. When the unit has preheated, place the sheet pan with the meat on Level 1 and the vegetables on Level 4. Close the oven door to begin cooking.

6. When cooking is complete, an instant-read thermometer inserted into the pork should read at least 145°F and the vegetables should be fork-tender.

7. Let the meat rest for about 5 minutes before slicing and serving.

Per serving: Calories: 282; Total Fat: 8g; Saturated Fat: 2g; Cholesterol: 74mg; Sodium: 77mg; Carbohydrates: 26g; Fiber: 3g; Protein: 26g

Pork Wellington with Garlic Green Beans

Though Wellingtons are notoriously intimidating to make, this one is easy as can be. I love being able to cook this dramatic and flavorful dish without worrying about the final product. Pork tenderloin is lean, healthy, and, of course, tender. It's tough to cook a beef Wellington to the correct doneness without poking holes in it with a meat thermometer. With pork, even if it's overcooked, it will remain moist in the pastry shell. The trick to a successful dish here is to make sure the tenderloin is wrapped tightly. The meat will shrink during cooking, and a tight wrap will help minimize space between the meat and puff pastry when you're ready to serve. —Kara Bleday

NUT-FREE

PREP TIME: 15 minutes
COOK TIME: 45 minutes

FUNCTION: Air Roast
TEMPERATURE: 350°F

ACCESSORIES: Ninja Sheet Pan

SUBSTITUTION: You can make this with different preserves. Other flavors that would be delicious with this recipe are raspberry or blueberry, spiced apple butter, or marmalade. I recommend avoiding applesauce as it contains too much water and will make the puff pastry soggy.

1 pound green beans, trimmed

2 tablespoons extra-virgin olive oil

2 garlic cloves, minced

Kosher salt and freshly ground black pepper, to taste

All-purpose flour, for dusting

1 frozen puff pastry sheet, thawed and rolled out to 12 by 15 inches

¼ cup apricot preserves

½ teaspoon dried thyme

4 thin slices prosciutto

1 (1½- to 2-pound) pork tenderloin, silver skin removed

2 tablespoons whole-grain mustard

2 tablespoons Dijon mustard

1 large egg, beaten with 1 tablespoon water

1. In a large bowl, toss the green beans with the olive oil, garlic, salt, and pepper. Set aside.

2. Dust a clean work surface with flour and lay out the puff pastry. Gently spread the apricot preserves over the middle 2 quarters. Sprinkle with the thyme and a pinch of salt and pepper.

3. Layer the prosciutto on top of the preserves lengthwise; you want the prosciutto to wrap around the whole tenderloin.

4. Place the tenderloin on a cutting board and pat dry with paper towels. Rub the whole-grain and Dijon mustards all over the meat and season it with salt and pepper. Place the tenderloin gently on the prosciutto, pushing in on both ends of the meat to ensure the tenderloin has even thickness throughout. Leave a 2-inch border of puff pastry on each end.

5. Fold one side of the puff pastry over the top of the tenderloin and roll to enclose the meat tightly. Brush a bit of the egg wash on the seam to seal. Turn the Wellington so it is seam-side down. Tightly close the ends and use the egg wash to seal completely. Finally, brush all over with the egg wash to promote even browning during cooking.

6. Place the Wellington on the sheet pan seam-side down. Place the green beans on both sides of the Wellington.

7. Install a wire rack on Level 2. Select AIR ROAST, set the temperature to 350ºF, and set the time to 45 minutes. Press START/STOP to begin preheating.

8. When the unit has preheated, place the sheet pan on the wire rack. Close the oven door to begin cooking.

9. Cooking is complete when the puff pastry is golden brown and an instant-read thermometer inserted into the pork reads at least 145ºF.

Per serving: *Calories: 869; Total Fat: 48g; Saturated Fat: 12g; Cholesterol: 166mg; Sodium: 799mg; Carbohydrates: 61g; Fiber: 5g; Protein: 50g*

Cuban-Style Pork Roast with "Fried" Sweet Plantains

SERVES 6 TO 8

This is a rendition of one of my favorite traditional Cuban dishes, Pernil Cubano con Maduros. Whenever I get the chance to visit my fiancé's family in Havana, it is one of the first meals his father prepares. Tender slow-roasted pork marinated in tangy mojo and accompanied by sweet plantains is one of my ultimate comfort foods. For the perfect pick-me-up on a dreary day, throw on some Cuban music, sip a mojito, and take a bite to get a little taste of this lively island nation. If you have any left over, it's delicious in tacos. —Kelly Gray

DAIRY-FREE, GLUTEN-FREE, NUT-FREE

PREP TIME: 15 minutes, plus overnight to marinate
COOK TIME: 2 hours 10 minutes

FUNCTION: Whole Roast, Air Fry
TEMPERATURE: 300°F, 400°F

ACCESSORIES: Air Fry Basket, Ninja Casserole Dish (9 by 13 inches)

1 small white onion, diced

5 garlic cloves, crushed

1 tablespoon dried oregano, preferably Mexican

1 tablespoon kosher salt

1 teaspoon freshly ground black pepper

2 cups freshly squeezed orange juice

1 cup freshly squeezed lime juice

3 pounds boneless pork shoulder

2 cups water

4 overripe (nearly black) plantains, peeled and sliced on the diagonal

Cooking oil spray

1. In a blender, combine the onion, garlic, oregano, salt, pepper, orange juice, and lime juice. Blend until frothy. Reserve 1 cup of marinade and pour the rest into a resealable bag. Add the pork, seal the bag, and make sure the meat is thoroughly coated. Refrigerate overnight.

2. Pour the contents of the bag (meat and liquid) into the casserole dish, add the water, and cover tightly with foil.

3. Install a wire rack on Level 1. Select WHOLE ROAST, set the temperature to 300°F, and set the time to 2 hours. Press START/STOP to begin preheating.

4. When the unit has preheated, place the covered casserole dish on the wire rack. Close the oven door to begin cooking.

5. When the pork is fork-tender, carefully remove the foil but leave the roast in the oven.

6. Select AIR FRY, select 2 LEVEL, set the temperature to 400°F, and set the time to 10 minutes.

7. Arrange the sliced plantains in the air fryer basket. Generously spray with cooking oil, then insert the air fryer basket on Level 3. Press START/STOP to begin cooking.

8. Cooking is complete when the plantains are caramelized and an instant-read thermometer inserted into the pork reads at least 205°F. Serve with the reserved mojo marinade.

Per serving: *Calories: 456; Total Fat: 8g; Saturated Fat: 3g; Cholesterol: 136mg; Sodium: 516mg; Carbohydrates: 44g; Fiber: 3g; Protein: 53g*

Mojito Mojo Pulled Pork Sandwiches

Pork butt is one of my favorite cuts. The amount of fat and marbling allows it to stay moist during cooking processes like the one in this recipe. Adding a braising liquid makes this dish bulletproof. The key is making sure the meat is so tender it's falling apart, so don't try and cut any corners here. Trust the process.
—Craig White

DAIRY-FREE, NUT-FREE

PREP TIME: 30 minutes, plus 2 hours or overnight to marinate
COOK TIME: 2 hours 30 minutes

FUNCTION: Air Roast
TEMPERATURE: 325°F

ACCESSORIES: Ninja Sheet Pan, 8-inch square baking pan

¼ cup white rum

Juice of 4 limes

Juice of 2 oranges

4 garlic cloves, minced

1 teaspoon ground cumin

4 tablespoons chopped fresh mint

4 tablespoons chopped fresh oregano

4 tablespoons chopped fresh cilantro

Kosher salt and freshly ground black pepper, to taste

2 pounds boneless pork butt, cut into 2-inch chunks

6 burger buns, split

Pickled jalapeño, dill pickle chips, thinly sliced red onion, and slaw, for serving

1. In a small bowl, combine the rum, lime juice, orange juice, garlic, cumin, mint, oregano, and cilantro. Season with salt and pepper.

2. Season the pork with salt and pepper and place it in the baking pan. Pour the marinade over the pork. Cover the pan with foil and marinate in the refrigerator for at least 2 hours or up to overnight.

3. Install the wire racks on Levels 1 and 3. Select AIR ROAST, select 2 LEVEL, set the temperature to 325°F, and set the time to 2 hours 30 minutes. Press START/STOP to begin preheating.

4. When the unit has preheated, place the covered pan on Level 3. Close the oven door to begin cooking.

5. When there are 5 minutes remaining, place the buns cut-side up on a sheet pan and place the sheet pan on Level 1.

6. When cooking is complete, remove the buns and pork from the oven.

7. Using two forks, pull apart and shred the pork. Place a big scoop of the meat on each bun bottom and top the sandwiches with the other half of the bun. Serve with the pickled jalapeño, dill pickle chips, thinly sliced red onion, and slaw as desired.

Per serving: Calories: 446; Total Fat: 20g; Saturated Fat: 7g; Cholesterol: 94mg; Sodium: 305mg; Carbohydrates: 28g; Fiber: 1g; Protein: 31g

Chorizo-Stuffed Poblano Peppers

SERVES 6 TO 8

To me, stuffed bell peppers are one of the most American dishes I can think of. I remember being a kid and loving them. So, you can imagine my surprise when I realized that they are not exclusive to the United States. Tons of countries have their own traditional stuffed peppers! This version is a love child of my two favorite versions, American and Mexican. In Mexico, chiles rellenos are poblano peppers stuffed with queso fresco (cheese), dipped in egg batter and then deep-fried. For the purpose of this recipe, I replaced the traditional white rice with cauliflower rice to make the dish healthier and easier to prepare on a busy weeknight. —Chelven Randolph

5 INGREDIENTS OR LESS, GLUTEN-FREE, NUT-FREE

PREP TIME: 10 minutes
COOK TIME: 40 minutes

FUNCTION: Air Roast
TEMPERATURE:
375°F, 450°F

ACCESSORIES: Air Fry Basket, Ninja Sheet Pan

VARIATION: This recipe is a great baseline for all sorts of variations you can play with. Try adding corn to the mixture or a different type of meat, such as ground pork or beef. Or top with salsa verde and sour cream after cooking for even more flavor.

1 pound chorizo
 sausage, diced

2 (12-ounce) bags
 cauliflower rice

1 (16-ounce) jar black
 bean salsa

2 cups shredded sharp
 cheddar cheese

8 poblano peppers, halved
 lengthwise and seeded

1. In a large bowl, stir together the chorizo, cauliflower rice, salsa, and 1½ cups of cheese until thoroughly combined. Fill each half pepper with the mixture evenly, about 1 cup per half. Arrange the stuffed peppers in the air fryer basket in a single layer.

2. Install a wire rack on Level 1. Select AIR ROAST, set the temperature to 375°F, and set the time to 35 minutes. Press START/STOP to begin preheating.

3. When the unit has preheated, place the sheet pan on the wire rack to catch any drippings, and insert the air fryer basket on Level 3. Close the oven door to begin cooking.

4. When cooking is complete, carefully remove the sheet pan and air fryer basket, and top each pepper with the remaining cheese.

CONTINUED ▶

5. Place the sheet pan back on the wire rack and the air fryer basket on Level 3. Select AIR ROAST, set the temperature to 450°F, and set the time to 5 minutes. Press START/STOP to begin.

6. When cooking is complete, let the peppers cool for about 5 minutes before serving.

Per serving: *Calories: 725; Total Fat: 55g; Saturated Fat: 25g; Cholesterol: 130mg; Sodium: 144mg; Carbohydrates: 17g; Fiber: 5g; Protein: 41g*

Mustard-and-Herb-Crusted Rack of Lamb with Warm Potato Salad

My first kitchen job was working for Chef Jody Adams at Rialto in Cambridge, Massachusetts. I remember cooking a lamb chop like this when I worked the grill station. We would start the lamb on the grill, get a good crust on it, then slather it in mustard, top it with bread crumbs, and finish it in the oven. I prefer my lamb chops cooked medium because I like that fat to render and the flavor to develop a little more, but a lot of people like their lamb rare. However you like your lamb, you're going to love this dish. Add it to your repertoire and prove to your family that you've got "chops" in the kitchen. —Craig White

NUT-FREE

PREP TIME: 30 minutes
COOK TIME: 20 to 30 minutes

FUNCTION: Air Roast
TEMPERATURE: 425°F, 400°F

ACCESSORIES: Ninja Roast Tray, 2 Ninja Sheet Pans

1 (1½-pound) rack of lamb

Kosher salt and freshly ground black pepper, to taste

2 tablespoons canola oil, divided

1½ pounds baby Yukon Gold potatoes, halved

¼ cup bread crumbs

2 tablespoons grated Parmesan cheese

1 teaspoon minced fresh thyme

1 teaspoon minced fresh rosemary

4 tablespoons Dijon mustard, divided

½ cup mayonnaise

¼ cup pitted kalamata olives, chopped

1 celery stalk, finely chopped

½ small red onion, finely chopped

2 tablespoons minced fresh dill

Grated zest and juice of 1 lemon

1. Install the wire racks on Levels 1 and 3. Select AIR ROAST, select 2 LEVEL, set the temperature to 425°F, and set the time to 30 minutes. Press START/STOP to begin preheating.

2. Place the lamb fat-side up on the roast tray set into a sheet pan. Season the lamb with salt and pepper, and coat it with 1 tablespoon of canola oil.

CONTINUED ▶

Mustard-and-Herb-Crusted Rack of Lamb with Warm Potato Salad continued

MAKE AHEAD: If you know you are going to be "in the weeds" the day you are cooking this, you could make the potato salad the day before and serve it cold. It will take on more flavor from the additional time in the dressing. If you like making your own bread crumbs and really want to be a rock star, you can make them the day before.

3. In a large bowl, toss the potatoes with remaining 1 tablespoon of canola oil and season with salt and pepper. Place in an even layer on the other sheet pan.

4. When the unit has preheated, place the sheet pan with the lamb on Level 3 and the potatoes on Level 1. Close the oven door to begin cooking.

5. In a small bowl, mix together the bread crumbs, Parmesan, thyme, rosemary, salt, and pepper.

6. When there are 20 minutes remaining, reduce the heat to 400°F and remove the lamb from the oven. Spread 3 tablespoons of mustard on the meat and press on the bread crumb mixture, coating evenly.

7. Return the lamb to the oven and continue cooking for 10 to 20 minutes, depending on how you like your lamb cooked.

8. When cooking is complete, remove the lamb and potatoes. Let the lamb rest for 5 to 10 minutes.

9. Place the potatoes in a large bowl. Add the remaining 1 tablespoon of mustard, the mayonnaise, olives, celery, onion, dill, and lemon zest and juice. Toss to combine.

10. Slice the lamb between the bones and serve with the potato salad.

Per serving: Calories: 848; Total Fat: 62g; Saturated Fat: 17g; Cholesterol: 126mg; Sodium: 596mg; Carbohydrates: 38g; Fiber: 6g; Protein: 37g

Air-Fried Fish Tacos, *page 138*

7

Seafood

Fish and Chips 136

Air-Fried Fish Tacos 138

"Fish in a Bag" 141

Parmesan-Crusted Tilapia and Garlic Asparagus 143

Tropical Mahi-Mahi and Vegetables 144

Soy and Maple Salmon with Carrots and Bok Choy 147

Shrimp Bake 149

Sheet Pan Baked Stuffed Shrimp 151

Sheet Pan Paella 153

Bacon-Stuffed Clams 156

Fish and Chips

SERVES 4

Fish and chips is a seafood favorite in many parts of the world, whether it be London, the coast of Maine, or the beaches of New Zealand. Each region has its own twist, from swapping the fries for potato chips to the type of fish used. Here, this classic gets a Ninja® Foodi™ makeover: The fish is air-fried instead of deep-fried, so you still get all the crunchy deliciousness with less oil. —Kenzie Swanhart

DAIRY-FREE, NUT-FREE

PREP TIME: 20 minutes
COOK TIME: 25 minutes

FUNCTION: Air Fry
TEMPERATURE: 400°F

ACCESSORIES: Air Fry Basket, Ninja Sheet Pan

VARIATION: I love using this technique to replicate a deep-fried beer batter. It's as great for chicken fingers and nuggets as it is for fish.

2 large eggs

1 cup ale beer

1 cup cornstarch

1 cup all-purpose flour

½ tablespoon chili powder

1 tablespoon ground cumin

1 teaspoon sea salt, plus more for seasoning

1 teaspoon freshly ground black pepper, plus more for seasoning

4 (5- to 6-ounce) cod fillets

Cooking oil spray

2 large russet potatoes, cut into ¼- to ½-inch-thick sticks

2 tablespoons vegetable oil

1. In a shallow bowl, whisk together the eggs and beer. In a medium bowl, whisk together the cornstarch, flour, chili powder, cumin, salt, and pepper.

2. Dip each cod fillet in the egg mixture, then dredge in the flour mixture, coating on all sides.

3. Coat the sheet pan with cooking spray. Evenly arrange the fish fillets on the pan and lightly spray each with cooking spray.

4. In a large bowl, toss the potatoes with the vegetable oil and season with salt and pepper.

5. Coat the air fryer basket with cooking spray. Evenly arrange the potatoes in the basket.

6. Install a wire rack on Level 3. Select AIR FRY, select 2 LEVEL, set the temperature to 400°F, and set the time to 25 minutes. Press START/STOP to begin preheating.

7. When the unit has preheated, place the sheet pan on the wire rack and insert the air fryer basket on Level 3. Close the oven door to begin cooking.

8. When cooking is complete, check for desired crispness. Cook for 5 minutes more if needed.

Per serving: *Calories: 373; Total Fat: 9g; Saturated Fat: 5g; Cholesterol: 113mg; Sodium: 603mg; Carbohydrates: 44g; Fiber: 3g; Protein: 28g*

Air-Fried Fish Tacos

SERVES 4

Tacos are one of my guilty pleasures, but these air-fried fish tacos in particular hold a special place in my heart. Light and flaky tilapia is tossed in spices and coated in a super crispy panko exterior—you honestly can't go wrong! They would be just perfect for your next Taco Tuesday and are a great way to get your family involved in the kitchen—have them help bread the fish and prepare the toppings, such as pico de gallo, diced avocado, and shredded lettuce.
—Caroline Schliep

30 MINUTES OR LESS, DAIRY-FREE, NUT-FREE

PREP TIME: 20 minutes
COOK TIME: 10 minutes

FUNCTION: Air Fry
TEMPERATURE: 425°F

ACCESSORIES: Air Fryer Basket

SUBSTITUTION: Can't find tilapia at the grocery store? You can substitute another whitefish, such as cod or haddock, or even substitute shrimp. If using shrimp, reduce the cooking time to 5 minutes.

1 pound tilapia fillets, cut into 1-inch-wide strips

Juice of 1 lime

1 (1-ounce) packet taco seasoning

½ cup all-purpose flour

2 large eggs

1 teaspoon sriracha hot sauce

2 cups panko bread crumbs

½ bunch fresh cilantro, minced

½ teaspoon kosher salt

¼ teaspoon freshly ground black pepper

Cooking oil spray

12 corn tortillas, warmed

1. Place the tilapia strips in a medium bowl. Drizzle them with the lime juice and sprinkle with the taco seasoning. Toss to evenly coat.

2. Prepare the breading station by laying out three shallow bowls. Put the flour in the first bowl. In the second bowl, whisk together the eggs and sriracha. In the third bowl, combine the panko bread crumbs, cilantro, salt, and pepper.

3. Lightly coat each fish strip in flour, then dip it in the egg mixture, gently shaking off any excess. Finally, coat each strip in the bread crumb mixture.

4. Coat the air fryer basket with cooking spray and arrange the breaded fish evenly in the basket, ensuring the fish is not overcrowded. Coat the fish strips with cooking spray.

5. Select AIR FRY, set the temperature to 425ºF, and set the time to 10 minutes. Press START/STOP to begin preheating.

6. When the unit has preheated, insert the air fryer basket on Level 3. Close the oven door to begin cooking.

7. When cooking is complete, serve the fish in the corn tortillas with the toppings of your choice.

Per serving: *Calories: 282; Total Fat: 5g; Saturated Fat: 1g; Cholesterol: 103mg; Sodium: 875mg; Carbohydrates: 30g; Fiber: 3g; Protein: 29g*

"Fish in a Bag"

So, why the quote marks around "Fish in a Bag"? Well, it's not exactly fish in a bag; it's fish in foil packets. But that doesn't exactly sound like, "Let me have some of that," does it? But why fish in a bag or fish in foil packets anyway? Why not just layer all the ingredients on a sheet pan and call it done? Because this way everyone gets their own personal portion, with the fish cooking up tender and moist on a bed of couscous and vegetables: the perfect potless meal. You'll need 8 (8-by-10-inch) sheets of foil to prepare this dish. —Sam Ferguson

---

NUT-FREE

PREP TIME: 20 minutes
COOK TIME: 20 minutes

FUNCTION: Air Roast
TEMPERATURE: 375°F

ACCESSORIES: Ninja Sheet Pan

VARIATION: Substitute salmon or any other fish of your choice.

Juice of 2 oranges (about 1½ cups)

1 cup chicken broth

1 cup white wine

2 cups Israeli couscous

Kosher salt and freshly ground black pepper, to taste

1 (16-ounce) bag frozen mixed vegetables

8 tablespoons chopped Niçoise olives, divided

8 (6-ounce) hearty whitefish fillets, such as cod or bass

8 tablespoons (1 stick) cold butter, cut into tablespoons

1. In a large bowl, combine the orange juice, broth, and wine.

2. Place 8 foil sheets on the countertop. Bend the corners inward to create a shallow bowl; this will prevent the ingredients from falling out during assembly.

3. Place ¼ cup of couscous on each foil sheet and season with salt and pepper. Place ½ cup of frozen vegetables on top of the couscous. Place ½ tablespoon of olives on the vegetables.

CONTINUED ▶

4. Place 1 fish fillet on the top, then sprinkle each with ½ tablespoon of olives. Smear gently to cover most of each piece of fish with the olives. Place 1 tablespoon of butter on top of each fish portion and season with salt and pepper.

5. Divide the orange juice mixture evenly between the packets, pouring it over the fish.

6. Lift the edges of the foil upward and inward, then fold the edges over one another and crimp to make a seal. Ensure the seal is tight so steam doesn't escape during cooking. Place the foil packets on the sheet pan.

7. Install a wire rack on Level 1. Select AIR ROAST, set the temperature to 375ºF, and set the time to 20 minutes. Press START/STOP to begin preheating.

8. When the unit has preheated, place the sheet pan on the wire rack. Close the oven door to begin cooking.

9. When cooking is complete, remove the sheet pan from the oven. Be careful to avoid steam when opening the foil packets. Serve.

Per serving: *Calories: 426; Total Fat: 14g; Saturated Fat: 7g; Cholesterol: 110mg; Sodium: 767mg; Carbohydrates: 37g; Fiber: 4g; Protein: 32g*

Parmesan-Crusted Tilapia and Garlic Asparagus

SERVES 6

I was looking for a way to enhance a mild-flavored fish with a topping that would be both delicious and filling. The salty Parmesan, bright-tasting parsley, and crunchy bread crumbs are a winning combination. —Meg Jordan

NUT-FREE

PREP TIME: 15 minutes
COOK TIME: 30 minutes

FUNCTION: Air Roast
TEMPERATURE: 375°F

ACCESSORIES: Ninja Sheet Pan

1 cup grated Parmesan cheese

3 tablespoons chopped fresh parsley

Kosher salt and freshly ground black pepper, to taste

½ cup panko bread crumbs

4 tablespoons (½ stick) unsalted butter, melted

6 (4-ounce) tilapia fillets

1 bunch asparagus, woody ends trimmed, cut into 1-inch pieces

1 tablespoon canola oil

1. Combine the Parmesan, parsley, salt and pepper, panko bread crumbs, and melted butter. Mix thoroughly to combine. Press the mixture onto the top of the tilapia fillets.

2. In a separate medium bowl, toss the asparagus and oil until evenly coated. Season with salt and pepper and toss again.

3. Arrange the fillets on the sheet pan with the asparagus around them. Install a wire rack on Level 3. Select AIR ROAST, set the temperature to 375°F, and set the time to 30 minutes. Press START/STOP to begin preheating.

4. When the unit has preheated, place the sheet pan on the wire rack. Close the oven door to begin cooking.

5. When cooking is complete, let the fish cool for 10 minutes before serving.

Per serving: Calories: 273; Total Fat: 16g; Saturated Fat: 8g; Cholesterol: 88mg; Sodium: 320mg; Carbohydrates: 6g; Fiber: 1g; Protein: 28g

Tropical Mahi-Mahi and Vegetables

SERVES 6

This recipe is a quick and easy way to liven up a weekday meal. A hint of lime and curry transforms this light fish, making it the perfect complement to tender roasted vegetables and sweet pineapple. If you like a little spice, add a pinch of red pepper flakes to the pineapple. Salty, spicy, tangy, and sweet, this dish covers all the bases and is truly a delight for the taste buds. —Kelly Gray

---

DAIRY-FREE, GLUTEN-FREE, NUT-FREE

PREP TIME: 15 minutes
COOK TIME: 25 to 30 minutes

FUNCTION: Air Fry
TEMPERATURE: 455°F

ACCESSORIES: Air Fry Basket, Ninja Sheet Pan

SUBSTITUTION: Can't find mahi-mahi fillets? Try swordfish steaks or salmon fillets.

---

2 cups baby carrots, halved

2 small russet potatoes, peeled and cut into ½-inch sticks

2 tablespoons crushed garlic

3 tablespoons canola oil, divided

1 small pineapple, peeled, cored, and cut into wedges

2 teaspoons curry powder, divided

6 (6-ounce) mahi-mahi fillets

Juice of 1 lime

Kosher salt and freshly ground black pepper, to taste

---

1. In a medium bowl, toss the carrots, potatoes, garlic, and 1 tablespoon of oil until evenly coated. Arrange the vegetables evenly in the air fryer basket.

2. In a separate bowl, toss the pineapple with 1 teaspoon of curry powder and arrange in the basket with the vegetables.

3. Install a wire rack on Level 1. Select AIR FRY, select 2 LEVEL, set the temperature to 455°F, and set the time to 30 minutes. Press START/STOP to begin preheating

4. When the unit has preheated, insert the air fryer basket on Level 3. Close the oven door to begin cooking.

5. While the vegetables are cooking, coat the fish fillets with the remaining 2 tablespoons of oil and the lime juice. Sprinkle with the remaining 1 teaspoon of curry, and season with salt and pepper. Place the fillets on the sheet pan.

6. When there are 20 minutes remaining, place the sheet pan on the wire rack. Close the oven door and continue cooking for 15 to 20 minutes.

7. Cooking is complete when an instant-read thermometer inserted in the fish reads 145°F. Serve the fish with the vegetables and pineapple.

Per serving: Calories: 333; Total Fat: 8g; Saturated Fat: 1g; Cholesterol: 92mg; Sodium: 422mg; Carbohydrates: 36g; Fiber: 4g; Protein: 30g

Soy and Maple Salmon with Carrots and Bok Choy

SERVES 8

Many people are attempting to minimize the amount of starch in their diet. At home, we incorporate some of that logic into our meals daily, such as with this recipe. Salmon is super versatile, and the result is always delicious. In this recipe, the sweet-and-salty marinade pairs perfectly with the vegetables. This dish is easy to assemble and even easier to enjoy! —Chelven Randolph

DAIRY-FREE, NUT-FREE

PREP TIME: 15 minutes, plus 20 minutes to 12 hours to marinate
COOK TIME: 15 minutes

FUNCTION: Air Roast
TEMPERATURE: 400°F

ACCESSORIES: Air Fry Basket, Ninja Roast Tray, Ninja Sheet Pan

⅓ cup pure maple syrup

3 tablespoons soy sauce

3 garlic cloves, minced

8 (6-ounce) skinless salmon fillets

1 pound baby carrots

8 heads baby bok choy, quartered lengthwise

Canola oil cooking spray

1 bunch scallions, green parts only, thinly sliced, for serving

1. In a small bowl, stir together the maple syrup, soy sauce, and garlic. Place the salmon fillets in a resealable bag and pour half of the marinade over the salmon, reserving the other half. Seal the bag and marinate in the refrigerator for at least 20 minutes and up to 12 hours.

2. Once the fish has marinated, nest the roast tray in a sheet pan. Lightly coat the roast tray with cooking spray. Arrange the salmon fillets on the roast tray.

3. In a large bowl, toss the carrots and bok choy with the reserved marinade. Evenly arrange the vegetables in the air fryer basket.

4. Install a wire rack on Level 1. Select AIR ROAST, select 2 LEVEL, set the temperature to 400°F, and set the time to 15 minutes. Press START/STOP to begin preheating.

CONTINUED ▶

5. When the unit has preheated, place the sheet pan and roast tray on the wire rack and insert the air fryer basket on Level 4. Close the oven door to begin cooking.

6. When cooking is complete, top the salmon with the scallions and serve alongside the carrots and bok choy.

Per serving: *Calories: 292; Total Fat: 11g; Saturated Fat: 2g; Cholesterol: 94mg; Sodium: 150mg; Carbohydrates: 11g; Fiber: 2g; Protein: 35g*

Shrimp Bake

When I was a kid, shrimp were the only seafood I liked. On holidays, we would always have store-bought shrimp cocktail, and I would devour it. Not much has changed since then, but I have figured out a few other ways that I like my shrimp. This preparation is super simple and a great alternative to the ubiquitous shrimp cocktail found at many family functions. —Craig White

30 MINUTES OR LESS, NUT-FREE

PREP TIME: 15 minutes
COOK TIME: 20 minutes

FUNCTION: Bake, Broil
TEMPERATURE: 350°F, HI

ACCESSORIES: 8-inch casserole dish or pie pan

SUBSTITUTION: Feel free to use white wine if you don't have sherry. When the shrimp are ready and hot out of the oven, pour a glass of the same wine for the perfect wine pairing!

1 pound (16- to 20-count) shrimp, peeled and deveined

6 tablespoons (¾ stick) unsalted butter, melted, divided

½ teaspoon Old Bay seasoning

1 tablespoon minced shallot

2 teaspoons chopped fresh parsley, divided

1 teaspoon minced garlic

Kosher salt and freshly ground black pepper, to taste

⅓ cup panko bread crumbs

¼ cup dry sherry

1 teaspoon minced fresh thyme

1 lemon, halved

1. In a large bowl, combine the shrimp, 3 tablespoons of melted butter, the Old Bay seasoning, shallot, 1 teaspoon of parsley, the garlic, salt, and pepper. Toss to coat the shrimp evenly.

2. In the casserole dish, arrange the shrimp so that they overlap about halfway on top of each other with the tails facing down. Pour any liquid from the bowl over shrimp.

3. In the same large bowl, mix together the remaining 3 tablespoons of melted butter, the panko bread crumbs, sherry, and thyme until well combined.

4. Sprinkle the panko bread crumb mixture evenly over the shrimp.

5. Install a wire rack on Level 3. Select BAKE, set the temperature to 350°F, and set the time to 15 minutes. Press START/STOP to begin preheating.

CONTINUED ▶

6. When the unit has preheated, place the casserole dish on the wire rack. Close the oven door to begin cooking.

7. After 15 minutes, select BROIL, set the temperature to HI, and press START/STOP to begin. Broil the shrimp for 3 to 5 minutes, until the bread crumbs are golden brown.

8. When cooking is complete, sprinkle the shrimp bake with the remaining 1 teaspoon of parsley and squeeze the lemon juice over the top before serving.

Per serving: Calories: 370; Total Fat: 25g; Saturated Fat: 15g; Cholesterol: 252mg; Sodium: 881mg; Carbohydrates: 10g; Fiber: 1g; Protein: 22g

Sheet Pan Baked Stuffed Shrimp

SERVES 4 TO 6

Garlic and lemon and shrimp and scallops—it's hard to go wrong! This dish is so packed with flavor that you'll have it in your holiday rotation in no time. My family has this every year for Christmas, and one of the best parts about it is being able to make it ahead of time. Prepare the stuffing up to 24 hours in advance and let it rest in the refrigerator. The extra time sitting will help the moisture soak into the bread crumbs and crackers and will make the whole dish taste richer and more developed. —Kara Bleday

---

NUT-FREE

PREP TIME: 20 minutes
COOK TIME: 40 minutes

FUNCTION: Reheat,
Air Roast
TEMPERATURE:
150°F, 350°F

ACCESSORIES: Ninja
Sheet Pan

PERFECT PARTNER:
Prepare this dish along
with Succotash (page 171).
The flavors will comple-
ment the rich stuffing and
provide a pop of color
for your plate. Install the
wire racks on Levels 1 and
3. Cook the shrimp and
stuffing as instructed on
Level 1. When 20 minutes
remain, place the suc-
cotash on Level 3 for
the remainder of the
cooking time.

8 tablespoons (1 stick)
unsalted butter

5 garlic cloves, pressed

2 sleeves Ritz butter
crackers, crushed

1 cup panko bread crumbs

⅓ cup freshly squeezed
lemon juice

¼ cup vermouth

½ bunch curly parsley,
chopped, plus more
for garnish

Kosher salt and
freshly ground black
pepper, to taste

6 ounces bay or sea
scallops, chopped

1 pound (16- to 20-count)
shrimp, peeled
and deveined

Lemon wedges, for serving

1. Place the butter and garlic on the sheet pan.

2. Install a wire rack on Level 2 and place the sheet pan on it. Select REHEAT, set the temperature to 150°F, and set the time to 5 minutes. Close the oven door and press START/STOP to begin. Cook until the butter is melted.

3. In a large bowl, gently toss the Ritz crumbs, panko bread crumbs, lemon juice, vermouth, and parsley to combine. Carefully tip the melted butter and garlic into the mixture and toss to combine. Taste and season with salt and pepper.

CONTINUED ▶

4. Add the chopped scallops to the crumb mixture and mix until well combined. (*Be sure not to taste the stuffing after the scallops are added.*)

5. Spread the stuffing evenly across the sheet pan used to melt the butter. Place the shrimp on top of the stuffing, arranging them however you like. I recommend alternating rows or linking two shrimp together at a time for a more dramatic presentation.

6. Select AIR ROAST, set the temperature to 350ºF, and set the time to 35 minutes. Press START/STOP to begin preheating.

7. When the unit has preheated, place the sheet pan on the wire rack. Close the door to begin cooking.

8. Cooking is complete when the shrimp and scallops are cooked through. This may vary depending on the size of the shrimp. Serve with lemon wedges and garnish with a sprinkle of chopped parsley.

Per serving: Calories: 458; Total Fat: 29g; Saturated Fat: 15g; Cholesterol: 214mg; Sodium: 822mg; Carbohydrates: 22g; Fiber: 1g; Protein: 23g

Sheet Pan Paella

SERVES 6 TO 8

When I was growing up in New Jersey, my dad's family would always celebrate large events at this amazing Spanish restaurant that served one of the best paellas I've ever had. This recipe takes me back to that restaurant and those memories, but it now stars as a one-pan meal! —Melissa Celli

DAIRY-FREE, GLUTEN-FREE, NUT-FREE

PREP TIME: 10 minutes
COOK TIME: 50 minutes

FUNCTION: Air Roast
TEMPERATURE:
400°F, 425°F

ACCESSORIES: Ninja Sheet Pan

PREP TIP: Make sure to wash and scrub the outside of the clams thoroughly with a stiff brush. Soak clams in clean water for about 20 minutes. Discard any that don't shut when tapped with two fingers and have broken or cracked shells.

- 2 tablespoons extra-virgin olive oil, divided
- 4 links chorizo sausage (about 12 ounces total), diced
- 1 pound boneless, skinless chicken thighs, cut into 1-inch pieces
- 1 small yellow onion, diced
- 1 red bell pepper, seeded and diced
- 2 tablespoons minced garlic
- 1 teaspoon paprika
- 1 teaspoon kosher salt, divided
- ¾ teaspoon freshly ground black pepper, divided
- 2 cups short-grain rice
- 5 cups chicken stock
- 1 teaspoon saffron threads
- ½ cup crushed or diced canned tomatoes
- ½ cup frozen green peas
- 8 ounces (16- to 20-count) shrimp, peeled and deveined
- 1 pound littleneck clams, scrubbed
- 2 tablespoons chopped fresh flat-leaf parsley
- Lemon wedges, for serving

1. Grease the sheet pan with 1 tablespoon of olive oil. Place the chorizo and chicken side by side on the pan.

2. Install a wire rack on Level 3. Select AIR ROAST, set the temperature to 400°F, and set the time to 50 minutes. Press START/STOP to begin preheating.

3. When the unit has preheated, place the sheet pan on the wire rack. Close the door to begin cooking.

CONTINUED ▶

4. After 10 minutes, remove the pan and add the onion, bell pepper, garlic, paprika, ½ teaspoon of salt, and ⅜ teaspoon of black pepper to the meat, and toss to coat. Return the pan to the oven to continue cooking.

5. Bake for 10 more minutes, stirring halfway through.

6. After 10 minutes, add the rice to the pan and toss to incorporate. Spread the mixture in an even layer. Return the pan to the oven to continue cooking.

7. Meanwhile, in a large microwafe-safe measuring cup, combine the chicken stock and saffron. Microwave on high for 2 minutes.

8. After the rice has cooked for 10 minutes, remove the pan and gently stir the stock mixture and tomatoes with their juices into the rice mixture until well combined. Carefully return the pan to the oven to continue cooking.

9. After 20 minutes, increase the oven temperature to 425°F and remove the pan from the oven. Sprinkle the peas over the rice. Nestle the shrimp into the mixture and arrange the clams evenly over the top. If all of the stock has been absorbed, drizzle 2 tablespoons water over the rice (if it seems dry, add 1 more tablespoon water). Drizzle the remaining 1 tablespoon of olive oil over the paella, and sprinkle with the remaining ½ teaspoon salt and remaining ⅜ teaspoon pepper. Carefully return the pan to the oven to continue cooking.

10. Bake until the clams have opened, 6 to 8 minutes. Remove the pan from the oven and garnish the paella with the chopped parsley. Serve with lemon wedges.

Per serving: Calories: 695; Total Fat: 28g; Saturated Fat: 10g; Cholesterol: 164mg; Sodium: 1478mg; Carbohydrates: 62g; Fiber: 3g; Protein: 42g

Bacon-Stuffed Clams

SERVES 6 TO 8

Who doesn't love bacon? Well, likely some vegetarians. Nevertheless, these bacon-stuffed clams would be a great choice for a cocktail party or as a simple appetizer before dinner. I jazz them up here with some smoked paprika and smoky chipotle-style hot sauce for an unexpected but kicked-up flavor.
—Melissa Celli

NUT-FREE

PREP TIME: 10 minutes
COOK TIME: 40 to 42 minutes

FUNCTION: Air Roast
TEMPERATURE: 400°F

ACCESSORIES: Ninja Sheet Pan

PREP TIP: Discard any open clams that don't shut when tapped with two fingers or any that have broken or cracked shells. Soak clams in clean water for about 20 minutes, then scrub the outside of the clams thoroughly with a stiff brush.

24 littleneck clams, scrubbed (see Prep tip)

6 ounces bacon, minced

½ cup minced red bell pepper

½ cup minced shallots

½ to ¾ cup Italian-style bread crumbs, divided

¼ cup grated Parmesan cheese

1 tablespoon chipotle hot sauce

1 teaspoon smoked paprika

½ teaspoon chili powder

½ teaspoon garlic powder

1 teaspoon kosher salt

½ teaspoon freshly ground black pepper

2 tablespoons chopped fresh parsley

Lemon wedges, for serving

1. Install a wire rack on Level 3. Select AIR ROAST, set the temperature to 400°F, and set the time to 5 minutes. Press START/STOP to begin preheating.

2. Place the clams on the sheet pan.

3. When the unit has preheated, place the sheet pan on the wire rack. Close the oven door to begin cooking. Roast the clams for 5 minutes, or until they open.

4. When cooking is complete, remove the pan from the oven. Discard any clams that have not opened. Remove the meat, reserving the shells. Drain any juice from the clams into a measuring cup, and pour ¼ cup of the liquid into a medium bowl. Mince the clam meat and place it in the bowl with the clam juice.

5. Put the bacon, bell pepper, and shallots on the same sheet pan. Place the sheet pan on the wire rack and close the oven door.

6. Select AIR ROAST, set the temperature to 400ºF, and set the time to 20 minutes. Press START/STOP to begin cooking.

7. When cooking is complete, the bacon should be crispy. In a large bowl, toss the mixture with ½ cup of bread crumbs, the Parmesan, hot sauce, paprika, chili powder, garlic powder, salt, pepper, and parsley. Add the clams and juice and toss to combine. If the mixture is very wet, add the remaining bread crumbs 1 tablespoon at a time. Fill each clamshell with about 1 tablespoon of the stuffing and place the shells on the sheet pan. Not all the shells will be used.

8. Place the sheet pan on the wire rack and close the oven door. Select AIR ROAST, set the temperature to 400ºF, and set the time to 17 minutes. Press START/STOP to begin cooking.

9. Roast the stuffed clams for 15 to 17 minutes. Serve with lemon wedges.

Per serving: Calories: 221; Total Fat: 13g; Saturated Fat: 5g; Cholesterol: 40mg; Sodium: 721mg; Carbohydrates: 10g; Fiber: 1g; Protein: 14g

Ratatouille, *page 160*

8

Vegetarian Sides and Mains

Ratatouille 160

Eggplant Parmesan "Lasagna" 162

Roasted Mushroom, Poblano, and Corn Enchiladas 164

Coconut Curried Tofu and Vegetables 167

Portabella Mushroom Parmesan and Spaghetti Squash 169

Succotash 171

Baked Macaroni and Cheese 173

Johnny's Corn Bread 175

Pesto Gnocchi with Roasted Vegetables 177

Ratatouille

SERVES 4

Ratatouille *is a great movie, and "Anyone can cook" is my favorite line from it. No truer words have ever been spoken. With a little patience, attention to detail, and of course, a little love, anyone can cook, and that "anyone" means you! This ratatouille is all about the prep and presentation as it is a visual showstopper. Take your time assembling this dish, and the juice will be worth the squeeze when you place it on the table and impress your family. "Anyone can cook, but only the fearless can be great."* —Craig White

DAIRY-FREE, GLUTEN-FREE, NUT-FREE, VEGAN

PREP TIME: 30 minutes
COOK TIME: 50 minutes

FUNCTION: Air Roast
TEMPERATURE: 400°F

ACCESSORIES: 9-inch deep-dish pie plate

PREP TIP:
A Japanese-style mandoline is the perfect tool for prepping the vegetables in this dish. It is widely used in commercial kitchens for tasks like this. Sliding vegetables down a mandoline will ensure even cuts every time. I highly recommend you add one to your kitchen tool arsenal if you want to step up your chef game.

1 (24-ounce) jar marinara sauce

2 summer squash

2 zucchini

2 Japanese eggplants

6 Roma tomatoes

4 tablespoons extra-virgin olive oil, divided

1 teaspoon dried herbes de Provence

Kosher salt and freshly ground black pepper, to taste

2 garlic cloves

¼ cup fresh basil leaves

¼ cup fresh parsley leaves

1. Spread the marinara evenly in the pie plate.

2. Cut the squash, zucchini, eggplants, and tomatoes into ¼-inch-thick slices. Even slices are key to ensure all the vegetables cook at the same time, so take care.

3. Taking one slice of summer squash, zucchini, eggplant, and tomato, arrange them concentrically about three-quarters of the way up each other, starting on the outside of the pie plate. Repeat this process with the vegetable slices, shingling them in the same order. When you get to the end of the dish, keep the process going in the opposite direction across the dish. This will give the vegetables a domino-looking affect. Repeat the process until the dish is full.

4. Drizzle the vegetables with 2 tablespoons of olive oil, and season them with the herbes de Provence, salt, and pepper. Cover the dish with foil.

5. Install a wire rack on Level 3. Select AIR ROAST, set the temperature to 400ºF, and set the time to 50 minutes. Press START/STOP to begin preheating.

6. When the unit has preheated, place the casserole dish on the wire rack. Close the oven door to begin cooking.

7. Mince the garlic and chop the basil and parsley. Place them in a small bowl, add the remaining 2 tablespoons of olive oil, and season with salt and pepper. Toss to combine and set aside.

8. After 40 minutes, remove the dish from the oven and remove the foil. Drizzle the herb mixture over the vegetables. Place the casserole dish back on the wire rack to continue cooking for the remaining 10 minutes.

9. When cooking is complete, remove the dish from the oven, and serve.

Per serving: Calories: 263; Total Fat: 15g; Saturated Fat: 2g; Cholesterol: 0mg; Sodium: 764mg; Carbohydrates: 32g; Fiber: 11g; Protein: 8g

Eggplant Parmesan "Lasagna"

SERVES 6 TO 8

My time at Ninja has pushed me to be creative with recipe development but still make sure the food is approachable. That task is harder than some would assume. There are only so many ways to reinvent chicken breasts or roasted vegetables. With this recipe, I tried to think back to my restaurant days of making staff meals. One thing we would usually have on hand is mozzarella sticks. They are fast, easy, and delicious. Sam used mozzarella sticks in a similar fashion in another recipe, and I thought it was ingenious. The result is a cool new take on a dish I hope you love as much as I do. —Chelven Randolph

NUT-FREE, VEGETARIAN

PREP TIME: 20 minutes
COOK TIME: 35 minutes

FUNCTION: Air Roast
TEMPERATURE: 375°F

ACCESSORIES: Ninja Casserole Dish (9 by 13 inches)

MAKE AHEAD: This is a great dish to make ahead of time! Build the base (through step 3) up to two days in advance and cover with plastic wrap. Refrigerate until you're ready to cook. The eggplant holds up well and will be just as delicious.

- 1 (15-ounce) container ricotta cheese
- 8 ounces Parmesan cheese, shredded or grated
- 1 bunch fresh parsley, chopped
- 2 (24-ounce) jars marinara sauce
- 2 globe eggplants, cut into discs and lightly salted
- 16 ounces mozzarella cheese, shredded
- 1 (16-ounce) package frozen mozzarella sticks

1. In a large bowl, mix together the ricotta, Parmesan, and parsley until well combined. Set aside.

2. Spoon a thin layer of marinara sauce across the bottom of the casserole dish.

3. Place an even layer of the salted eggplant discs on bottom of the dish. Using the back of a spoon, spread a layer of the ricotta mixture on top of the eggplant. Top with more marinara sauce, then sprinkle with some shredded mozzarella. Repeat until three-quarters of the dish is filled. Cover the dish with foil.

4. Install a wire rack on Level 1. Select AIR ROAST, set the temperature to 375°F, and set the time to 25 minutes. Press START/STOP to begin preheating.

5. When the unit has preheated, place the casserole dish on the wire rack. Close the oven door to begin cooking.

6. When cooking is complete, remove the dish from the oven and remove the foil. Arrange the frozen mozzarella sticks evenly on top.

7. Select AIR ROAST, set the temperature to 375°F, and set the time to 10 minutes. Press START/STOP to begin preheating.

8. When the unit has preheated, place the casserole dish on the wire rack. Close the oven door to begin cooking.

9. When cooking is complete, remove the dish from the oven. Let the lasagna cool for 5 to 10 minutes before serving.

Per serving: *Calories: 835; Total Fat: 51g; Saturated Fat: 26g; Cholesterol: 153mg; Sodium: 1831mg; Carbohydrates: 44g; Fiber: 8g; Protein: 51g*

Roasted Mushroom, Poblano, and Corn Enchiladas

SERVES 8 TO 12

One of my favorite dishes to make for dinner during the week is enchiladas. I like green enchilada sauce better than red, because it's milder, but if you prefer red enchilada sauce, go for it! The best part is that the filling is so interchangeable. Have some leftover roasted chicken or seared tofu? Throw it in! —Melissa Celli

NUT-FREE, VEGETARIAN

PREP TIME: 10 minutes
COOK TIME: 35 minutes

FUNCTION: Air Roast
TEMPERATURE: 400°F

ACCESSORIES: Ninja Sheet Pan

SUBSTITUTION: Red enchilada sauce works just as well in this recipe. Swap out the green enchilada sauce for the same amount of red.

- **8 ounces white mushrooms, sliced**
- **2 poblano peppers, seeded and diced**
- **2 ears corn, shucked and kernels cut from cobs**
- **1 medium white onion, diced**
- **¼ cup canola oil**
- **1 teaspoon chili powder**
- **1 teaspoon garlic powder**
- **1 teaspoon ground cumin**
- **1 teaspoon smoked paprika**
- **2 tablespoons freshly squeezed lime juice**
- **2 cups shredded mozzarella cheese, divided**
- **Kosher salt and freshly ground black pepper, to taste**
- **2 (10-ounce) cans green enchilada sauce, divided**
- **6 to 8 fajita-size flour tortillas**
- **Chopped fresh cilantro, for garnish**
- **Lime wedges, for serving**

1. In a large bowl, toss together the mushrooms, peppers, corn kernels, onion, canola oil, chili powder, garlic powder, cumin, and paprika until the vegetables are well coated. Arrange the vegetables on the sheet pan in a single layer.

2. Install a wire rack on Level 3. Select AIR ROAST, set the temperature to 400°F, and set the time to 20 minutes. Press START/STOP to begin preheating.

3. When the unit has preheated, place the sheet pan on the wire rack. Close the oven door to begin cooking.

4. When cooking is complete, remove the pan from the oven and let the vegetables cool.

5. Drain off any liquid from the pan. Transfer the roasted vegetables to a large bowl and add the lime juice and 1 cup of mozzarella. Season with salt and pepper and stir to combine.

6. Pour 1 can of enchilada sauce in the bottom of the casserole dish.

7. Lay out the tortillas and place up to ¼ cup of filling in the center of each. Roll up the tortillas and place them seam-side down in the dish. Pour the remaining 1 can of enchilada sauce over the enchiladas and top with the remaining 1 cup of mozzarella. Cover with foil.

8. Select AIR ROAST, set the temperature to 400°F, and set the time to 15 minutes. Press START/STOP to begin preheating.

9. When the unit has preheated, place the sheet pan on the wire rack. Close the oven door to begin cooking.

10. When there are 5 minutes remaining, remove the foil and continue to cook to brown the top.

11. When cooking is complete, remove the pan from the oven and garnish with the cilantro. Serve with lime wedges.

Per serving: *Calories: 324; Total Fat: 16g; Saturated Fat: 5g; Cholesterol: 22mg; Sodium: 551mg; Carbohydrates: 34g; Fiber: 4g; Protein: 12g*

Coconut Curried Tofu and Vegetables

SERVES 6 TO 8

Admittedly, I used to hate tofu. I did not like the texture or flavor, and I wondered why people didn't just eat meat! Little did I know. As my culinary career progressed, I came to understand not only the appeal of various forms of tofu but also the enormous versatility it offers. This recipe uses firm tofu because it holds its shape better than other styles of tofu. —Chelven Randolph

DAIRY-FREE, NUT-FREE, VEGAN

PREP TIME:
20 minutes, plus
30 minutes to marinate
COOK TIME: 25 minutes

FUNCTION: Air Fry
TEMPERATURE: 400°F

ACCESSORIES: Air Fry Basket, Ninja Sheet Pan

VARIATION: If you are looking for more protein, substitute diced chicken for the tofu. When using chicken, make double the amount of marinade and reserve half so that you can use it for the vegetables without fear of cross-contamination.

2 tablespoons soy sauce

1 tablespoon maple syrup

2 tablespoons curry powder

1 pound firm tofu, cut into 1-inch cubes

¼ cup unsweetened shredded coconut

1 head cauliflower, cut into 1-inch florets

1 (15-ounce) can chickpeas, drained and rinsed

1 bunch (about 12 ounces) kale, stemmed and chopped

1 (13-ounce) can coconut cream

Canola oil cooking spray

1. In a bowl, combine the soy sauce, maple syrup, and curry powder. Place the tofu cubes in a resealable bag and pour in the marinade. Seal the bag and let the tofu marinate for 30 minutes at room temperature.

2. Put the coconut in a medium bowl. Remove the tofu cubes from the bag, reserving the marinade, and dredge the tofu in the coconut.

3. Put the cauliflower, chickpeas, and kale in large bowl. Add the reserved marinade and the coconut cream. Stir until well mixed.

4. Lightly coat the air fryer basket with cooking spray. Evenly arrange the coconut-coated tofu cubes in the basket. Using a slotted spoon, transfer the cauliflower mixture to the sheet pan, reserving the excess coconut sauce.

CONTINUED ▶

5. Install a wire rack on Level 1. Select AIR FRY, select 2 LEVEL, set the temperature to 400°F, and set the time to 25 minutes. Press START/STOP to begin prehearing.

6. When the unit has preheated, place the sheet pan on the wire rack and insert the air fryer basket on Level 4. Close the oven door to begin cooking.

7. When cooking is complete, transfer the tofu to a serving dish. Top with the cauliflower mixture and drizzle with the reserved coconut sauce. Serve immediately.

Per serving: *Calories: 467; Total Fat: 32g; Saturated Fat: 21g; Cholesterol: 0mg; Sodium: 470mg; Carbohydrates: 33g; Fiber: 12g; Protein: 22g*

Portabella Mushroom Parmesan and Spaghetti Squash

SERVES 4 TO 6

I love this alternative to chicken Parmesan and find that during the winter, I often need a light alternative to the heavy meals I've been making. I adore the meaty flavor of portabella mushrooms, and by using the AIR FRY function in the Ninja® Foodi™ XL Pro Air Oven, I'm able to get a really delicious and crispy crust. Served over tender spaghetti squash, this is the perfect replacement for a typically heavy Italian dinner. Serve it with garlic bread and a fresh arugula salad. —Kara Bleday

NUT-FREE, VEGETARIAN

PREP TIME: 15 minutes
COOK TIME: 45 minutes

FUNCTIONS: Air Fry
TEMPERATURE: 400°F

ACCESSORIES: Air Fry Basket, Ninja Sheet Pan

- 1 spaghetti squash, halved lengthwise and seeded
- Extra-virgin olive oil, for brushing the squash
- 1 teaspoon garlic salt
- 1 teaspoon paprika
- ¼ teaspoon freshly ground black pepper, plus more to taste
- ½ teaspoon kosher salt, plus more to taste
- 6 small portabella mushrooms, stemmed
- 1 cup all-purpose flour
- 3 large eggs, beaten
- 2 cups bread crumbs
- Cooking oil spray
- 1½ cups jarred spaghetti sauce
- 2 cups shredded mozzarella cheese

1. Line the sheet pan with parchment paper. Place the spaghetti squash halves cut-side up on the pan and brush the flesh with olive oil.

2. Install a wire rack on Level 1. Select AIR FRY, set the temperature to 400°F, and set the time to 45 minutes. Press START/STOP to begin preheating.

3. When the unit has preheated, place the sheet pan on the wire rack. Close the oven door to begin cooking.

4. Meanwhile, clean the mushrooms by wiping them with a wet cloth. Use a spoon to scoop out and discard the gills.

CONTINUED ▶

Portabella Mushroom Parmesan and Spaghetti Squash continued

VARIATION: If the spaghetti squash is too difficult to cut in half (some are harder than others), prick it all over with a fork and coat with oil. Place it whole on the prepared sheet pan and increase the cooking time to 1 hour. Begin cooking the mushroom caps with 15 minutes remaining. Be careful when cutting the cooked spaghetti squash—it will be hot! And don't forget to remove the seeds.

5. Set up your breading station: Line up three shallow bowls. Put the flour in one bowl, the eggs in the second, and the bread crumbs in the third. One at a time, coat the mushroom caps in flour, then dip them in the eggs, and finally, coat them in the bread crumbs. Place the mushrooms in the air fryer basket in a single layer. Spray them all over with cooking spray to promote even browning during cooking.

6. After the squash has cooked for 25 minutes, insert the air fryer basket on Level 3.

7. When there are 5 minutes remaining, remove the basket and spoon a bit of spaghetti sauce on each mushroom cap, then sprinkle with the mozzarella. Return the basket to the oven to continue cooking for the remaining 5 minutes.

8. When cooking is complete, remove the spaghetti squash from the oven and carefully use a fork to remove the flesh from the rind. It will pull apart like spaghetti strands. Season the squash with salt and pepper and serve with the browned portabella Parmesan.

Per serving: *Calories: 380; Total Fat: 16g; Saturated Fat: 8g; Cholesterol: 91mg; Sodium: 927mg; Carbohydrates: 39g; Fiber: 6g; Protein: 22g*

Succotash

SERVES 4 TO 6

To me, corn and tomatoes signify summer is here. When I was a kid in New Jersey, I remember my parents buying fresh corn from farm stands. The sweetness of the fresh corn is something I'll never forget. This quick and easy recipe combines fresh corn and other vegetables to create a beautiful dish to serve at a summer barbecue. —Meg Jordan

GLUTEN-FREE, NUT-FREE, VEGETARIAN

PREP TIME: 15 minutes
COOK TIME: 20 minutes

FUNCTION: Air Roast
TEMPERATURE: 350°F

ACCESSORIES: 2 Ninja Sheet Pans

VARIATION: A lot of succotash recipes traditionally include bacon. If you'd like to add some, before making the succotash, air-fry a few slices on a sheet pan at 350°F for 10 to 12 minutes, checking it often so it doesn't overcook. Crumble the crispy bacon over the cooked succotash before serving.

Cooking oil spray

10 cups fresh corn kernels (from about 12 ears)

2½ cups cherry tomatoes, halved

8 garlic cloves, minced

2 small onions, chopped

2 cups frozen lima beans

8 tablespoons (1 stick) unsalted butter, cut into small cubes

Kosher salt and freshly ground black pepper, to taste

Thinly sliced fresh basil, for garnish

1. Lightly coat the sheet pans with cooking spray.

2. Divide the corn, cherry tomatoes, garlic, onions, lima beans, and butter cubes between the two pans. Season with salt and pepper and thoroughly mix to combine.

3. Install the wire racks on Levels 1 and 3. Select AIR ROAST, select 2 LEVEL, set the temperature to 350ºF, and set the time to 20 minutes. Press START/STOP to begin preheating.

4. When the unit has preheated, place a sheet pan on each wire rack. Close the oven door to begin cooking.

5. After 10 minutes, open the oven and stir the vegetables. Close the oven door to continue cooking.

6. When cooking is complete, garnish the succotash with the basil and serve.

Per serving: Calories: 642; Total Fat: 29g; Saturated Fat: 15g; Cholesterol: 61mg; Sodium: 740mg; Carbohydrates: 91g; Fiber: 16g; Protein: 18g

Baked Macaroni and Cheese

Is there anything more comforting than mac and cheese? This version is different because it is made on the Ninja Sheet Pan, which means it is the perfect combination of creamy and cheesy, with the maximum amount of crispy crunchy topping! For this version made on the Ninja Sheet Pan, the pasta doesn't need to be boiled first, and it still results in the perfect combination of creamy and cheesy! —Kenzie Swanhart

NUT-FREE, VEGETARIAN

PREP TIME: 15 minutes
COOK TIME: 1 hour

FUNCTION: Bake
TEMPERATURE: 375°F

ACCESSORIES: Ninja Casserole Dish (9 by 13 inches)

SUBSTITUTION: Panko is a Japanese-style bread crumb. If you do not have panko in your pantry, you can use regular unseasoned bread crumbs or crushed butter crackers.

VARIATION: Amp up this dish by adding small raw broccoli florets, shredded buffalo chicken, or crumbled crispy bacon in step 2.

1 cup cottage cheese

2 cups whole milk

1 teaspoon Dijon mustard

½ teaspoon dry mustard

¼ teaspoon garlic powder

¼ teaspoon onion powder

Pinch ground cayenne pepper

Kosher salt and freshly ground black pepper, to taste

1 pound elbow macaroni

8 ounces sharp cheddar cheese, shredded

8 ounces mozzarella cheese, shredded, divided

½ cup grated Parmesan cheese

Cooking oil spray

½ cup panko bread crumbs

2 tablespoons unsalted butter, melted

1. In a blender or food processor, combine the cottage cheese, milk, Dijon and dry mustards, garlic powder, onion powder, cayenne, salt, and pepper. Blend until smooth.

2. In a large bowl, combine the cottage cheese mixture, elbow macaroni, cheddar, half of the mozzarella, and the Parmesan until well mixed.

3. Coat the casserole dish with cooking spray. Arrange the pasta mixture in the dish. Cover tightly with foil.

CONTINUED ▶

4. Install a wire rack on Level 4. Select BAKE, set the temperature to 375ºF, and set the time to 60 minutes. Press START/STOP to begin preheating.

5. When the unit has preheated, place the casserole dish on the wire rack. Close the oven door to begin cooking.

6. Meanwhile, in a small bowl, combine the panko with the melted butter and the remaining half of the mozzarella.

7. After 30 minutes, remove the casserole dish from the oven and remove the foil. Stir gently and spread the bread crumb mixture evenly on top.

8. Return the casserole dish to the oven and continue cooking for the remaining 30 minutes, or until golden brown.

9. When cooking is complete, let the macaroni and cheese cool for 10 minutes before serving.

Per serving: *Calories: 540; Total Fat: 25g; Saturated Fat: 13g; Cholesterol: 75mg; Sodium: 634mg; Carbohydrates: 51g; Fiber: 2g; Protein: 28g*

Johnny's Corn Bread

SERVES 8

Shout-out to my friend Johnny for the assist on this recipe. He and I were line cooks in the same restaurant. Fast-forward 10 years and I'm stealing his recipes for a cookbook! Johnny now owns a catering company and takeout food business, and every Friday people come from all over the greater Boston area to get his corn bread with fried chicken. So, JB, thanks for the recipe inspiration! —Sam Ferguson

NUT-FREE, VEGETARIAN

PREP TIME: 10 minutes
COOK TIME: 40 minutes

FUNCTION: Bake
TEMPERATURE: 315°F

ACCESSORIES: Ninja Casserole Dish (9 by 13 inches)

FREEZER FRIENDLY: When cooking is complete, remove the corn bread from the casserole dish and cut it into your desired portion sizes. Wrap each portion tightly in plastic wrap and freeze for up to 2 to 3 months. The corn bread portions should defrost in as little as 20 minutes.

3 cups whole milk

½ cup canola oil, plus more for greasing

3 large eggs

¼ cup dark molasses

2¼ cups all-purpose flour

2¼ cups cornmeal

⅓ cup sugar

1 tablespoon baking powder

1 cup shredded sharp cheddar cheese

1 teaspoon kosher salt

1. In a large bowl, whisk together the milk, oil, eggs, and molasses until smooth and well incorporated.

2. Add the flour, cornmeal, sugar, baking powder, cheddar, and salt to the bowl and whisk well to combine. There should be no clumps of dry ingredients in the mixture.

3. Grease the casserole dish with canola oil. Pour the corn bread batter into the dish.

4. Install a wire rack on Level 3. Select BAKE, set the temperature to 315°F, and set the time to 40 minutes. Press START/STOP to begin preheating.

5. When the unit has preheated, place the casserole dish on the wire rack. Close the oven door to begin cooking.

6. When cooking is complete, let the corn bread cool for 5 minutes before removing it from the dish and serving.

Per serving: Calories: 609; Total Fat: 26g; Saturated Fat: 6g; Cholesterol: 93mg; Sodium: 310mg; Carbohydrates: 78g; Fiber: 5g; Protein: 16g

Pesto Gnocchi with Roasted Vegetables

SERVES 4 TO 6

If you are looking for a dish that is super simple, family friendly, and perfect to throw together after a long workday, this recipe is for you! —Caroline Schliep

30 MINUTES OR LESS, VEGETARIAN

PREP TIME: 10 minutes
COOK TIME: 20 minutes

FUNCTION: Bake
TEMPERATURE: 425°F

ACCESSORIES: 2 Ninja Sheet Pans

VARIATION: Want something a little more comforting? Use Alfredo sauce instead of pesto and broccoli florets instead of zucchini.

Cooking oil spray

1 pound potato gnocchi, boiled and drained

1 pint cherry tomatoes

1 small zucchini, halved lengthwise and cut into ¼-inch-thick half moons

1 red bell pepper, seeded and cut into thin strips

1 yellow bell pepper, seeded and cut into thin strips

1 red onion, sliced

1 cup basil pesto

¼ cup grated Parmesan cheese

Fresh basil leaves, for garnish

1. Coat the sheet pan with cooking spray and set aside.

2. In a large bowl, combine the gnocchi, tomatoes, zucchini, bell peppers, and onion with the pesto until evenly coated. Divide the mixture between the two pans and spread in an even layer.

3. Install the wire racks on Levels 1 and 3. Select BAKE, select 2 LEVEL, set the temperature to 425°F, and set the time to 20 minutes. Press START/STOP to begin preheating.

4. When the unit has preheated, place a sheet pan on each wire rack. Close the oven door to begin cooking.

5. After 10 minutes, remove the sheet pans and use tongs to toss the mixture. Spread the mixture into an even layer and return the sheet pan to the oven. Close the oven door to continue cooking for the remaining 10 minutes.

6. When cooking is completed, sprinkle with the Parmesan and garnish with the basil leaves. Serve immediately.

Per serving: Calories: 223; Total Fat: 9g; Saturated Fat: 5g; Cholesterol: 24mg; Sodium: 448mg; Carbohydrates: 30g; Fiber: 4g; Protein: 6g

Sweet-and-Spicy Candied Nuts, *page 180*

9

Entertaining

Sweet-and-Spicy Candied Nuts 180

Party Snack Mix 181

Mediterranean Veggie Platter 183

Crab BLT Dip and Crostini 185

Cheesy Cranberry Pull-Apart Bread 187

Honey Mustard Spiral Ham with Sweet-and-Spicy Carrots 189

Meatball Parmesan al Forno 192

Parmesan-Crusted Beef with Bacon Potatoes 194

New England Hot Dish 196

Roasted Leg of Lamb with Vegetable Medley 198

Salt-Brined Turkey Breast with Quinoa Stuffing 201

Shellfish Newburg Casserole 203

Corn Bread, Sausage, and Pear Stuffing 205

Roasted Carrots with Honey and Dill Butter 207

Heirloom Tomato Pie 209

Salt Potatoes 211

Thanksgiving Side Dishes 212

Sweet Potato Casserole 214

Cauliflower Gratin 216

Root Vegetables and Potatoes au Gratin 218

Liz's Spoon Bread 220

Sheet Pan Pies, Two Ways 222

Sweet-and-Spicy Candied Nuts

SERVES 6 TO 8

These nuts are a Christmas staple in my household. They are great on a salad, added to a cheese board, or just in a bowl put out for people to munch on. Fair warning: these will go fast so you might want to roast a double batch and keep a tray for yourself. —Craig White

DAIRY-FREE, GLUTEN-FREE, 30 MINUTES OR LESS, VEGAN

PREP TIME: 5 minutes
COOK TIME: 23 minutes

FUNCTION: Air Roast
TEMPERATURE: 350°F

ACCESSORIES: Ninja Sheet Pan

SUBSTITUTION: If you don't have herbes de Provence, you can use dried thyme, basil, or rosemary. The dried herbs are a big flavor pop in this recipe, but if you aren't a big fan of these flavors, you can leave them out.

1 cup pecans
1 cup walnuts
1 cup almonds
¼ cup maple syrup
¼ cup granulated sugar
2 tablespoons light brown sugar
¼ teaspoon cayenne pepper
1 tablespoon dried herbes de Provence
1 teaspoon kosher salt

1. In a large bowl, mix together the pecans, walnuts, almonds, maple syrup, granulated sugar, brown sugar, cayenne pepper, herbes de Provence, and salt until well combined and the nuts are coated.

2. Line the sheet pan with parchment paper. Pour the nuts onto the pan and spread them into an even layer.

3. Install a wire rack on Level 3. Select AIR ROAST, set the temperature to 350ºF, and set the time to 23 minutes. Press START/STOP to begin preheating.

4. When the unit has preheated, place the sheet pan on the wire rack. Close the oven door to begin cooking.

5. Every 8 minutes through the cooking time, open the oven door and stir the nuts. When cooking is complete, remove the nuts from the oven and let cool completely.

Per serving: Calories: 429; Total Fat: 35g; Saturated Fat: 3g; Cholesterol: 0mg; Sodium: 197mg; Carbohydrates: 27g; Fiber: 6g; Protein: 9g

Party Snack Mix

SERVES 16

Every Christmas my grandma and I would make this delicious party snack by the gallons. It's so simple and satisfying; mix, bake, and you can check one item off the list when you're entertaining. Short on time? Make up to 1 week ahead and store in an airtight container until you're ready to enjoy. Leftovers are perfect for lunchboxes and movie nights. —Kelly Gray

PREP TIME: 10 minutes
COOK TIME: 45 minutes

FUNCTIONS: Bake
TEMPERATURE: 315°F

ACCESSORIES: 2 Ninja Sheet Pans

VARIATION: Customize your snack mix by using different snacks, cereals, and seasonings.

3 cups whole-wheat cereal

3 cups corn cereal

3 cups rice cereal

1 cup pretzel sticks

1 cup bagel chips

1 cup lightly salted roasted peanuts

1 cup cheese crackers

8 tablespoons (1 stick) unsalted butter, melted

3 tablespoons Worcestershire sauce

2 teaspoons seasoned salt

1 teaspoon garlic powder

1. In a large bowl, combine the whole-wheat cereal, corn cereal, rice cereal, pretzel sticks, bagel chips, peanuts, and cheese crackers.

2. In a small bowl, mix together the melted butter, Worcestershire sauce, salt, and garlic powder. Pour the mixture over the dry ingredients and mix until they are thoroughly coated.

3. Divide the mixture between the two sheet pans, spreading it into an even layer.

4. Install the wire racks on Levels 1 and 3. Select BAKE, set the temperature to 315ºF, and set the time to 45 minutes. Press START/STOP to begin preheating.

5. When the unit has preheated, place the sheet pans on the wire racks. Close the oven door to begin cooking.

CONTINUED ▶

6. When there are 23 minutes remaining, remove the pans from the oven and place on trivets or a wooden cutting board. Stir the contents of each pan and spread each back into an even layer. Return the pans to the oven and continue cooking for the remaining 23 minutes, or until the party mix is slightly toasted and fragrant.

7. When cooking is complete, remove the pans from the oven and let the mix cool completely.

Per serving: *Calories: 201; Total Fat: 11g; Saturated Fat: 5g; Cholesterol: 15mg; Sodium: 288mg; Carbohydrates: 21g; Fiber: 1g; Protein: 5g*

Mediterranean Veggie Platter

SERVES 8

Elevate the boring old vegetable tray at your next party, picnic, or potluck with a delicious Mediterranean twist. Curried roasted vegetables, warm pitas, and creamy toasted feta cheese will have everyone thinking you put a lot of hard work into what is actually a simple appetizer. Premade Greek dolmas and olive tapenade are an easy addition to this platter, making it a well-rounded pleasure for the palate. —Kelly Gray

---

NUT-FREE, VEGETARIAN

PREP TIME: 20 minutes
COOK TIME: 20 minutes

FUNCTION: Air Fry
TEMPERATURE: 400°F

ACCESSORIES: Air Fry Basket, Ninja Sheet Pan

PERFECT PARTNER: Pair this with Spanakopita Star (page 67) next time you're entertaining.

---

1 head cauliflower, cut into 1-inch florets

1 bunch asparagus, woody ends trimmed

5 baby bell peppers, halved and seeded

1 tablespoon curry powder

1 tablespoon canola oil

Kosher salt and freshly ground black pepper, to taste

1 (5-ounce) block feta cheese

5 pitas, quartered

1 (8-ounce) can Greek dolmas (stuffed grape leaves)

1 (6-ounce) jar olive tapenade

Chopped fresh parsley, for garnish

1. In a large bowl, combine the cauliflower, asparagus, bell peppers, curry powder, canola oil, salt, and black pepper. Toss to coat the vegetables. Arrange the mixture in the air fryer basket.

2. Place the block of feta on the sheet pan.

3. Install a wire rack on Level 1. Select AIR FRY, select 2 LEVEL, set the temperature to 400ºF, and set the time to 20 minutes. Press START/STOP to begin preheating.

4. When the unit has preheated, place the sheet pan on the wire rack and insert the air fryer basket on Level 3.

CONTINUED ▶

5. After 10 minutes, remove the sheet pan and add the pita quarters to it. Remove the basket and move the wire rack to Level 3. Insert the air fryer basket on Level 1 and place the sheet pan on the wire rack. Close the oven door to continue cooking.

6. When cooking is complete, the feta should be brown and the inside soft and spreadable. Place the feta on a platter and top with the tapenade. Arrange the warm vegetables, dolmas, and pitas around it. Garnish the vegetables with parsley before serving.

Per serving: Calories: 189; Total Fat: 9g; Saturated Fat: 3g; Cholesterol: 16mg; Sodium: 473mg; Carbohydrates: 23g; Fiber: 7g; Protein: 8g

Crab BLT Dip and Crostini

SERVES 6 TO 8

When it comes to hosting, there is nothing better than putting out a delicious, warm dip for guests to help themselves to. Truth be told, if you make a delicious dip like this one and you invite me over, you will more than likely find me holding court next to said dip. Station it next to the punch bowl and I may never leave. This recipe is a combination of one of my favorite sandwiches (BLT) and one of my favorite dips (crab dip). I cannot stress enough how addictively good this is. I suggest making two! —Chelven Randolph

30 MINUTES OR LESS, NUT-FREE

PREP TIME: 10 minutes
COOK TIME: 20 minutes

FUNCTION: Bake
TEMPERATURE: 375°F

ACCESSORIES: Ninja Casserole Dish (9 by 13 inches), Ninja Sheet Pan

MAKE AHEAD: This recipe is perfect to prepare the day before and store in the refrigerator until ready to cook. Just follow step 1, then cover the dish with plastic wrap and refrigerate. The next day, proceed from step 2.

1 pound lump crabmeat

1 pound whipped cream cheese

1 cup mayonnaise

½ teaspoon onion powder

½ teaspoon smoked paprika

1 cup thinly sliced scallions, white and green parts

2 cups shredded Monterey Jack cheese, divided

2 tablespoons canola oil

1 loaf French bread, thinly sliced

10 bacon slices, cooked until crisp, crumbled (about 1 cup)

1 cup shredded iceberg lettuce

1 cup diced tomatoes

1. In a large bowl, mix together the crabmeat, cream cheese, mayonnaise, onion powder, paprika, scallions, and 1 cup of shredded cheese until well combined. Evenly spread the mixture on the bottom of the casserole dish. Top with the remaining 1 cup of cheese.

2. Lightly brush the oil on one side of the bread slices. Arrange the bread in a single layer on the sheet pan, oil-side up.

CONTINUED ▶

3. Install the wire racks on Level 1 and 3. Select BAKE, select 2 LEVEL, set the temperature to 375ºF, and set the time to 20 minutes. Press START/STOP to begin preheating.

4. When the unit has preheated, place the casserole dish on the Level 1 wire rack and the sheet pan on the Level 3 wire rack. Close the oven door to begin cooking.

5. After 10 minutes, remove the sheet pan. Close the oven door and continue cooking the dip.

6. When cooking is complete, top the dip with the crumbled bacon, lettuce, and tomatoes. Serve alongside the toasted bread. Serve immediately.

Per serving: Calories: 982; Total Fat: 71g; Saturated Fat: 25g; Cholesterol: 185mg; Sodium: 1342mg; Carbohydrates: 45g; Fiber: 3g; Protein: 40g

Cheesy Cranberry Pull-Apart Bread

SERVES 16

This is a simple yet delicious appetizer that would be great for your next holiday party. Who doesn't love bread that's been doused in butter, stuffed full with cheese and cranberry sauce, and baked until the cheese is super-soft and melty and the bread is nice and crunchy? Because the bread is cut before cooking, once it has baked all you have to do is chuck it on a plate and let your guests devour it while it's still warm. It's really the perfect handheld bite. —Caroline Schliep

30 MINUTES OR LESS, NUT-FREE, VEGETARIAN

PREP TIME: 10 minutes
COOK TIME: 20 minutes

FUNCTION: Whole Roast
TEMPERATURE: 350°F

ACCESSORY: Ninja Sheet Pan

VARIATION: For a pizza pull-apart loaf, exchange the Brie for mozzarella, the rosemary for oregano and basil, and the cranberry sauce for marinara and add your favorite toppings, like Italian sausage or pepperoni.

1 (20-ounce) loaf oval sourdough bread

12 tablespoons (1½ sticks) butter, melted

2 tablespoons minced fresh rosemary

2 tablespoons minced fresh parsley

2 tablespoons minced garlic

2 (15-ounce) can whole-berry cranberry sauce

2 (8-ounce) wheel Brie cheese, cut into ¼-inch slices

½ cup shredded Parmesan cheese

1. Using a serrated knife, cut a 1-inch square grid pattern into the loaf, leaving the bottom ½ inch of the loaf uncut. Put it on a sheet of foil.

2. In a small bowl, mix together the melted butter, rosemary, parsley, and garlic. Using a silicone brush, brush the bread with the butter mixture, making sure to get in between every piece.

3. Stuff the buttered bread with the cranberry sauce and Brie slices and sprinkle with the Parmesan. Loosely wrap the bread in foil. Place it on the sheet pan.

CONTINUED ▶

4. Install a wire rack on Level 4. Select WHOLE ROAST, set the temperature to 350°F, and set the time to 20 minutes. Press START/STOP to begin preheating.

5. When the unit has preheated, place the sheet pan on the wire rack. Close the oven door to begin cooking.

6. After 10 minutes, remove the pan from the oven and remove the foil. Return the sheet pan to the oven and continue cooking for the remaining 10 minutes.

7. When cooking is complete, the cheese should be melty and the bread toasted and golden brown. Serve warm.

Per serving: Calories: 363; Total Fat: 18g; Saturated Fat: 11g; Cholesterol: 54mg; Sodium: 532mg; Carbohydrates: 40g; Fiber: 1g; Protein: 11g

Honey Mustard Spiral Ham with Sweet-and-Spicy Carrots

SERVES 8

My Aunt Dee is known for making a ham for most holidays—Christmas, Easter, you name it (besides Thanksgiving, of course!). She loves to take advantage of the points from her local supermarket to get a free spiral-cut ham. This type of ham is great because it is fully cooked and presliced, making it super convenient. Naturally, it makes for great sandwiches the day after, as well.
—Melissa Celli

DAIRY-FREE, GLUTEN-FREE, NUT FREE

PREP TIME: 20 minutes
COOK TIME: 1 hour 20 minutes

FUNCTION: Air Roast
TEMPERATURE: 325°F, 300°F

ACCESSORIES: Ninja Casserole Dish (9 by 13 inches)

SUBSTITUTION: If the ham did not come with a glaze packet, whisk together 1 cup brown sugar, ½ cup freshly squeezed orange juice, ¼ cup honey, and ¼ cup Dijon mustard. Use this mixture in place of the glaze packet in step 4.

1 (7- to 10-pound) spiral-cut ham with glaze packet (see Substitution tip)

3 tablespoons freshly squeezed orange juice

½ teaspoon ground cayenne pepper

¼ teaspoon ground ginger

1 teaspoon kosher salt

2 (12-ounce) bags baby carrots

2 tablespoons Dijon mustard

2 tablespoons whole-grain mustard

¼ cup water

1. Install a wire rack on Level 1. Select AIR ROAST, set the temperature to 325°F, and set the time to 1 hour 20 minutes. Press START/STOP to begin preheating.

2. Remove the ham from its packaging (set the glaze packet aside) and place the ham sliced-side up in the casserole dish.

3. When the unit has preheated, place the casserole dish on the wire rack. Close the oven door to begin cooking.

CONTINUED ▶

4. Meanwhile, in a medium bowl, combine the contents of the glaze packet with the orange juice and whisk until combined. Remove ½ cup of the glaze and set aside. Add the cayenne, ginger, and salt to the glaze in the bowl and stir to combine. Add the carrots and toss to coat in the glaze.

5. When there are 50 minutes remaining, remove the dish from the oven. Arrange the carrots on the pan around the ham. Place the casserole dish back on the wire rack and continue cooking.

6. To the reserved glaze, whisk in the Dijon mustard, whole-grain mustard, and water.

7. When there are 30 minutes remaining, remove the ham from the oven and drizzle the mustard glaze over the top, making sure to get in between the slices.

8. Reduce the oven temperature to 300°F, place the ham back in the oven, and continue cooking for the remaining time.

9. When cooking is complete, remove the ham from the oven and let cool for 5 to 10 minutes. Use a slotted spoon to remove the carrots from the dish. Slice the ham and serve it along with the carrots.

Per serving: Calories: 547; Total Fat: 23g; Saturated Fat: 7g; Cholesterol: 226mg; Sodium: 3212mg; Carbohydrates: 13g; Fiber: 3g; Protein: 74g

Meatball Parmesan al Forno

SERVES 6 TO 8

The best meatballs I have ever had were from a restaurant I worked at in West Hollywood called Mozza. The recipe and method were so simple, I still don't understand how they were that amazing. Al forno just means that the meatballs have been baked in an oven. (Chefs are great at making things sound fancier than they are.) This dish is a nod to Nancy at Mozza and to one of my favorite sandwiches, the meatball sub. No party is complete without meatballs, and these meatballs are sure to be a crowd-pleaser. —Craig White

NUT-FREE

PREP TIME: 20 minutes
COOK TIME: 35 minutes

FUNCTION:
Air Roast, Broil
TEMPERATURE: 400°F, HI

ACCESSORIES: Ninja Casserole Dish (9 by 13 inches), Ninja Roast Tray, Ninja Sheet Pan

SUBSTITUTION: You can use lean ground beef, chicken, or turkey if you can't find meat loaf mix or want to make the recipe a little leaner.

- ½ cup Italian-style bread crumbs
- ¼ cup whole milk
- 2 pounds ground meat loaf mix (ground beef, pork, and veal)
- 1½ cups grated Parmesan cheese, divided
- 2 large eggs, beaten
- 1 teaspoon garlic powder
- 1 teaspoon red pepper flakes
- 1 tablespoon Italian seasoning
- Kosher salt and freshly ground black pepper, to taste
- 1 (24-ounce) jar marinara sauce
- ½ cup beef stock
- 8 ounces mozzarella cheese
- Fresh basil leaves, torn, for garnish

1. In a large bowl, stir together the bread crumbs and milk and let sit for 5 minutes.

2. After the bread crumbs and milk have sat for 5 minutes, add the meat loaf mix, ¾ cup of Parmesan, the eggs, garlic powder, red pepper flakes, Italian seasoning, salt, and pepper to the bowl. Mix well to thoroughly combine.

3. Using a ¼-cup measure, fill it with the meat loaf mixture, then roll it into balls. Place the meatballs on the roast tray nested in a sheet pan.

4. Install a wire rack on Level 3. Select AIR ROAST, set the temperature to 400ºF, and set the time to 30 minutes. Press START/STOP to begin preheating.

5. When the unit has preheated, place the sheet pan and roast tray on the wire rack. Close the oven door to begin cooking.

6. Meanwhile, combine the marinara sauce and beef stock in the casserole dish.

7. After 15 minutes, remove the sheet pan and roast tray from the oven and place the meatballs, browned-side down, in the sauce in the casserole dish. Place the casserole dish on the wire rack and continue cooking.

8. When cooking is complete, remove the dish and sprinkle the meatballs with the mozzarella and remaining ½ cup of Parmesan.

9. Select BROIL, set the temperature to HI, and set the time to 5 minutes. Press START/STOP to begin.

10. Place the casserole dish on the wire rack and broil until the cheese is melted and starting to brown. Garnish with the basil before serving.

Per serving: Calories: 579; Total Fat: 33g; Saturated Fat: 15g; Cholesterol: 213mg; Sodium: 1245mg; Carbohydrates: 18g; Fiber: 2g; Protein: 51g

Parmesan-Crusted Beef with Bacon Potatoes

SERVES 8

This recipe reminds me of my Great-Aunt Ginny. She was basically the Down East Maine version of Julia Child. One of my fondest childhood food memories was going over to her house for family gatherings and getting a spoonful of molasses as a treat. She'd use the prospect of molasses as leverage for my good behavior, rewarding me with the sugary treat only as I was practically on my way out the door to go home. —Sam Ferguson

NUT-FREE

PREP TIME: 15 minutes
COOK TIME: 55 minutes

FUNCTION: Air Roast
TEMPERATURE: 400°F, 360°F

ACCESSORIES: Air Fry Basket, Ninja Roast Tray, Ninja Sheet Pan

PREP TIP: The fastest and most effective way to remove rosemary leaves from the stem is to hold the stem at the top with one hand, place your thumb and index finger of your other hand just below the top, and then pull downward with medium force. This will remove most or all leaves from the stem in mere seconds.

1 (4-pound) beef roast (whole tenderloin or sirloin roast)

8 tablespoons (½ cup) canola oil, divided

Kosher salt and freshly ground black pepper, to taste

3 pounds fingerling or baby red potatoes, halved

8 bacon slices, cut into ½-inch pieces

1 cup grated Parmesan cheese

1 cup plain bread crumbs

¼ cup chopped fresh parsley

2 tablespoons chopped fresh rosemary

1. Place the beef roast on the roast tray nested in a sheet pan. Pour 2 tablespoons of canola oil on the roast and rub it evenly all over the meat. Season the beef with salt and pepper.

2. Install a wire rack on Level 1. Select AIR ROAST, set the temperature to 400°F, and set the time to 55 minutes. Press START/STOP to begin preheating.

3. When the unit has preheated, place the sheet pan and roast tray on the wire rack. Close the oven door to begin cooking.

4. Meanwhile, in a large bowl, combine the potatoes, bacon, 2 tablespoons of canola oil, salt, and pepper. Mix well to coat the potatoes.

5. In a medium bowl, combine the Parmesan, bread crumbs, remaining 4 tablespoons of canola oil, the parsley, rosemary, salt, and pepper. Mix well to combine.

6. When there are 35 minutes remaining, remove the sheet pan and roast tray from the oven. Carefully pack the bread crumb mixture on the top and sides of the beef. Transfer the potatoes to the air fryer basket.

7. Place the sheet pan and roast tray back on the wire rack, and insert the air fryer basket on Level 3. Set the temperature to 360°F, and close the oven door to continue cooking.

8. When cooking is complete, remove the beef from the oven and let it rest for up to 10 minutes. Leave the potatoes in the oven to stay warm while the beef rests. After 10 minutes, slice the beef and serve with the potatoes.

Per serving: *Calories: 714; Total Fat: 37g; Saturated Fat: 10g; Cholesterol: 169mg; Sodium: 597mg; Carbohydrates: 32g; Fiber: 3g; Protein: 61g*

New England Hot Dish

SERVES 20

If you're from the Midwest, I'm sorry for stealing your comfort food. But this recipe is so warming and satisfying that I now consider New England Hot Dish a Yankee staple. I wanted to develop a recipe that would resonate with our midwestern community but still maintain a uniquely New England identity. Baked beans and clam chowder in the same dish? You never thought you'd love it (you will, please trust me). —Sam Ferguson

NUT-FREE

PREP TIME: 15 minutes
COOK TIME: 55 minutes

FUNCTION: Air Roast
TEMPERATURE: 375°F

ACCESSORIES: 2 Ninja Casserole Dishes (9 by 13 inches)

PREP TIP: This recipe makes a *lot* of food. To yield only one casserole (easily plenty for 6 people), cut all the ingredients in half.

VARIATION: If you want to top these with cheese (good idea), add 1 cup of shredded cheese of your choice to the top of each casserole dish for the last 10 minutes of cooking.

- **4 pounds 90% lean ground beef, divided**
- **2 teaspoons onion powder, divided**
- **2 teaspoons garlic powder, divided**
- **Kosher salt and freshly ground black pepper, to taste**
- **2 (16-ounce) cans Boston baked beans, divided**
- **2 (16-ounce) bags frozen mixed vegetables, divided**
- **2 (28-ounce) cans New England clam chowder, divided**
- **2 pounds frozen tater tots, divided**
- **2 (12-ounce) packages frozen clam strips, divided**

1. Place 2 pounds of ground beef in each casserole dish and press into an even layer to cover the bottom of the dish. Season the meat in each dish with 1 teaspoon of onion powder, 1 teaspoon of garlic powder, salt, and pepper.

2. Install the wire racks on Levels 1 and 3. Select AIR ROAST, select 2 LEVEL, set the temperature to 375ºF, and set the time to 55 minutes. Press START/STOP to begin preheating.

3. When the unit has preheated, place a casserole dish on each wire rack. Close the oven door to begin cooking.

4. When there are 40 minutes remaining, remove the casserole dishes from the oven.

5. Evenly pour 1 can of baked beans over the top of the ground beef in one casserole dish. In a medium bowl, stir 1 bag of frozen vegetables together with 1 can of clam chowder, then use a spatula to spread the mixture evenly over the baked beans. Place 1 pound of tater tots and 1 package of clam strips on top of the vegetables, ensuring they are evenly spread out. Repeat for the other casserole.

6. Place the casserole dishes back on the wire racks and close the oven door to resume cooking.

7. When cooking is complete, remove the casserole dishes from the oven and serve.

Per serving: *Calories: 393; Total Fat: 12g; Saturated Fat: 5g; Cholesterol: 87mg; Sodium: 865mg; Carbohydrates: 35g; Fiber: 6g; Protein: 34g*

Roasted Leg of Lamb with Vegetable Medley

SERVES 8 TO 10

Leg of lamb is one of my favorite meat cuts as you can marinate it to your liking. Traditionally, I'm a fan of the classic garlic-and-rosemary combination, which I've included in this recipe. Paired with vegetables, the Ninja® Foodi™ XL Pro Air Oven gives you a complete meal for a large family gathering or your next dinner party. —Meg Jordan

GLUTEN-FREE, NUT-FREE

PREP TIME: 20 minutes, plus 1 hour to marinate
COOK TIME: 1 hour

FUNCTIONS: Whole Roast
TEMPERATURE: 400°F

ACCESSORIES: Air Fry Basket, Ninja Roast Tray, Ninja Sheet Pan

- 12 garlic cloves
- 3 tablespoons fresh rosemary
- ¼ cup chicken stock, plus more as needed
- 4 tablespoons (½ stick) unsalted butter, melted
- 2 teaspoons kosher salt, divided
- 2 teaspoons freshly ground black pepper, divided
- 1 (3-pound) bone-in leg of lamb
- 2 tablespoons canola oil
- 3 carrots, cut into 1-inch pieces
- 2 medium yellow onions, cut into 1-inch pieces
- 8 ounces Brussels sprouts, stems trimmed, halved lengthwise

1. In a blender or food processor, combine the garlic, rosemary, chicken stock, melted butter, 1 teaspoon of salt, and 1 teaspoon of pepper. Blend until a paste forms. If it is too thick, add a little more stock.

2. Place the lamb on a cutting board and season with the garlic mixture. Refrigerate the lamb for 1 hour to marinate.

3. Meanwhile, in a large bowl, drizzle the canola oil over the carrots, onions, and Brussels sprouts and season with the remaining 1 teaspoon salt and 1 teaspoon of pepper. Toss to coat the vegetables. Place the vegetables in the air fryer basket in a single layer.

4. Once the lamb has marinated, install a wire rack on Level 1. Select WHOLE ROAST, select 2 LEVEL, set the temperature to 400ºF, and set the time to 60 minutes. Press START/STOP to begin preheating.

5. When the unit has preheated, place the lamb on the roast tray nested into a sheet pan and place on the wire rack. Insert the air fryer basket on Level 4. Close the oven door to begin cooking.

6. Cooking is complete when an instant-read thermometer inserted into the lamb reads 130ºF to 140ºF (for medium-rare). Remove the lamb and vegetables from the oven. Let the lamb rest at least 10 minutes before slicing and serving alongside the roasted vegetables.

Per serving: *Calories: 341; Total Fat: 24g; Saturated Fat: 10g; Cholesterol: 82mg; Sodium: 236mg; Carbohydrates: 8g; Fiber: 2g; Protein: 22g*

Salt-Brined Turkey Breast with Quinoa Stuffing

SERVES 6 TO 8

I love a good ol' Thanksgiving-inspired meal any time of year. To me, it is so reminiscent of quality time spent with friends and family. It takes a lot of prep to cook a whole turkey, though, and who wants to do that in the middle of spring? You could substitute a whole chicken, but for this recipe, I use the whole turkey breast you can find in your local grocer's meat or freezer section. If you are making this recipe, give yourself enough lead time, as the dry brine will take a few days to absorb all the flavors. —Chelven Randolph

DAIRY-FREE, NUT-FREE

PREP TIME: 20 minutes, plus 3 days to brine
COOK TIME: 1 hour 20 minutes

FUNCTION: Whole Roast
TEMPERATURE: 425°F, 375°F

ACCESSORIES: Ninja Roast Tray, Ninja Sheet Pan, 9-inch square casserole dish

SUBSTITUTION: Butternut squash is a great substitute for the sweet potatoes in this dish and does not require any changes to the cook time. Try folding diced apples into the stuffing, as well.

2 tablespoons kosher salt

1 tablespoon sugar

1 teaspoon dried sage, divided

1 (5-pound) turkey breast

2 cups cooked quinoa

2 cups cubed peeled sweet potatoes (1-inch cubes)

½ cup dried cranberries

3 cups chicken stock

1 tablespoon chopped fresh rosemary

1 tablespoon chopped fresh thyme

1. In small bowl, combine the salt, sugar, and 1 teaspoon of sage. Rub this all over the turkey breast, then place the turkey in a resealable bag. Refrigerate for 3 days, flipping over the bag once a day.

2. When ready to cook, remove the turkey from the bag and pat it dry with paper towels. Place the turkey on the roast tray and nest the roast tray in the sheet pan. Let the turkey sit at room temperature while you prepare the stuffing.

3. In a casserole dish, combine the quinoa, sweet potatoes, cranberries, chicken stock, rosemary, and thyme. Stir well and cover the dish with foil.

CONTINUED ▶

4. Install a wire rack on Level 1. Select WHOLE ROAST, set the temperature to 425°F, and set the time to 20 minutes. Press START/STOP to begin preheating.

5. When the unit has preheated, place the sheet pan with the turkey on the wire rack. Close the oven door to begin cooking.

6. After 20 minutes, install another wire rack on Level 3 and place the casserole dish on it. Close the oven door. Select WHOLE ROAST, select 2 LEVEL, set the temperature to 375°F, and set the time to 60 minutes. Press START/STOP to begin cooking.

7. When cooking is complete, remove the turkey and quinoa stuffing. Uncover the quinoa and fluff it with a fork. An instant-read thermometer inserted into the turkey should read 165°F. Loosely cover the turkey with foil and let it rest for about 10 minutes. Slice and serve alongside the stuffing.

Per serving: Calories: 316; Total Fat: 10g; Saturated Fat: 3g; Cholesterol: 79mg; Sodium: 740mg; Carbohydrates: 26g; Fiber: 3g; Protein: 30g

Shellfish Newburg Casserole

SERVES 6 TO 8

When I was growing up on the coast of Maine, lobster was typically steamed and then served in the shell with drawn butter. Lobster Newburg is a higher-brow way to prepare it—picked lobster meat simmered in a delicate cream sauce, usually served on toast points. Here, I'm inspired by that fancy dish, but take a casual approach. If you have a shellfish that you particularly love, go ahead and sub it in for one of the seafood ingredients listed. —Sam Ferguson

NUT-FREE

PREP TIME: 10 minutes
COOK TIME: 40 minutes

FUNCTION: Bake
TEMPERATURE: 360°F

ACCESSORIES: Ninja Casserole Dish (9 by 13 inches)

PREP TIP: Don't forget to remove the small side muscle from the scallops. This is the little muscle that connects the bivalve to its shell. Once cooked, this piece becomes tough and chewy—so be sure to pull it off each scallop before cooking.

PERFECT PARTNER: Pair this dish with Succotash (page 171) or Heirloom Tomato Pie (page 209).

- 2 cups heavy cream
- 1 (8-ounce) package cream cheese, at room temperature
- ¼ cup dry sherry
- 2 teaspoons smoked paprika
- 2 (8-ounce) containers lump crabmeat
- 1 pound sea scallops
- 1 pound shrimp, peeled and deveined
- 8 ounces whitefish fillets, such as cod, cut into 2-inch pieces
- Kosher salt, to taste
- 4 large egg yolks
- Juice of 1 lemon
- 5 English muffins, torn into 2-inch pieces

1. In a large bowl, whisk together the cream, cream cheese, sherry, and paprika until smooth.

2. Add the crabmeat, scallops, shrimp, and fish, and season with salt. Mix well to combine. Pour the mixture into the casserole dish.

3. Install a wire rack on Level 3. Select BAKE, set the temperature to 360ºF, and set the time to 40 minutes. Press START/STOP to begin preheating.

4. When the unit has preheated, place the casserole dish on the wire rack. Close the oven door to begin cooking.

CONTINUED ▶

5. When there are 15 minutes remaining, remove the casserole dish from the oven. Stir the egg yolks and lemon juice into the casserole. Place the English muffin pieces on top, pushing down lightly to partially submerge the bread.

6. Return the casserole dish to the wire rack. Close the oven door to continue cooking.

7. When cooking is complete, let the casserole cool for 5 minutes before serving.

Per serving: Calories: 697; Total Fat: 42g; Saturated Fat: 24g; Cholesterol: 457mg; Sodium: 1356mg; Carbohydrates: 30g; Fiber: 3g; Protein: 48g

Corn Bread, Sausage, and Pear Stuffing

SERVES 10 TO 15

I brought this stuffing to a Friendsgiving hosted by a guy I was dating to try to impress him. I had attempted this stuffing before and reworked it a few times, and this version was the best. He had mentioned that he really loved a good corn bread stuffing, so I had this recipe up my sleeve. Well, it worked, as that guy is now my boyfriend! With the XL Pro Air Oven, you can make side dishes for your next party or holiday meal that will be sure to wow. —Meg Jordan

NUT-FREE

PREP TIME: 20 minutes
COOK TIME: 45 minutes

FUNCTION: Bake
TEMPERATURE: 350°F

ACCESSORIES: Ninja Casserole Dish (9 by 13 inches)

Unsalted butter, at room temperature, for greasing

2½ pounds prepared corn bread, cut into 1-inch cubes (about 13 cups)

1 medium yellow onion, diced

4 celery stalks, cut into ½-inch pieces

2 green pears, cored and cut into ½-inch pieces

1½ pounds precooked ground Italian sausage

6 garlic cloves, minced

2 tablespoons dried sage

2 large eggs, beaten

2 cups chicken broth, plus more as needed

Chopped fresh parsley, for garnish

1. Grease the casserole dish with butter and set aside.

2. In a large bowl, mix together the corn bread, onion, celery, pears, sausage, garlic, sage, eggs, and chicken broth until well incorporated. If the corn bread mixture feels very dry to the touch, slowly add in more chicken broth until it feels slightly wet. Transfer the corn bread mixture to the prepared casserole dish.

3. Install a wire rack on Level 3. Select BAKE, set the temperature to 350°F, and set the time to 45 minutes. Press START/STOP to begin preheating.

CONTINUED ▶

Corn Bread, Sausage, and Pear Stuffing continued

4. When the unit has preheated, place the casserole dish on the wire rack. Close the oven door to begin cooking.

5. When cooking is complete, the top of the corn bread will be golden brown. Remove the dish from the oven and let the stuffing cool for 10 minutes. Garnish with parsley and serve.

Per serving: *Calories: 586; Total Fat: 28g; Saturated Fat: 9g; Cholesterol: 122mg; Sodium: 1502mg; Carbohydrates: 61g; Fiber: 4g; Protein: 23g*

Roasted Carrots with Honey and Dill Butter

SERVES 4 TO 6

I didn't learn about flavored butters until culinary school. After that, my life changed! Butter itself is, in my opinion, a great fat to utilize in cooking. Add some herbs and spices to butter, and you can really take proteins and vegetables to another level. Carrots are my favorite vegetable, and for this recipe, I wanted to highlight the sweetness of the carrots with the honey and fresh flavor of dill. —Meg Jordan

---

30 MINUTES OR LESS, GLUTEN-FREE, NUT-FREE, VEGETARIAN

PREP TIME: 10 minutes
COOK TIME: 20 minutes

FUNCTION: Air Roast
TEMPERATURE: 400°F

ACCESSORIES: Ninja Sheet Pan

VARIATION: Flavored butters are so easy to make and can add a major punch of flavor to almost any dish. Try other herbs and spices, such as rosemary, thyme, or smoked paprika to create your own.

---

4 tablespoons (½ stick) unsalted butter, at room temperature

3 tablespoons chopped fresh dill

2 tablespoons honey

Kosher salt and freshly ground black pepper, to taste

2 pounds carrots, halved lengthwise

2 teaspoons canola oil

1. In a small bowl, mix together the butter, dill, honey, salt, and pepper.

2. In a large bowl, toss the carrots with the oil. Place the carrots on the sheet pan in an even layer.

3. Install a wire rack on Level 3. Select AIR ROAST, set the temperature to 400°F, and set the time to 20 minutes. Press START/STOP to begin preheating.

4. When the unit has preheated, place the sheet pan on the wire rack. Close the oven door to begin cooking.

5. After 10 minutes, open the oven and stir the carrots. Close the oven door to resume cooking.

6. When cooking is complete, remove the carrots from the oven, immediately toss them with the honey-dill butter, and serve.

Per serving: Calories: 247; Total Fat: 14g; Saturated Fat: 8g; Cholesterol: 31mg; Sodium: 197mg; Carbohydrates: 30g; Fiber: 6g; Protein: 2g

Heirloom Tomato Pie

SERVES 4 TO 6

This fresh summer dish—an ode to artist and author Susan Branch—has always been a staple at warm-weather barbeques. I love how baking the tomatoes brings out their natural sweetness, and the bread crumbs and Parmesan on top add a nice crust and texture. On particularly warm days, this layered dish can be cooled and served straight from the refrigerator. Pack it for a picnic or even spoon it over warm linguine for a warm pasta salad. There's nothing here that will spoil, and it transports well in its pan. —Kara Bleday

---

30 MINUTES OR LESS, NUT-FREE, VEGETARIAN

PREP TIME: 10 minutes
COOK TIME: 20 minutes

FUNCTION: Air Roast
TEMPERATURE: 450°F

ACCESSORIES: 8-inch square baking pan or pie plate

PREP TIP: This dish is best when made with fresh, tender, and colorful heirloom tomatoes. The natural sweetness of the tomatoes will complement the tender basil and tart balsamic vinegar. Choose heirloom tomatoes in a variety of colors; when you cut into the pie, they make for a beautiful layered presentation.

- **4 large ripe heirloom tomatoes**
- **4 tablespoons extra-virgin olive oil, divided**
- **2 roasted red peppers, seeded and sliced**
- **10 fresh basil leaves**
- **Kosher salt and freshly ground black pepper, to taste**
- **3 tablespoons balsamic vinegar, divided**
- **¼ cup panko bread crumbs**
- **¼ cup grated Parmesan cheese**

1. Slice the tomatoes ¼ to ½ inch thick. Set aside.

2. Drizzle 1 tablespoon of olive oil in the bottom of the baking pan.

3. Place an even layer of tomatoes—about one-third of the slices—on the bottom of the pan. Make sure the whole bottom is covered; overlapping is fine. Place half of the roasted red pepper slices over the tomatoes and top with a layer of 5 basil leaves. Season with salt and pepper and drizzle with 1 tablespoon of olive oil and 1 tablespoon of balsamic vinegar. Repeat with another layer of tomatoes, roasted red pepper, basil, salt, pepper, balsamic vinegar, and olive oil. Top the pie with the remaining one-third of tomato slices and remaining olive oil and balsamic vinegar. Drizzle with the remaining 1 tablespoon of vinegar and sprinkle the panko bread crumbs and Parmesan on top.

CONTINUED ▶

4. Install a wire rack on Level 3. Select AIR ROAST, set the temperature to 450ºF, and set the time to 20 minutes. Press START/STOP to begin preheating.

5. When the unit has preheated, place the sheet pan on the wire rack. Close the oven door to begin cooking.

6. When cooking is complete, remove the tomato pie from the oven. Serve warm or cooled.

Per serving: *Calories: 315; Total Fat: 26g; Saturated Fat: 3g; Cholesterol: 5mg; Sodium: 300mg; Carbohydrates: 17g; Fiber: 3g; Protein: 5g*

Salt Potatoes

SERVES 6

This side dish is as dramatic as it is delicious. The cut potatoes, roasted on a bed of kosher salt, are full of flavor inside and crispy outside. The salt bed provides a tender baking surface that allows airflow around the potatoes while seasoning them both inside and out. Though this is a great dish to make in the Ninja Sheet Pan, it's also possible to prepare the potatoes in a long and low ovenproof serving dish, making it a beautiful addition to the table. —Kara Bleday

5 INGREDIENTS OR LESS, DAIRY-FREE, GLUTEN-FREE, NUT-FREE, VEGAN

PREP TIME: 10 minutes
COOK TIME: 35 minutes

FUNCTION: Air Roast
TEMPERATURE: 450°F

ACCESSORIES: Ninja Sheet Pan

VARIATION: To add another layer (or three!) of flavor, nestle some whole herbs or aromatics among the potatoes and on top of the salt. Choose herbs based on the flavors you'll be using for the main dish: Sage, rosemary, whole garlic cloves, or thyme are always a great choice for potatoes.

2 pounds baby potatoes   2 cups kosher salt

1. Cut the potatoes in half or in quarters so that each piece is no bigger than 1½ inches.

2. Cover the bottom of the sheet pan with the salt in an even layer. Arrange the potatoes in an even layer on top of the salt.

3. Install a wire rack on Level 2. Select AIR ROAST, set the temperature to 450°F, and set the time to 35 minutes. Press START/STOP to begin preheating.

4. When the unit has preheated, place the sheet pan on the wire rack. Close the door to begin cooking.

5. When cooking is complete, remove the sheet pan from the oven and check for doneness. Cooking is complete when the potatoes are brown and crispy outside and soft and creamy inside.

Per serving: Calories: 116; Total Fat: 0g; Saturated Fat: 0g; Cholesterol: 0mg; Sodium: 376mg; Carbohydrates: 26g; Fiber: 3g; Protein: 3g

Thanksgiving Side Dishes

SERVES 4

Is there anything more stressful when you are entertaining than ensuring that the whole meal is ready at the same time? This was always a challenge at my house on Thanksgiving—we never had enough space in the oven to cook the turkey and sides. I developed this recipe to save your next Thanksgiving. While your bird is roasting in your regular oven, use the Ninja® Foodi™ XL Pro Air Oven to cook five sides at once! Say goodbye to spending the whole day in the kitchen and hello to dinner! —Kenzie Swanhart

NUT-FREE

PREP TIME: 30 minutes
COOK TIME: 16 minutes

FUNCTION: Air Roast
TEMPERATURE: 350°F

ACCESSORIES: 2 Ninja Sheet Pans

PREP TIP: When entertaining, do as much prep as possible in advance. The night before or morning of, chop the potatoes, dice the onion, measure out seasoning, and so on. It makes the actual cooking that much faster and leaves you more time to spend with your guests.

Cooking oil spray

1 (16.3-ounce) tube large biscuits (8 biscuits)

12 ounces frozen cranberries

½ cup granulated sugar

⅓ cup fresh orange juice

2 tablespoons cornstarch

1½ pounds (about 2 medium) sweet potatoes, peeled and chopped

¾ cup whole milk, divided

2 tablespoons unsalted butter, at room temperature

2 tablespoons light brown sugar

½ teaspoon vanilla extract

Kosher salt and freshly ground black pepper, to taste

1 (10.5-ounce) can cream of mushroom soup

1 teaspoon soy sauce

4 cups cooked cut green beans

2 Yukon Gold potatoes, sliced ⅛ inch thick

½ cup heavy cream

½ cup grated Parmesan cheese

1 small garlic clove, finely chopped

1 teaspoon chopped fresh thyme

½ cup mini marshmallows

⅓ cup crispy fried onions

¼ cup shredded Gruyère cheese

1. Lightly coat the sheet pans with cooking spray.

2. Arrange the biscuits down the middle of each sheet pan lengthwise, dividing each pan into two sections.

3. In a medium bowl, mix together the cranberries, granulated sugar, orange juice, and cornstarch, and set aside.

4. Put the sweet potatoes in a medium microwave-safe bowl and cover with plastic wrap. Microwave on high for about 12 minutes, or until soft. Add ¼ cup of milk, the butter, brown sugar, and vanilla. Season with salt and pepper. Mash the potatoes with a fork to combine and set aside.

5. In another medium bowl, combine the cream of mushroom soup, remaining ½ cup of milk, soy sauce, and green beans. Season with salt and pepper. Set aside.

6. In another medium microwave-safe bowl, place the Yukon Gold potatoes, cream, Parmesan, garlic, and thyme. Season with salt and pepper and stir to combine. Microwave on high for about 6 minutes, or until softened. Set aside.

7. Pour the cranberry mixture on one side of one of the sheet pans. Spread the sweet potatoes over the other side of the pan and sprinkle them with the marshmallows.

8. Pour the green bean mixture on one side of the other sheet pan and sprinkle them with the fried onions. Spread the Yukon Gold potato mixture over the other side of the pan and sprinkle with the Gruyère.

9. Install the wire racks on Levels 1 and 3. Select AIR ROAST, select 2 LEVEL, set the temperature to 350°F, and set the time to 16 minutes. Press START/STOP to begin preheating.

10. When the unit has preheated, place a sheet pan on each wire rack. Close the oven door to begin cooking.

11. When cooking is complete, the biscuits will be golden brown. Remove the pans from the oven and let the dishes cool for 5 minutes before serving.

Per serving: *Calories: 1155; Total Fat: 38g; Saturated Fat: 17g; Cholesterol: 72mg; Sodium: 1256mg; Carbohydrates: 184g; Fiber: 16g; Protein: 26g*

Sweet Potato Casserole

SERVES 8 TO 10

Sweet potato casserole is one of my all-time favorite Thanksgiving side dishes and should be passed around at everyone's table. It's one of those dishes that you wait to eat all year, and if you don't bring it to the family gathering, you have made a big mistake. I mean how can you go wrong when you mash sweet potatoes with brown sugar, butter, and cinnamon and top them with ooey-gooey marshmallows and crunchy pecans? There are never any leftovers of this dish. —Caroline Schliep

PREP TIME: 10 minutes
COOK TIME: 33 minutes

FUNCTION: Bake, Broil
TEMPERATURE: 400°F, HI

ACCESSORIES: Ninja Casserole Dish (9 by 13 inches), Ninja Sheet Pan

PREP TIP: Don't have room to cook your potatoes in the oven due to all your other holiday sides taking up space? Boil them on the stove instead and proceed from step 4.

3 pounds sweet potatoes, peeled and cut into 1-inch cubes

½ cup water

Kosher salt, to taste

1 cup packed light brown sugar

3 tablespoons butter, melted

1½ teaspoons ground cinnamon

1 cup hot milk

2 cups mini marshmallows

½ cup pecans, chopped

1. Divide the sweet potatoes between two large pieces of foil, placing them in the center. Pour the water over the potatoes and season with salt. Wrap the foil around the potatoes, creating two pouches, and seal tightly. Place the foil packets on the sheet pan.

2. Install a wire rack on Level 3. Select BAKE, set the temperature to 400°F, and set the time to 30 minutes. Press START/STOP to begin preheating.

3. When the unit has preheated, place the sheet pan on the wire rack. Close the oven door to begin cooking.

4. When cooking is complete, carefully transfer the potatoes to a large bowl. Add the brown sugar, butter, cinnamon, and milk. Use a fork or potato masher to mash the sweet potatoes to your desired consistency.

5. Transfer the potatoes to the casserole dish. Top them with the marshmallows and pecans.

6. Select BROIL, set the temperature to HI, and set the time to 3 minutes. Press START/STOP to begin.

7. Place the casserole dish on the wire rack and close the oven door to begin cooking.

8. Cooking is done when the marshmallows are golden brown. Remove the dish from the oven and let cool slightly before serving.

Per serving: Calories: 376; Total Fat: 10g; Saturated Fat: 4g; Cholesterol: 14mg; Sodium: 96mg; Carbohydrates: 70g; Fiber: 5g; Protein: 5g

Cauliflower Gratin

SERVES 6

I made this dish for a group of friends one wintery weekend night and was surprised at how much they all loved it. It was one of those meals where I didn't know what to make; I was mostly focused on roasting the perfect chicken, so when it came time for a vegetable side, I reached for the cauliflower and a little cream and cheese, and I pulled this dish out of my you-know-what.
—Sam Ferguson

NUT-FREE, VEGETARIAN

PREP TIME: 15 minutes
COOK TIME: 35 minutes

FUNCTION: Air Roast
TEMPERATURE: 360°F

ACCESSORIES: Ninja Sheet Pan

PERFECT PARTNER: This is a great companion to Parmesan-Crusted Beef with Bacon Potatoes (page 194). Cook this recipe first, then cover it with foil while the beef and potatoes cook. Then, while the beef is resting, throw this dish back into the oven for 5 or 10 minutes to reheat before serving.

1 cup whole milk

1½ cups heavy cream, divided

¼ cup cornstarch

1 (2-pound) head cauliflower, cut into 2-inch florets

Kosher salt and freshly ground black pepper, to taste

1 cup plain bread crumbs

1½ cups shredded Parmesan cheese, divided

1. Pour the milk and 1 cup of cream into a microwave-safe glass bowl. Cover the bowl with plastic wrap, then microwave on high for 3 minutes. Add the cornstarch and whisk well until slightly thickened.

2. In a large bowl, combine the cauliflower, salt, pepper, bread crumbs, and 1 cup of Parmesan. Pour in the warmed milk and cream, and toss well to mix everything together.

3. Transfer the mixture to the sheet pan and spread it out so it evenly covers the surface of the pan. Pour the remaining ½ cup of cream evenly over the top.

4. Install a wire rack on Level 3. Select AIR ROAST, set the temperature to 360°F, and set the time to 35 minutes. Press START/STOP to begin preheating.

5. When the unit has preheated, place the sheet pan on the wire rack. Close the oven door to begin cooking.

6. When there are 5 minutes remaining, sprinkle the remaining ½ cup of Parmesan over the top of the cauliflower, then close the oven door to resume cooking.

7. When cooking is complete, remove the cauliflower gratin from the oven and let cool for at least 5 minutes before serving.

Per serving: *Calories: 464; Total Fat: 32g; Saturated Fat: 19g; Cholesterol: 107mg; Sodium: 695mg; Carbohydrates: 32g; Fiber: 4g; Protein: 15g*

Root Vegetables and Potatoes au Gratin

SERVES 8

There is something classic about cheesy potatoes au gratin. I decided to kick it up a level and change the traditional dish by adding hearty root vegetables—sweet potatoes, carrots, and parsnips—as well as some fresh herbs. I especially love the nutty flavor Asiago cheese brings. If you have a mandoline, this is a great time to use it. —Melissa Celli

NUT-FREE, VEGETARIAN

PREP TIME: 20 minutes
COOK TIME: 1 hour 10 minutes

FUNCTION: Air Roast
TEMPERATURE: 360°F

ACCESSORIES: 8-inch baking dish

MAKE AHEAD: Slice the potatoes and vegetables ahead of time and store covered in cold water in the refrigerator for 1 to 2 days. Drain and pat dry when ready to use.

- 3 tablespoons unsalted butter
- 1 medium onion, diced
- 2 tablespoons chopped fresh rosemary, divided
- 2 tablespoons all-purpose flour
- 3 cups light cream
- 5 ounces Asiago cheese, grated, divided
- 2 cups shredded cheddar cheese, divided
- 2 cups shredded mozzarella cheese, divided
- Kosher salt and freshly ground black pepper, to taste
- 1 russet potato, peeled and sliced ⅛ inch thick
- 1 sweet potato, peeled and sliced ⅛ inch thick
- 3 large carrots, sliced ⅛ inch thick
- 3 large parsnips, peeled and sliced ⅛ inch thick
- ¼ cup chopped fresh chives

1. In a small saucepan over medium heat, melt the butter, then add the onion and sauté for about 5 minutes, or until translucent. Add 1 tablespoon of rosemary, then whisk in the flour. Continue whisking until a light brown paste forms (called a roux). Add the cream a little at a time, whisking to dissolve the roux into the cream before adding more.

2. Bring to a boil, then reduce to a simmer and add ½ cup of Asiago, whisking constantly. Then, ½ cup at a time until melted, add 1½ cups of cheddar and 1½ cups of mozzarella, whisking constantly to combine, ensuring nothing is stuck to the bottom of the pan. Season with salt and pepper. Remove the pan from the heat.

3. Ladle a little of the sauce on the bottom of the baking dish, swirling to coat it. Layer the russet potato, sweet potato, carrots, and parsnip slices in an overlapping pattern to cover the bottom of the dish. Ladle some cheese sauce over the vegetables, season with salt and pepper, and top with a sprinkling of rosemary. Repeat these layers until all the vegetables, cheese sauce, and rosemary have been used. Cover the dish with foil.

4. Install a wire rack on Level 3. Select AIR ROAST, set the temperature to 360°F, and set the time to 1 hour, 10 minutes. Press START/STOP to begin preheating.

5. When the unit has preheated, place the casserole dish on the wire rack. Close the oven door to begin cooking.

6. When there are 10 minutes remaining, remove the foil and top the vegetables with the remaining grated Asiago, remaining ½ cup of cheddar, and remaining ½ cup of mozzarella.

7. Continue cooking for another 8 to 10 minutes, until the cheese on top is golden brown.

8. When cooking is complete, remove the dish from the oven. Let cool slightly, then garnish with the chives and serve.

Per serving: Calories: 599; Total Fat: 43g; Saturated Fat: 25g; Cholesterol: 137mg; Sodium: 649mg; Carbohydrates: 33g; Fiber: 5g; Protein: 23g

Liz's Spoon Bread

SERVES 8

This recipe is one of my childhood favorites from time spent with family and friends so close they might as well be in Cape Cod. My second-mom, Liz, would always make this crowd-pleaser as a side dish though everyone consumed it like a main. Fluffy and moist with crispy, caramelized edges, this spoon bread can be enjoyed as leftovers for days. This twist on her classic recipe is an ode to Liz and all the shared laughter with everyone in beautiful Wellfleet. —Kelly Gray

---

GLUTEN-FREE, NUT-FREE, VEGETARIAN

PREP TIME: 20 minutes
COOK TIME: 30 to 35 minutes

FUNCTIONS: Bake
TEMPERATURE: 350°F

ACCESSORIES: 2-quart casserole dish

VARIATION: Customize your spoon bread by using whatever ingredients you have on hand. Like spice? Add diced jalapeños or green chiles.

Cooking oil spray

1 cup grated Parmesan cheese, divided

4 cups whole milk, divided

½ teaspoon kosher salt

1 cup yellow cornmeal

3 tablespoons unsalted butter

1 cup half-and-half

4 large eggs

1 bunch scallions, white and green parts, chopped

½ cup corn kernels

1. Coat the casserole dish with cooking spray. Sprinkle the bottom of the dish with 3 tablespoons of Parmesan and set aside.

2. In a medium saucepan over medium heat, heat 2 cups of milk and the salt until bubbles begin to form around the edges of the pan. Slowly sprinkle in the cornmeal, stirring occasionally.

3. Reduce the heat to low and cook until the mixture is smooth and creamy. Remove the pan from the heat and add the remaining ¾ cup and 1 tablespoon of Parmesan and the butter. Stir until well incorporated and the butter is melted. Let cool for 10 minutes.

4. After 10 minutes, combine the cornmeal mixture, the remaining 2 cups of milk, the half-and-half, and eggs in a blender. Blend for about 30 seconds, or until mixed and smooth. Add the scallions and corn, pulse a few times, and pour the mixture into the prepared casserole dish.

5. Install a wire rack on Level 2. Select BAKE, set the temperature to 350ºF, and set the time to 30 minutes. Press START/STOP to begin preheating.

6. When the unit has preheated, place the casserole dish on the wire rack. Close the oven door to begin cooking.

7. When the cooking is complete, the spoon bread should be puffy and golden on top. If necessary, cook for up to 5 minutes longer. Serve immediately.

Per serving: *Calories: 305; Total Fat: 18g; Saturated Fat: 10g; Cholesterol: 139mg; Sodium: 424mg; Carbohydrates: 23g; Fiber: 2g; Protein: 13g*

Sheet Pan Pies, Two Ways

SERVES 16

Hands down, my favorite thing about the Ninja® Foodi™ XL Pro Air Oven is the ability to cook on two levels at the same time without needing to fuss with the food. This is a huge advantage when it comes to entertaining and both time and oven space are at a premium. With this recipe, you get two for the price of one: two delicious yet simple pies cooked at once. These pies will make the perfect addition to any get-together, but I love them on Thanksgiving. In fact, you can prep the fillings in advance, assemble right before dinner, and let the pies cook while you eat. Then dessert is ready just in time! —Kenzie Swanhart

VEGETARIAN

PREP TIME: 45 minutes
COOK TIME: 45 minutes

FUNCTION: Bake
TEMPERATURE: 350°F

ACCESSORIES: 2 Ninja Sheet Pans

SUBSTITUTION: Turbinado sugar is partially refined sugar that has a golden color and a subtle caramel flavor. If you do not have turbinado sugar, you can replace it with 2 tablespoons brown sugar and 2 tablespoons granulated sugar.

Cooking oil spray

All-purpose flour, for dusting, plus 4 teaspoons

5 refrigerated rolled piecrusts

5 pounds apples, peeled, cored, and sliced ¼ inch thick

½ cup granulated sugar

4 teaspoons flour

2 tablespoons freshly squeezed lemon juice

1 cup (2 sticks) unsalted butter, melted, divided

1 tablespoon ground cinnamon

Kosher salt, to taste

1 cup packed light brown sugar

1 cup light corn syrup

2 teaspoons vanilla extract

5 large eggs, divided, 1 lightly beaten

1½ cups pecan halves, toasted

¼ cup turbinado sugar (see Substitution tip)

1. Lightly coat the sheet pans with cooking spray.

2. Lightly flour a clean work surface. Unroll 2 piecrusts and stack them on top of each other. Dust a rolling pin with flour and roll out the layered dough into a large rectangle. Place the dough on one of the sheet pans and gently press the crust into the pan so it comes up the sides and hangs over slightly. Repeat with 2 more piecrusts. Place both sheet pans in the refrigerator to chill until ready to use.

3. In a large bowl, combine the apples, granulated sugar, flour, lemon juice, ½ cup of melted butter, cinnamon, and a pinch of salt. Set aside.

4. In another large bowl, whisk together the brown sugar, corn syrup, remaining ½ cup of melted butter, vanilla, 4 eggs, and a pinch of salt until smooth. Fold in the pecans and set aside.

5. Remove both baking sheets from the refrigerator. Prick the crusts all over with a fork.

6. Fill one crust with the pecan filling and the other with the apple filling.

7. Unroll the remaining piecrust on a lightly floured work surface and roll it out into a large rectangle the size of a sheet pan. Place it on top of the apple filling.

8. Crimp the edges of both pies and brush the edges and top crust of the apple pie with the beaten egg. Sprinkle the apple pie crust with the turbinado sugar and cut decorative slits in the top crust.

9. Install the wire racks on Levels 1 and 3. Select BAKE, select 2 LEVEL, set the temperature to 350°F, and set the time to 45 minutes. Press START/STOP to begin preheating.

10. When the unit has preheated, place the sheet pans on the wire racks. Close the oven door to begin cooking.

11. Cooking is complete when both pies are set and the crust on the apple pie is golden brown. Let cool slightly before serving.

PERFECT PARTNER: Make Thanksgiving prep a little easier by pairing this recipe with Thanksgiving Side Dishes (page 212), and use your XL Pro Air Oven to cook most of the meal!

Per serving: Calories: 735; Total Fat: 38g; Saturated Fat: 15g; Cholesterol: 89mg; Sodium: 335mg; Carbohydrates: 98g; Fiber: 6g; Protein: 6g

Peanut Butter and Jelly Crumble Bars, *page 232*

10

Desserts

Salted Butter Pecan Cookies 226

Double Chocolate Chip Walnut Biscotti 228

Sheet Pan Cookie Bars, Two Ways 230

Peanut Butter and Jelly Crumble Bars 232

Sheet Pan Key Lime Pie Bars 235

Fudgy Layered Brownies 237

Hazelnut and Pretzel Brownies 239

Cookie and Candy Layer Cake 242

Razzleberry Hand Pies 244

Pumpkin-Spiced Latte Bread Pudding 247

Salted Butter Pecan Cookies

Can't decide if you want a sweet or salty snack? Now you don't have to—this recipe will solve both cravings. Rich butter cookies, with either melty butterscotch chips or crunchy toffee bits, topped with a pop of salt, are the perfect indulgence. With the Ninja® Foodi™ XL Pro Air Oven, these cookies are ready so quickly, you won't mind being asked to make them over and over, for a special occasion or just because it's 3 o'clock. —Kelly Gray

VEGETARIAN

PREP TIME: 25 minutes
COOK TIME: 10 minutes

FUNCTIONS: Bake
TEMPERATURE: 350°F

ACCESSORIES: 2 Ninja Sheet Pans

VARIATION: Truly anything goes with these cookies, so substitute using your favorite add-ins. Sometimes I substitute chocolate chips or use a blend of both chips and toffee bits.

- 1½ cups pecan halves
- 1⅓ cups granulated sugar, divided
- ⅓ cup packed dark brown sugar
- 12 tablespoons (1½ sticks) unsalted butter, at room temperature
- 1¾ teaspoons kosher salt, divided
- ½ teaspoon baking soda
- 1 tablespoon vanilla extract
- 1 large egg
- 2 cups all-purpose flour
- 1½ cups toffee bits or butterscotch chips

1. Spread the pecans in a single layer on the sheet pan.

2. Install a wire rack on Level 2. Select BAKE, set the temperature to 350°F, and set the time to 6 minutes. Press START/STOP to begin preheating.

3. When the unit has preheated, place the sheet pan on the wire rack. Close the oven door to begin cooking.

4. When cooking is complete, remove the pan from the oven. Let the pecans cool, then chop them.

5. In a large bowl, combine 1 cup of granulated sugar, the brown sugar, butter, ½ teaspoon of salt, the baking soda, and vanilla. Using a hand mixer or stand mixer, beat until smooth and creamy.

6. Add the egg and continue to beat until creamy and well incorporated. Scrape down the sides of the bowl with a spatula. Add the flour, toffee bits, and pecans. Mix until fully incorporated.

7. In a small bowl, combine the remaining ⅓ cup of granulated sugar and 1¼ teaspoons of salt.

8. Using a spoon, scoop 1- to 1½-inch dough balls. Roll each in the sugar-and-salt mixture, then place them on the sheet pans about 1 inch apart (about 12 cookies per pan). Gently press down on each dough ball to form 2-inch rounds.

9. Install the wire racks on Levels 1 and 3. Select BAKE, select 2 LEVEL, set the temperature to 350°F, and set the time to 10 minutes. Press START/STOP to begin preheating.

10. When the unit has preheated, place a sheet pan on each wire rack. Close the oven door to begin cooking.

11. Cooking is complete when the cookies are crisp and brown at the edges and soft in the center. Carefully remove the sheet pans and place on trivets for the cookies to cool before serving.

Per serving (1 cookie): Calories: 244; Total Fat: 13g; Saturated Fat: 5g; Cholesterol: 28mg; Sodium: 135mg; Carbohydrates: 31g; Fiber: 1g; Protein: 3g

Double Chocolate Chip Walnut Biscotti

MAKES 16 BISCOTTI

I have very fond memories of my grandmother dipping store-bought biscotti in her coffee in the mornings. All I could smell was the anise used in the biscotti. As I learned how to bake, I started making her my biscotti, and she eventually stopped buying them. She loved when I drizzled them with white chocolate—a way to jazz them up! —Melissa Celli

VEGETARIAN

PREP TIME: 10 minutes
COOK TIME: 45 minutes

FUNCTION: Bake
TEMPERATURE: 325°F

ACCESSORIES: 2 Ninja Sheet Pans

VARIATION: This recipe lends itself well to different variations. For orange-chocolate biscotti, omit the walnuts and add in the zest and juice of 1 orange with the vanilla and eggs. For white chocolate and cranberry biscotti, omit the walnuts and chocolate chips and add in ½ cup dried cranberries and 1 cup white chocolate chips.

1 cup sugar

8 tablespoons (1 stick) unsalted butter or margarine, at room temperature

1 teaspoon vanilla extract

2 large eggs

2½ cups all-purpose flour

3 tablespoons unsweetened cocoa powder

1 tablespoon baking powder

1 teaspoon kosher salt

1 cup mini semisweet chocolate chips

½ cup chopped walnuts

1. In large bowl, beat the sugar and butter with a hand mixer on medium speed, or mix with a spoon. Beat in the vanilla and eggs until smooth. Stir in the flour, cocoa powder, baking powder, and salt. Stir in the chocolate chips and walnuts.

2. Divide the dough between the sheet pans. Shape each dough half into a 10-by-3-inch rectangle.

3. Place the wire racks on Levels 1 and 3. Select BAKE, select 2 LEVEL, set the temperature to 325°F, and set the time to 45 minutes. Press START/STOP to begin preheating.

4. When the unit has preheated, place a sheet pan on each wire rack. Close the oven door to begin cooking.

5. When there are 20 minutes remaining, check to see that a toothpick inserted in the center of each rectangle comes out clean. Press START/STOP to pause cooking. Remove the sheet pans from the oven and let cool for 10 minutes.

6. Transfer the rectangles to a cutting board, and using a sharp knife, cut each crosswise into 8 equal slices. Place the slices cut-side down on the sheet pans. Place the sheet pans back on the wire racks and close the oven door. Press START/STOP to continue cooking.

7. Bake for about 10 minutes, or until golden brown and dry on top. Turn over the biscotti and bake for about 10 minutes longer, or until golden brown and dry. Remove the sheet pans from the oven and place on wire racks to cool.

Per serving (1 biscotto): Calories: 259; Total Fat: 12g; Saturated Fat: 6g; Cholesterol: 39mg; Sodium: 85mg; Carbohydrates: 36g; Fiber: 2g; Protein: 4g

Sheet Pan Cookie Bars, Two Ways

MAKES 24 BARS

One of my favorite ways to use a sheet pan is to do two tasks at once—you can make a sheet pan meal with a protein and veggies or even two desserts at once! In this recipe I am making two different-flavored cookie bars on one pan, but you can use this same method with a variety of desserts and sides (check out Thanksgiving Side Dishes, page 212). Cookie bars are a quick and fun dessert for any occasion, and I am sure these will become a staple in your house!
—Kenzie Swanhart

30 MINUTES OR LESS, VEGETARIAN

PREP TIME: 15 minutes
COOK TIME: 20 minutes

FUNCTION: Bake
TEMPERATURE: 350°F

ACCESSORIES: Ninja Sheet Pan

VARIATION: Switch up the flavor of these cookie bars by using different add-ins. Try candy-coated chocolate instead of chocolate chips, or add 2 tablespoons instant espresso powder with the butter. Or make a glaze by whisking together 1 cup powdered sugar, 2 tablespoons hot water, and ½ teaspoon vanilla to drizzle over the cooled bars.

- 1 cup (2 sticks) unsalted butter, at room temperature
- 1 cup firmly packed light brown sugar
- 1 cup granulated sugar
- 3 large eggs
- 1½ teaspoons vanilla extract
- ¾ teaspoon baking soda
- ¾ teaspoon kosher salt
- 3 cups all-purpose flour
- 1 cup chocolate chips
- 1 cup white chocolate chips
- 1 cup crushed salted macadamia nuts

1. Using a hand mixer or stand mixer, beat the butter, brown sugar, and granulated sugar until smooth. Add the eggs and vanilla and mix until well combined.

2. In a large bowl, stir the baking soda and salt into the flour. Slowly add the flour to the wet ingredients, mixing until just combined.

3. Transfer half of the dough to another large bowl. Fold the chocolate chips into the dough in one bowl and the white chocolate chips and macadamia nuts into the dough in the other bowl.

4. Line the sheet pan with parchment paper. Spread the chocolate chip cookie dough onto half of the sheet pan. Spread the white chocolate and macadamia dough on the other half of the pan. Use a spatula or your fingers to spread out each evenly.

5. Install a wire rack on Level 3. Select BAKE, set the temperature to 350ºF, and set the time to 20 minutes. Press START/STOP to begin preheating.

6. When the unit has preheated, place the sheet pan on the wire rack. Close the oven door to begin cooking.

7. When cooking is complete, remove the sheet pan from the oven and place on a wire rack to cool. Cut into 24 bars.

Per serving (1 bar): *Calories: 314; Total Fat: 17g; Saturated Fat: 8g; Cholesterol: 45mg; Sodium: 113mg; Carbohydrates: 39g; Fiber: 1g; Protein: 4g*

Peanut Butter and Jelly Crumble Bars

MAKES 16 BARS

When I was growing up, my neighbor made these bars all the time. And once you see how quick and effortless they are to make, I'm sure you will, too. One of the things I like so much about this dessert is that you can throw it together at the last minute because all the ingredients are already in the pantry and refrigerator. This recipe is also great for those who are intimidated by baking. These are also great to make with the kids as it's supposed to have that messy rustic look to it. —Caroline Schliep

VEGETARIAN

PREP TIME: 15 minutes
COOK TIME: 30 minutes

FUNCTION: Bake
TEMPERATURE: 350°F

ACCESSORY: Ninja Sheet Pan

VARIATION: You can easily customize this recipe by using raspberry jam, blackberry jam, or even orange preserves instead of the strawberry jam.

1½ cups (3 sticks) unsalted butter, at room temperature

1½ cups packed light brown sugar

½ cup granulated sugar

2¾ cups old-fashioned rolled oats

2 cups all-purpose flour

1 teaspoon vanilla extract

1 teaspoon kosher salt

1 teaspoon baking powder

1 (18-ounce) jar strawberry jam

½ cup peanut butter

1. Using a hand mixer or stand mixer, beat together the butter, brown sugar, and granulated sugar until smooth.

2. Add the oats, flour, vanilla, salt, and baking powder and stir until thoroughly combined.

3. Transfer two-thirds of the crumb mixture to the sheet pan and press it into an even, flat layer (it should go about three-quarters of the way up the side of the pan).

4. Spread the jam evenly over the crust, leaving a ½-inch border along the edges. Use a ½-tablespoon measuring spoon to dollop the peanut butter evenly on top of the jam.

5. Sprinkle the remaining crumb mixture over the top.

6. Install a wire rack on Level 3. Select BAKE, set the temperature to 350ºF, and set the time to 30 minutes. Press START/STOP to begin preheating.

7. When the unit has preheated, place the sheet pan on the wire rack. Close the oven door to begin cooking.

8. When cooking is complete, remove the pan from the oven and let cool completely before cutting into squares.

Per serving (1 bar): *Calories: 507; Total Fat: 23g; Saturated Fat: 12g; Cholesterol: 46mg; Sodium: 126mg; Carbohydrates: 72g; Fiber: 3g; Protein: 6g*

Sheet Pan Key Lime Pie Bars

MAKES 16 BARS

Key lime pie is one of those classic desserts, combining sweet and sour flavors with a delicious graham cracker crust. And you can't forget about the dollop (or two) of whipped cream on top. Because this is such a popular dessert, I wanted to develop a quick and simple sheet pan version so it can really be a crowd-pleaser instead of just your typical 8-slice pie. And you can even get a little bit of a workout squeezing all those limes before you stuff your face with too many slices. —Caroline Schliep

---

NUT-FREE, VEGETARIAN

PREP TIME: 15 minutes, plus 1 hour to chill
COOK TIME: 22 minutes

FUNCTION: Bake
TEMPERATURE: 350°F

ACCESSORY: Ninja Sheet Pan

VARIATION: Feel free to use the citrus of your choosing, such as oranges, grapefruit, or even lemons, instead of the limes.

- 8 tablespoons (1 stick) unsalted butter, melted
- 3 cups graham cracker crumbs
- ½ cup sugar
- 2 (14-ounce) cans sweetened condensed milk
- 2 large eggs
- 2 tablespoons grated lime zest
- 1¼ cups freshly squeezed or bottled key lime juice
- ½ teaspoon kosher salt
- Whipped cream (optional)

1. Line the sheet pan with parchment paper. Make a diagonal cut in each corner of parchment so it can lay flat. Set aside.

2. In a large bowl, mix together the melted butter, graham cracker crumbs, and sugar.

3. Pour the crumb mixture onto the prepared sheet pan, and use the bottom of a glass to press the crust into an even, flat layer.

4. Install a wire rack on Level 3. Select BAKE, set the temperature to 350°F, and set the time to 22 minutes. Press START/STOP to begin preheating.

5. When the unit has preheated, place the sheet pan on the wire rack. Close the oven door to begin cooking.

CONTINUED ▶

6. Meanwhile, in a medium bowl, whisk together the sweetened condensed milk, eggs, lime zest, lime juice, and salt. Set aside.

7. When there are 12 minutes remaining, remove the sheet pan from the oven and pour the filling over the crust, using a spatula to spread it into an even layer. Place the sheet pan back on the wire rack and close the oven door to continue cooking.

8. When cooking is complete, remove the pan from the oven and let cool completely. Once cooled, place the sheet pan in the refrigerator to chill for at least 1 hour.

9. Once chilled, cut into squares and serve with whipped cream (if using).

Per serving (1 bar): *Calories: 316; Total Fat: 12g; Saturated Fat: 7g; Cholesterol: 55mg; Sodium: 182mg; Carbohydrates: 47g; Fiber: 1g; Protein: 6g*

Fudgy Layered Brownies

SERVES 12

My mom made these brownies for almost every bake sale when I was growing up, and they were always the first to sell out. There's no competition for the tender brownie bottom and decadent fudge-and-marshmallow topping. Though these may seem like a labor of love, they're a snap to make, and they turn any day into a special occasion. I love the way the Ninja® Foodi™ XL Pro Air Oven gently melts the butter and chocolate. This technique allows you to use a higher-quality chocolate to bring the flavor of the brownies to the next level. —Kara Bleday

NUT-FREE

PREP TIME: 30 minutes, plus 1 hour to chill
COOK TIME: 45 minutes

FUNCTION: Bake
TEMPERATURE: 350°F

ACCESSORIES:
2 oven-safe bowls, Ninja Casserole Dish

FREEZER FRIENDLY: Cut the chilled brownies and individually wrap them in plastic wrap. Freeze for 2 to 3 weeks. When you're ready to eat, enjoy them frozen or thaw at room temperature for about 30 minutes. Do not microwave them to defrost or the topping will melt.

For the brownie layer
- 4 ounces unsweetened baking chocolate, broken into small pieces
- 1 cup (2 sticks) unsalted butter, at room temperature, plus more for greasing
- 4 large eggs
- 2 cups granulated sugar
- 1 cup all-purpose flour
- 1 tablespoon vanilla extract

For the topping
- 4 ounces unsweetened baking chocolate, broken into small pieces
- 1 cup (2 sticks) unsalted butter, at room temperature
- 4 cups powdered sugar
- 2 large eggs
- 1 tablespoon vanilla extract
- 3 to 4 cups mini marshmallows

1. **To make the brownie layer:** Put the chocolate and butter in an oven-safe bowl.

2. Install a wire rack on Level 3. Select BAKE, set the temperature to 350°F, and set the time to 5 minutes. Press START/STOP to begin preheating.

3. When unit has preheated, place the bowl on the wire rack. Close the oven door to begin cooking.

4. Meanwhile, in a large bowl, use a hand mixer or stand mixer to combine the eggs, granulated sugar, flour, and vanilla.

CONTINUED ▶

5. When cooking is complete, remove the bowl from the oven and stir the chocolate and butter until well combined. Pour the chocolate mixture into the batter and mix to combine.

6. Grease the baking pan with butter (or cooking spray). Pour the brownie batter into the pan and spread it into an even layer.

7. Select BAKE, set the temperature to 350°F, and set the time to 35 minutes. Press START/STOP to begin preheating.

8. When the unit has preheated, place the sheet pan on the wire rack. Close the oven door to begin cooking.

9. When cooking is complete, remove the pan from the oven and let cool completely.

10. **To make the topping:** Put the chocolate and butter in an oven-safe bowl.

11. Leave the wire rack on Level 3. Select BAKE, set the temperature to 350°F, and set the time to 5 minutes. Press START/STOP to begin preheating.

12. When unit has preheated, place the bowl on the wire rack. Close the oven door to begin cooking.

13. When cooking is complete, remove the bowl from the oven and stir the chocolate and butter until well combined.

14. Pour the chocolate mixture into a large bowl and add the powdered sugar, eggs, and vanilla. Mix until well combined. Stir in the marshmallows.

15. Spread the topping onto the cooled brownies. Chill in the refrigerator for at least 1 hour before cutting.

Per serving (1 brownie): *Calories: 771; Total Fat: 43g; Saturated Fat: 26g; Cholesterol: 175mg; Sodium: 56mg; Carbohydrates: 90g; Fiber: 3g; Protein: 7g*

Hazelnut and Pretzel Brownies

SERVES 10 TO 15

I have a major sweet tooth, and I love chocolate! I'm also a big fan of sweet-and-salty combinations, and this recipe definitely delivers. The hazelnut spread and pretzel bits taste like a chocolate-covered pretzel—but even better. With the XL Pro Air Oven, I can cook two layers of these delicious brownies and maybe share them if I'm feeling nice! —Meg Jordan

---

VEGETARIAN

PREP TIME: 20 minutes
COOK TIME: 35 minutes

FUNCTION: Bake
TEMPERATURE: 350°F

ACCESSORIES: 2 (8-inch square) baking pans

1 cup (2 sticks) unsalted butter, at room temperature, plus more for greasing

1½ cups sugar

1 teaspoon vanilla extract

4 large eggs

½ cup hazelnut spread, plus more for topping

1¾ cups all-purpose flour

½ cup unsweetened cocoa powder

½ teaspoon kosher salt

1 cup mini pretzels, crushed into small pieces, plus more for topping

1. Grease the baking pans with butter and set aside.

2. In a stand mixer with the paddle attachment, beat the butter, sugar, and vanilla on medium speed until smooth. Reduce the mixer speed to low. Add the eggs one at a time, incorporating each completely before adding the next egg. Add the hazelnut spread and mix on low speed for 30 seconds, or until fully incorporated.

3. Turn the mixer off and use a spatula to scrape down the sides of the bowl. Add the flour, cocoa powder, and salt, and mix on low speed until well combined. Using a spatula, stir in the crushed pretzels. Divide the batter evenly between the two baking pans.

4. Install the wire racks on Levels 1 and 3. Select BAKE, select 2 LEVEL, set the temperature to 350ºF, and set the time to 35 minutes. Press START/STOP to begin preheating.

CONTINUED ▶

5. When the unit has preheated, place a baking pan on each wire rack. Close the oven door to begin cooking.

6. Cooking is complete when a toothpick inserted in the center of the brownies comes out clean. Remove the pans from the oven and let cool completely. Spread a thin layer of hazelnut spread on top of the brownies and sprinkle with additional crushed pretzel pieces.

Per serving (1 brownie): *Calories: 493; Total Fat: 26g; Saturated Fat: 17g; Cholesterol: 123mg; Sodium: 146mg; Carbohydrates: 62g; Fiber: 3g; Protein: 7g*

Cookie and Candy Layer Cake

SERVES 10

This recipe is so easy, even the most reluctant baker can do it. I used to work with a line cook who loved sugar; she would make a recipe similar to this every time it was her turn to make family meal. I always admired this recipe because it was simple, was easy to modify, and took no more than 10 minutes to prep and assemble. —Sam Ferguson

VEGETARIAN

PREP TIME: 10 minutes, plus 2 hours to chill
COOK TIME: 45 minutes

FUNCTION: Bake
TEMPERATURE: 350°F

ACCESSORIES: 9-inch round springform cake pan

SUBSTITUTION: This recipe is perfect with almost any candy substitution that you want. It's as simple as replacing the candy with whatever combinations you'd like!

Cooking oil spray

3 (16-ounce) packages prepared chocolate chip cookie dough

2 (2-ounce) Snickers bars, cut into 1-inch pieces

2 (2-ounce) 3 Musketeers bars, cut into 1-inch pieces

2 (2-ounce) Peppermint Patties, cut into 2-inch pieces

2 (2-ounce) packages Peanut M&M's

1 (15-ounce) jar vanilla frosting

1. Cut a piece of parchment paper or foil into a circle that is approximately the same diameter as the bottom of the cake pan. Place the parchment paper or foil in the bottom of the pan. Cut a long strip of parchment paper or foil and wrap it along the inside wall of the pan. Use a light spray of oil as "glue" to keep the parchment paper or foil against the wall of the pan.

2. Place 1 package of cookie dough in the bottom of the pan. Press the dough so that it covers the bottom in an even layer.

3. Cover the dough with half of the Snickers bars, half of the 3 Musketeers bars, half of the Peppermint Patties, and half of the Peanut M&M's in an even layer.

4. Repeat the layers with the second package of cookie dough and the remaining candy.

5. Press the third package of cookie dough on top to form the cake.

6. Install a wire rack on Level 3. Select BAKE, set the temperature to 350ºF, and set the time to 45 minutes. Press START/STOP to begin preheating.

7. When the unit has preheated, place the sheet pan on the wire rack. Close the oven door to begin cooking.

8. When cooking is complete, let the cake cool in the refrigerator for at least 2 hours.

9. Release the springform pan and invert the cake onto a cutting board or cake plate to remove. Turn the cake right-side up and spread the frosting evenly over the top and sides of the cake. Cut and serve.

Per serving: *Calories: 988; Total Fat: 46g; Saturated Fat: 16g; Cholesterol: 13mg; Sodium: 476mg; Carbohydrates: 140g; Fiber: 3g; Protein: 8g*

Razzleberry Hand Pies

SERVES 6

I use frozen fruit daily while testing blenders in the Ninja Test Kitchen. I love using frozen fruit in other applications because I can keep it in the freezer and it's there whenever I need it. Smoothies, sorbets, jams, frozen drinks, muffins, pies—you name it—frozen fruit is a great option. It's perfect for these hand pies with the bonus of being so easy to put together. —Craig White

---

NUT-FREE, VEGETARIAN

PREP TIME: 15 minutes
COOK TIME: 25 minutes

FUNCTION: Bake
TEMPERATURE: 350°F

ACCESSORIES: Ninja Sheet Pan

SUBSTITUTION: When fresh berries are at their peak, feel free to substitute them for the frozen berries in this recipe.

---

1 (7.5-ounce) roll store-bought pie dough

½ cup frozen blackberries

½ cup frozen raspberries

1 teaspoon freshly squeezed lemon juice

1 teaspoon vanilla extract

3 tablespoons granulated sugar, plus 2 teaspoons

1 tablespoon cornstarch

¼ teaspoon ground cinnamon

2 tablespoons whole milk

1. Unroll the pie dough and use a 4½-inch round biscuit cutter to cut 4 circles of dough, then reroll the scrap dough to the same thickness and cut out 2 more circles of dough.

2. In a small bowl, combine the blackberries and raspberries with the lemon juice and vanilla, and toss to coat the berries. This will help the sugar mixture stick.

3. In another small bowl, mix 3 tablespoons of sugar, the cornstarch, and cinnamon until there are no clumps. Add the mixture to the bowl with the berries, and toss to coat.

4. Line the sheet pan with parchment paper. Place the circles of pie dough on the pan and brush each with the milk. Divide the filling evenly among the dough circles.

5. Fold the pie dough over the filling and seal the edges with your fingers. Crimp the edges with a fork.

6. Using a paring knife, poke a hole in the top of each pie. Brush the tops with milk and sprinkle with the remaining 2 teaspoons of sugar.

7. Install a wire rack on Level 3. Select BAKE, set the temperature to 350ºF, and set the time to 25 minutes. Press START/STOP to begin preheating.

8. When the unit has preheated, place the sheet pan on the wire rack. Close the oven door to begin cooking.

9. Halfway through cooking, open the door and rotate the sheet pan. Close the oven door to continue cooking.

10. When cooking is complete, remove the pan from the oven and let the hand pies cool.

Per serving: Calories: 212; Total Fat: 9g; Saturated Fat: 3g; Cholesterol: 1mg; Sodium: 148mg; Carbohydrates: 31g; Fiber: 2g; Protein: 2g

Pumpkin-Spiced Latte Bread Pudding

SERVES 6 TO 8

The fall season means pumpkin everything. And there is nothing more ubiquitous than the pumpkin-spiced latte. I made this dessert years ago when I was in the restaurant industry as an homage to those who love that warm, delicious drink. —Chelven Randolph

NUT-FREE, VEGETARIAN

PREP TIME: 15 minutes
COOK TIME: 30 minutes

FUNCTION: Bake
TEMPERATURE: 350°F

ACCESSORIES: 9-inch casserole dish

PERFECT PARTNER: For me, nothing goes better with bread pudding than ice cream. With this pumpkin-spiced latte bread pudding, I prefer butter pecan or coffee ice cream, but vanilla is always a safe bet.

1 cup pumpkin puree (not pumpkin pie filling)

1 cup packed dark brown sugar

3 large eggs

1 cup whole milk

½ cup heavy cream

½ cup cold brew coffee or espresso

1 tablespoon vanilla extract

2 teaspoons pumpkin pie spice

4 cups cubed day-old crusty bread, preferably French bread (but any kind works)

8 tablespoons (1 stick) unsalted butter, melted

Cooking oil spray

1. Mix together the pumpkin puree, brown sugar, eggs, milk, cream, coffee, vanilla, and pumpkin pie spice.

2. In a large bowl, toss the bread with the butter. Pour over the pumpkin mixture and fold until the bread is coated.

3. Lightly coat the casserole dish with cooking spray. Pour the bread mixture into the dish.

4. Install a wire rack on Level 3. Select BAKE, set the temperature to 350°F, and set the time to 30 minutes. Press START/STOP to begin preheating.

5. When the unit has preheated, place the casserole dish on the wire rack. Close the oven door to begin cooking.

6. When cooking is complete, the top of the bread pudding will be golden brown. Remove the dish from the oven and let cool slightly before serving.

Per serving: Calories: 732; Total Fat: 41g; Saturated Fat: 24g; Cholesterol: 247mg; Sodium: 285mg; Carbohydrates: 81g; Fiber: 3g; Protein: 11g

Ninja® Foodi™ XL Pro Air Oven
CHARTS

Air Fry Chart

INGREDIENT	AMOUNT	PREPARATION	OIL	TEMP	ONE-LEVEL COOK TIME* (MINUTES)	TWO-LEVEL COOK TIME** (MINUTES)
FROZEN FOOD						
Chicken nuggets	Up to 4 lbs	None	None	400°F	15-20	30-35
Fish fillets (breaded)	Up to 20 fillets	None	None	400°F	10-15	20-25
Fish sticks	Up to 2 lbs	None	None	375°F	11-15	23-28
French fries	Up to 4 lbs	None	None	390°F	19-22	38-40
Mozzarella sticks	Up to 4 lbs	None	None	375°F	8-10	15-18
Pizza rolls	Up to 3 lbs (2 boxes)	None	None	375°F	9-12	18-25
Popcorn shrimp	Up to 2 lbs	None	None	390°F	8-11	15-17
Tater tots	Up to 4 lbs	None	None	360°F	15-18	25-28

CONTINUED ▶

INGREDIENT	AMOUNT	PREPARATION	OIL	TEMP	ONE-LEVEL COOK TIME* (MINUTES)	TWO-LEVEL COOK TIME** (MINUTES)
POULTRY, FISH, MEAT						
Chicken drumsticks	12 drumsticks	Pat dry, season as desired	Toss with 2T oil	400°F	22-27	45-50
Chicken thighs	8 thighs (8-10 oz each)	Pat dry, season as desired	Toss with 2T oil	375°F	25-28	45-48
Chicken wings	Up to 4 lbs	Pat dry	1T oil	390°F	18-22	35-40
Crab cakes	10-12 cakes (6 oz each)	None	Brush with 1T oil	400°F	12-17	23-28
Salmon fillets	8-10 fillets (6-8 oz each)	None	Brush with 2T oil	400°F	13-18	25-28
Sausage	Up to 20 sausage	None	None	390°F	8-10	8-10

INGREDIENT	AMOUNT	PREPARATION	OIL	TEMP	ONE-LEVEL COOK TIME* (MINUTES)	TWO-LEVEL COOK TIME** (MINUTES)
VEGETABLES						
Asparagus	4 bunches	Trim stems	2T oil	400°F	13-15	23-25
Beets	3 lbs	Peel, cut into ½" cubes	2T oil	400°F	18-23	35-40
Bell peppers (for roasting)	8 peppers	Quarter; remove seeds	2T oil	400°F	15-20	30-35
Broccoli	Up to 3 lbs	Cut into 1"-2" florets	2T oil	375°F	13-17	26-30
Brussels sprouts	Up to 4 lbs	Halve; remove stems	1T oil	425°F	13-17	26-30
Cauliflower	Up to 3 lbs	Cut into 1"-2" florets	2T oil	375°F	12-18	24-30
Green beans	1½ lbs	Trim	2T oil	425°F	13-18	25-28
Hand-cut fries	Up to 4 lbs	Soak, pat dry	2T oil	375°F	22-28	38-42

CONTINUED ▶

INGREDIENT	AMOUNT	PREPARATION	OIL	TEMP	ONE-LEVEL COOK TIME* (MINUTES)	TWO-LEVEL COOK TIME** (MINUTES)
Kale (for chips)	8 oz	Tear into pieces; remove stems	None	325°F	8-11	15-18
Mushrooms	2 lbs	Rinse; thinly slice	2T oil	400°F	23-28	25-30
Potatoes, russet	3 lbs	Cut into 1" wedges	2T oil	390°F	23-28	45-50
Potatoes, russet	2 lbs	Hand-cut fries, soak 20 mins in cold water, pat dry	3T oil	390°F	18-23	35-40
Potatoes, sweet	2 lbs	Hand-cut fries, soak 20 mins in cold water, pat dry	3T oil	390°F	15-20	30-35
Zucchini	2 lbs	Quarter lengthwise, then cut into 1" pieces	1T oil	390°F	10-14	20-24

*When cooking foods on one level, cut the ingredient amount by 50% for best results

**Two-Level air fry times are based on using two air fryer baskets. You can air fry on two levels using an air fryer basket and a sheet pan with roasting tray, but cook times and air fry quality may vary. For best results, we recommend purchasing a second air fryer basket at ninjaaccessories.com

Dehydrate Chart

INGREDIENT	PREPARATION	TEMP	TIME (HOURS)
FRUITS & VEGETABLES			
Apples	Cut in ⅛" slices, core, rinse in lemon water, pat dry	135°F	5-6
Asparagus	Cut in 1" pieces	135°F	5-6
Bananas	Peel, cut in ⅜" slices	135°F	7-8
Beets	Peel, cut in ⅛" slices	135°F	5-6
Fresh herbs	Rinse, pat dry, remove stems	135°F	4
Ginger root	Peel, cut in ⅜" slices	135°F	5-6
Mangoes	Peel, pit, cut in ⅜" slices	135°F	5-6
Mushrooms	Clean with soft brush (don't rinse)	135°F	5-6
Pineapple	Peel, cut in ⅜"-½" slices, core	135°F	4-5
Strawberries	Cut in half or ½" slices	135°F	4-5
Tomatoes	Cut in ⅜" slices or grate	135°F	5-6

CONTINUED ▶

INGREDIENT	PREPARATION	TEMP	TIME (HOURS)
MEAT, POULTRY, FISH			
Beef jerky	Cut in ¼" slices, remove all fat, marinate overnight	155°F	5-6
Chicken jerky	Cut in ¼" slices, remove all fat, marinate overnight	155°F	5-6
Salmon jerky	Cut in ¼" slices, marinate overnight	155°F	5-6
Turkey jerky	Cut in ¼" slices, remove all fat, marinate overnight	155°F	5-6

MEASUREMENT CONVERSIONS

VOLUME EQUIVALENTS (LIQUID)

US Standard	US Standard (ounces)	Metric (approximate)
2 tablespoons	1 fl. oz.	30 mL
¼ cup	2 fl. oz.	60 mL
½ cup	4 fl. oz.	120 mL
1 cup	8 fl. oz.	240 mL
1½ cups	12 fl. oz.	355 mL
2 cups or 1 pint	16 fl. oz.	475 mL
4 cups or 1 quart	32 fl. oz.	1 L
1 gallon	128 fl. oz.	4 L

OVEN TEMPERATURES

Fahrenheit (F)	Celsius (C) (approximate)
250°F	120°C
300°F	150°C
325°F	165°C
350°F	180°C
375°F	190°C
400°F	200°C
425°F	220°C
450°F	230°C

VOLUME EQUIVALENTS (DRY)

US Standard	Metric (approximate)
⅛ teaspoon	0.5 mL
¼ teaspoon	1 mL
½ teaspoon	2 mL
¾ teaspoon	4 mL
1 teaspoon	5 mL
1 tablespoon	15 mL
¼ cup	59 mL
⅓ cup	79 mL
½ cup	118 mL
⅔ cup	156 mL
¾ cup	177 mL
1 cup	235 mL
2 cups or 1 pint	475 mL
3 cups	700 mL
4 cups or 1 quart	1 L

WEIGHT EQUIVALENTS

US Standard	Metric (approximate)
½ ounce	15 g
1 ounce	30 g
2 ounces	60 g
4 ounces	115 g
8 ounces	225 g
12 ounces	340 g
16 ounces or 1 pound	455 g

INDEX

A

Air-Fried Fish Tacos, 138–139
Air fry function, 3, 5, 7, 8, 10
Air fryer baskets, 9, 14
Air roast function, 3, 4, 7, 8
Apples
    Sheet Pan Pies, Two Ways,
      222–223
    Spiced Apple Sheet Pan
      Pancake, 40–41
Artichoke hearts
    Cheesy Spinach and Artichoke
      Pinwheels, 73–74
Asparagus
    Asparagus, Ham, and Cheese
      Puff Pastry Bundles, 70–71
    Mediterranean Veggie Platter,
      183–184
    Parmesan-Crusted Tilapia and
      Garlic Asparagus, 143
    Quiche, Two Ways, 30–31
Avocados
    Crab and Avocado Rangoon,
      82–83

B

Bacon. *See also* Canadian bacon
    Bacon and Kale Ranch Dip,
      55–56
    Bacon-Stuffed Clams, 156–157
    Barbecue Meat Loaf and Crispy
      Ranch Potatoes, 117–118
    Crab BLT Dip and Crostini,
      185–186
    Jalapeño Poppers, 79
    Loaded Air-Fried Potato
      Wedges, 77–78
    Parmesan-Crusted Beef with
      Bacon Potatoes, 194–195
    Toad in a Hole with Crispy
      Bacon, 26–27
Bagel function, 3, 6, 7
Baked Chicken Tacos, 104–105
Baked Macaroni and Cheese,
    173–174
Bake function, 5, 7
Baking pans, 14

Barbecue Meat Loaf and Crispy
    Ranch Potatoes, 117–118
Beans
    French-Inspired Chicken Stew,
      106
    New England Hot Dish,
      196–197
    Succotash, 171
Beef
    Barbecue Meat Loaf and
      Crispy Ranch Potatoes,
      117–118
    Carne Asada Street Tacos, 114
    Chili-Lime Beef Jerky, 87
    Garlic-Crusted Flank Steak
      with Roasted Vegetables,
      115–116
    Meatball Parmesan al Forno,
      192–193
    New England Hot Dish,
      196–197
    Parmesan-Crusted Beef with
      Bacon Potatoes, 194–195
    Philly Cheesesteak Egg Rolls, 75
Beer
    Soft Pretzel Sticks with Beer
      Cheese Dip, 59–61
Berries. *See also* Jams and
    preserves
    Cheesy Cranberry Pull-Apart
      Bread, 187–188
    Lemon-Blueberry Crunch
      Coffee Cake, 49–50
    Razzleberry Hand Pies,
      244–245
    Salt-Brined Turkey Breast with
      Quinoa Stuffing, 201–202
    Thanksgiving Side Dishes,
      212–213
Bok choy
    Soy and Maple Salmon with
      Carrots and Bok Choy,
      147–148
Breads
    in Brown Sugar and Cinnamon
      French Toast Bake, 37–38
    Cheesy Cranberry Pull-Apart
      Bread, 187–188
    Cheesy Sausage Bread, 62–63

    in Cheesy Spinach and
      Artichoke Pinwheels, 73–74
    in Corn Bread, Sausage, and
      Pear Stuffing, 205–206
    in Crab BLT Dip and Crostini,
      185–186
    in "Fried" Chicken Po' Boys with
      Remoulade Coleslaw, 97–98
    in Italian Eggs in Purgatory
      with Garlic Bread, 28–29
    Johnny's Corn Bread, 175
    Liz's Spoon Bread, 220–221
    in Mojito Mojo Pulled Pork
      Sandwiches, 126–127
    in Mushroom and Swiss Bagel
      Pudding, 35–36
    Prosciutto, Chive, and
      Parmesan Scones, 47–48
    in Pumpkin-Spiced Latte
      Bread Pudding, 247
    in Shellfish Newburg
      Casserole, 203–204
    Soft Pretzel Sticks with Beer
      Cheese Dip, 59–61
    in Sweet and Savory Breakfast
      Stratas, 32–34
    in Thanksgiving Side Dishes,
      212–213
    in Toad in a Hole with Crispy
      Bacon, 26–27
Broil function, 5, 7
Brown Sugar and Cinnamon
    French Toast Bake, 37–38
Brussels sprouts
    Garlic-Crusted Flank Steak
      with Roasted Vegetables,
      115–116
    Roasted Leg of Lamb with
      Vegetable Medley, 198–199

C

Canadian bacon
    Sweet and Savory Breakfast
      Stratas, 32–34
Carne Asada Street Tacos, 114
Carrots
    French-Inspired
      Chicken Stew, 106

Honey Mustard Spiral Ham
with Sweet-and-Spicy
Carrots, 189–190
Roasted Carrots with Honey
and Dill Butter, 207
Roasted Leg of Lamb with
Vegetable Medley, 198–199
Root Vegetables and Potatoes
au Gratin, 218–219
Tropical Mahi-Mahi and
Vegetables, 144–145
Casserole dishes, 14
Cauliflower
Cauliflower Gratin, 216–217
Chorizo-Stuffed Poblano
Peppers, 129–130
Coconut Curried Tofu and
Vegetables, 167–168
Mediterranean Veggie Platter,
183–184
Celery
Corn Bread, Sausage, and Pear
Stuffing, 205–206
Mustard-and-Herb-Crusted
Rack of Lamb with Warm
Potato Salad, 131–132
Cereal
Party Snack Mix, 181–182
Cheese. *See also* Cream cheese;
Ricotta cheese
Asparagus, Ham, and Cheese
Puff Pastry Bundles, 70–71
Bacon and Kale Ranch Dip,
55–56
Bacon-Stuffed Clams, 156–157
Baked Chicken Tacos, 104–105
Baked Macaroni and Cheese,
173–174
Barbecue Meat Loaf and
Crispy Ranch Potatoes,
117–118
Cauliflower Gratin, 216–217
Cheesy Chicken Casserole, 109
Cheesy Cranberry Pull-Apart
Bread, 187–188
Cheesy Sausage Bread, 62–63
Cheesy Spinach and Artichoke
Pinwheels, 73–74
Chorizo-Stuffed Poblano
Peppers, 129–130
Crab BLT Dip and Crostini,
185–186
Creamy Spinach Chicken
Cordon Bleu, 94–95

Eggplant Parmesan "Lasagna,"
162–163
French Onion Ring Soup
Fritters, 80–81
Garlic-Crusted Flank Steak
with Roasted Vegetables,
115–116
Green Chicken Enchiladas,
107–108
Heirloom Tomato Pie,
209–210
Italian Eggs in Purgatory with
Garlic Bread, 28–29
Jalapeño Corn Dip with
Homemade Tortilla Chips,
57–58
Jalapeño Poppers, 79
Johnny's Corn Bread, 175
Kung Pao Chicken Totchos, 85
Loaded Air-Fried Potato
Wedges, 77–78
Margherita Pizza, 65–66
Meatball Parmesan al Forno,
192–193
Mediterranean Veggie Platter,
183–184
Mexican-Inspired Turkey Meat
Loaf with Chili-Rubbed
Street Corn, 110–111
Mushroom and Swiss Bagel
Pudding, 35–36
Mustard-and-Herb-Crusted
Rack of Lamb with Warm
Potato Salad, 131–132
Parmesan-Crusted Beef with
Bacon Potatoes, 194–195
Parmesan-Crusted Tilapia and
Garlic Asparagus, 143
Pesto Gnocchi with Roasted
Vegetables, 177
Philly Cheesesteak Egg Rolls, 75
Portabella Mushroom
Parmesan and Spaghetti
Squash, 169–170
Potato Crisps with Creamy
Pesto Dip, 76
Prosciutto, Chive, and
Parmesan Scones, 47–48
Quiche, Two Ways, 30–31
Roasted Mushroom, Poblano,
and Corn Enchiladas,
164–165
Root Vegetables and Potatoes
au Gratin, 218–219

Soft Pretzel Sticks with Beer
Cheese Dip, 59–61
Spanakopita Star, 67–69
Sweet and Savory Breakfast
Stratas, 32–34
Thanksgiving Side Dishes,
212–213
Chicken
Baked Chicken Tacos, 104–105
Cheesy Chicken Casserole, 109
Creamy Spinach Chicken
Cordon Bleu, 94–95
French-Inspired Chicken Stew,
106
"Fried" Chicken Po' Boys with
Remoulade Coleslaw, 97–98
Green Chicken Enchiladas,
107–108
Honey Mustard Chicken with
Pretzel Crust and Crispy
Potato Wedges, 102–103
Korean-Style Fried Chicken,
92–93
Kung Pao Chicken Totchos, 85
Orange and Rosemary
Chicken with Sweet
Potatoes, 90–91
Sheet Pan Chicken Fajitas,
99–100
Sheet Pan Paella, 153–154
Soy-Braised Chicken Wings, 86
Chickpeas
Coconut Curried Tofu and
Vegetables, 167–168
Chiles
Baked Chicken Tacos, 104–105
Green Chicken Enchiladas,
107–108
Jalapeño Corn Dip with
Homemade Tortilla Chips,
57–58
Mexican-Inspired Turkey Meat
Loaf with Chili-Rubbed
Street Corn, 110–111
Chili-Lime Beef Jerky, 87
Chocolate
Chocolate, Nut Butter, and Oat
Breakfast Bars, 42–43
Cocoa Breakfast Popovers,
44–45
Cookie and Candy Layer Cake,
242–243
Double Chocolate Chip Walnut
Biscotti, 228–229

Chocolate (*continued*)
Fudgy Layered Brownies, 237–238
Hazelnut and Pretzel Brownies, 239–240
Sheet Pan Cookie Bars, Two Ways, 230–231
Chorizo-Stuffed Poblano Peppers, 129–130
Clams
Bacon-Stuffed Clams, 156–157
New England Hot Dish, 196–197
Sheet Pan Paella, 153–154
Cocoa Breakfast Popovers, 44–45
Coconut Curried Tofu and Vegetables, 167–168
Cod
Fish and Chips, 136–137
"Fish in a Bag," 141–142
Shellfish Newburg Casserole, 203–204
Coffee
Pumpkin-Spiced Latte Bread Pudding, 247
Coleslaw
"Fried" Chicken Po' Boys with Remoulade Coleslaw, 97–98
Control panel, 4–6
Cookie and Candy Layer Cake, 242–243
Cooking sprays, 9
Corn
Jalapeño Corn Dip with Homemade Tortilla Chips, 57–58
Liz's Spoon Bread, 220–221
Mexican-Inspired Turkey Meat Loaf with Chili-Rubbed Street Corn, 110–111
Roasted Mushroom, Poblano, and Corn Enchiladas, 164–165
Succotash, 171
Corn Bread, Sausage, and Pear Stuffing, 205–206
Cottage cheese
Baked Macaroni and Cheese, 173–174
Crabmeat
Crab and Avocado Rangoon, 82–83
Crab BLT Dip and Crostini, 185–186

Shellfish Newburg Casserole, 203–204
Cream cheese
Bacon and Kale Ranch Dip, 55–56
Brown Sugar and Cinnamon French Toast Bake, 37–38
Cheesy Spinach and Artichoke Pinwheels, 73–74
Crab and Avocado Rangoon, 82–83
Creamy Spinach Chicken Cordon Bleu, 94–95
Jalapeño Poppers, 79
Potato Crisps with Creamy Pesto Dip, 76
Shellfish Newburg Casserole, 203–204
Creamy Spinach Chicken Cordon Bleu, 94–95
Cuban-Style Pork Roast with "Fried" Sweet Plantains, 124–125

D

Dairy-free
Air-Fried Fish Tacos, 138–139
Carne Asada Street Tacos, 114
Chili-Lime Beef Jerky, 87
Coconut Curried Tofu and Vegetables, 167–168
Cuban-Style Pork Roast with "Fried" Sweet Plantains, 124–125
Fish and Chips, 136–137
French-Inspired Chicken Stew, 106
Honey-Garlic Glazed Pork Tenderloin with Roasted Vegetables, 119–120
Honey Mustard Spiral Ham with Sweet-and-Spicy Carrots, 189–190
Korean-Style Fried Chicken, 92–93
Mojito Mojo Pulled Pork Sandwiches, 126–127
Ratatouille, 160–161
Salt-Brined Turkey Breast with Quinoa Stuffing, 201–202
Salt Potatoes, 211
Sheet Pan Chicken Fajitas, 99–100
Sheet Pan Paella, 153–154

Soy and Maple Salmon with Carrots and Bok Choy, 147–148
Soy-Braised Chicken Wings, 86
Sweet-and-Spicy Candied Nuts, 180
Toad in a Hole with Crispy Bacon, 26–27
Tropical Fruit Leather, 54
Tropical Mahi-Mahi and Vegetables, 144–145
Dehydrate function, 6, 7
Desserts
Cookie and Candy Layer Cake, 242–243
Double Chocolate Chip Walnut Biscotti, 228–229
Fudgy Layered Brownies, 237–238
Hazelnut and Pretzel Brownies, 239–240
Peanut Butter and Jelly Crumble Bars, 232–233
Pumpkin-Spiced Latte Bread Pudding, 247
Razzleberry Hand Pies, 244–245
Salted Butter Pecan Cookies, 226–227
Sheet Pan Cookie Bars, Two Ways, 230–231
Sheet Pan Key Lime Pie Bars, 235–236
Sheet Pan Pies, Two Ways, 222–223
Dips
Bacon and Kale Ranch Dip, 55–56
Crab BLT Dip and Crostini, 185–186
Jalapeño Corn Dip with Homemade Tortilla Chips, 57–58
Potato Crisps with Creamy Pesto Dip, 76
Soft Pretzel Sticks with Beer Cheese Dip, 59–61
Double Chocolate Chip Walnut Biscotti, 228–229

E

Eggplants
Eggplant Parmesan "Lasagna," 162–163
Ratatouille, 160–161

Egg roll wrappers
Philly Cheesesteak
Egg Rolls, 75
Eggs
Brown Sugar and Cinnamon
French Toast Bake, 37–38
Italian Eggs in Purgatory with
Garlic Bread, 28–29
Mushroom and Swiss Bagel
Pudding, 35–36
Quiche, Two Ways, 30–31
Sheet Pan Pies, Two Ways,
222–223
Shellfish Newburg Casserole,
203–204
Sweet and Savory Breakfast
Stratas, 32–34
Toad in a Hole with Crispy
Bacon, 26–27
Equipment, 14, 16

F

Fish
Air-Fried Fish Tacos, 138–139
Fish and Chips, 136–137
"Fish in a Bag," 141–142
Parmesan-Crusted Tilapia and
Garlic Asparagus, 143
Shellfish Newburg Casserole,
203–204
Soy and Maple Salmon with
Carrots and Bok Choy,
147–148
Tropical Mahi-Mahi and
Vegetables, 144–145
5 ingredients or less
Chorizo-Stuffed Poblano
Peppers, 129–130
Margherita Pizza, 65–66
Mushroom and Swiss Bagel
Pudding, 35–36
Potato Crisps with Creamy
Pesto Dip, 76
Salt Potatoes, 211
Tropical Fruit Leather, 54
Freezer staples, 19, 21
French-Inspired Chicken Stew,
106
French Onion Ring Soup Fritters,
80–81
"Fried" Chicken Po' Boys with
Remoulade Coleslaw, 97–98
Fudgy Layered Brownies,
237–238

G

Garlic-Crusted Flank Steak with
Roasted Vegetables, 115–116
Gluten-free
Bacon and Kale Ranch Dip,
55–56
Baked Chicken Tacos, 104–105
Chorizo-Stuffed Poblano
Peppers, 129–130
Creamy Spinach Chicken
Cordon Bleu, 94–95
Cuban-Style Pork Roast with
"Fried" Sweet Plantains,
124–125
French-Inspired Chicken Stew,
106
Honey-Garlic Glazed Pork
Tenderloin with Roasted
Vegetables, 119–120
Honey Mustard Spiral Ham
with Sweet-and-Spicy
Carrots, 189–190
Kung Pao Chicken Totchos, 85
Liz's Spoon Bread, 220–221
Loaded Air-Fried Potato
Wedges, 77–78
Mexican-Inspired Turkey Meat
Loaf with Chili-Rubbed
Street Corn, 110–111
Orange and Rosemary
Chicken with Sweet
Potatoes, 90–91
Potato Crisps with Creamy
Pesto Dip, 76
Ratatouille, 160–161
Roasted Carrots with Honey
and Dill Butter, 207
Roasted Leg of Lamb with
Vegetable Medley, 198–199
Salt Potatoes, 211
Sheet Pan Paella, 153–154
Succotash, 171
Sweet-and-Spicy Candied
Nuts, 180
Tropical Fruit Leather, 54
Tropical Mahi-Mahi and
Vegetables, 144–145
Green beans
Honey-Garlic Glazed Pork
Tenderloin with Roasted
Vegetables, 119–120
Pork Wellington with Garlic
Green Beans, 122–123
Thanksgiving Side Dishes,
212–213
Green Chicken Enchiladas,
107–108

H

Ham. *See also* Canadian bacon;
Prosciutto
Asparagus, Ham, and
Cheese Puff Pastry
Bundles, 70–71
Creamy Spinach Chicken
Cordon Bleu, 94–95
Honey Mustard Spiral Ham
with Sweet-and-Spicy
Carrots, 189–190
Quiche, Two Ways, 30–31
Hazelnut and Pretzel Brownies,
239–240
Heirloom Tomato Pie, 209–210
Honey-Garlic Glazed Pork
Tenderloin with Roasted
Vegetables, 119–120
Honey Mustard Chicken with
Pretzel Crust and Crispy
Potato Wedges, 102–103
Honey Mustard Spiral Ham with
Sweet-and-Spicy Carrots,
189–190

I

Ingredient staples, 16–19, 21
Italian Eggs in Purgatory with
Garlic Bread, 28–29

J

Jalapeño Corn Dip with
Homemade Tortilla Chips,
57–58
Jalapeño Poppers, 79
Jams and preserves
Cocoa Breakfast Popovers,
44–45
Peanut Butter and Jelly
Crumble Bars, 232–233
Pork Wellington with Garlic
Green Beans, 122–123
Sweet and Savory Breakfast
Stratas, 32–34
Johnny's Corn Bread, 175

K

Kale
 Bacon and Kale Ranch Dip, 55–56
 Coconut Curried Tofu and Vegetables, 167–168
Korean-Style Fried Chicken, 92–93
Kung Pao Chicken Totchos, 85

L

Lamb
 Mustard-and-Herb-Crusted Rack of Lamb with Warm Potato Salad, 131–132
 Roasted Leg of Lamb with Vegetable Medley, 198–199
Lemon-Blueberry Crunch Coffee Cake, 49–50
Limes
 Sheet Pan Key Lime Pie Bars, 235–236
Liz's Spoon Bread, 220–221
Loaded Air-Fried Potato Wedges, 77–78

M

Mahi-Mahi and Vegetables, Tropical, 144–145
Mangos
 Tropical Fruit Leather, 54
Margherita Pizza, 65–66
Marshmallows
 Fudgy Layered Brownies, 237–238
 Sweet Potato Casserole, 214–215
 Thanksgiving Side Dishes, 212–213
Meals
 cooking complete, 2, 20
 sheet pan creations, 15
Meatball Parmesan al Forno, 192–193
Mediterranean Veggie Platter, 183–184
Mexican-Inspired Turkey Meat Loaf with Chili-Rubbed Street Corn, 110–111
Mojito Mojo Pulled Pork Sandwiches, 126–127

Mushrooms
 Mushroom and Swiss Bagel Pudding, 35–36
 Portabella Mushroom Parmesan and Spaghetti Squash, 169–170
 Roasted Mushroom, Poblano, and Corn Enchiladas, 164–165
Mustard-and-Herb-Crusted Rack of Lamb with Warm Potato Salad, 131–132

N

New England Hot Dish, 196–197
Ninja®Foodi™ XL Pro Air Oven
 about, 2–3
 accessories, 14
 cleaning, 10–11
 control panel, 4–6
 converting conventional oven recipes for, 8
 frequently asked questions, 9–11
 steps for using, 6–7
Nut butters
 Chocolate, Nut Butter, and Oat Breakfast Bars, 42–43
Nut-free
 Air-Fried Fish Tacos, 138–139
 Asparagus, Ham, and Cheese Puff Pastry Bundles, 70–71
 Bacon and Kale Ranch Dip, 55–56
 Bacon-Stuffed Clams, 156–157
 Baked Chicken Tacos, 104–105
 Baked Macaroni and Cheese, 173–174
 Barbecue Meat Loaf and Crispy Ranch Potatoes, 117–118
 Brown Sugar and Cinnamon French Toast Bake, 37–38
 Carne Asada Street Tacos, 114
 Cauliflower Gratin, 216–217
 Cheesy Cranberry Pull-Apart Bread, 187–188
 Cheesy Sausage Bread, 62–63
 Cheesy Spinach and Artichoke Pinwheels, 73–74
 Chili-Lime Beef Jerky, 87
 Chorizo-Stuffed Poblano Peppers, 129–130

 Cocoa Breakfast Popovers, 44–45
 Coconut Curried Tofu and Vegetables, 167–168
 Corn Bread, Sausage, and Pear Stuffing, 205–206
 Crab and Avocado Rangoon, 82–83
 Crab BLT Dip and Crostini, 185–186
 Creamy Spinach Chicken Cordon Bleu, 94–95
 Cuban-Style Pork Roast with "Fried" Sweet Plantains, 124–125
 Eggplant Parmesan "Lasagna," 162–163
 Fish and Chips, 136–137
 "Fish in a Bag," 141–142
 French-Inspired Chicken Stew, 106
 French Onion Ring Soup Fritters, 80–81
 "Fried" Chicken Po' Boys with Remoulade Coleslaw, 97–98
 Fudgy Layered Brownies, 237–238
 Garlic-Crusted Flank Steak with Roasted Vegetables, 115–116
 Green Chicken Enchiladas, 107–108
 Heirloom Tomato Pie, 209–210
 Honey-Garlic Glazed Pork Tenderloin with Roasted Vegetables, 119–120
 Honey Mustard Chicken with Pretzel Crust and Crispy Potato Wedges, 102–103
 Honey Mustard Spiral Ham with Sweet-and-Spicy Carrots, 189–190
 Italian Eggs in Purgatory with Garlic Bread, 28–29
 Jalapeño Corn Dip with Homemade Tortilla Chips, 57–58
 Jalapeño Poppers, 79
 Johnny's Corn Bread, 175
 Korean-Style Fried Chicken, 92–93
 Liz's Spoon Bread, 220–221

Loaded Air-Fried Potato
  Wedges, 77–78
Margherita Pizza, 65–66
Meatball Parmesan al Forno,
  192–193
Mediterranean Veggie Platter,
  183–184
Mexican-Inspired Turkey Meat
  Loaf with Chili-Rubbed
  Street Corn, 110–111
Mojito Mojo Pulled Pork
  Sandwiches, 126–127
Mushroom and Swiss Bagel
  Pudding, 35–36
Mustard-and-Herb-Crusted
  Rack of Lamb with Warm
  Potato Salad, 131–132
New England Hot Dish, 196–197
Orange and Rosemary
  Chicken with Sweet
  Potatoes, 90–91
Parmesan-Crusted Beef with
  Bacon Potatoes, 194–195
Parmesan-Crusted Tilapia and
  Garlic Asparagus, 143
Philly Cheesesteak Egg Rolls, 75
Pork Wellington with Garlic
  Green Beans, 122–123
Portabella Mushroom
  Parmesan and Spaghetti
  Squash, 169–170
Potato Crisps with Creamy
  Pesto Dip, 76
Prosciutto, Chive, and
  Parmesan Scones, 47–48
Pumpkin-Spiced Latte Bread
  Pudding, 247
Quiche, Two Ways, 30–31
Ratatouille, 160–161
Razzleberry Hand Pies,
  244–245
Roasted Carrots with Honey
  and Dill Butter, 207
Roasted Leg of Lamb with
  Vegetable Medley, 198–199
Roasted Mushroom, Poblano,
  and Corn Enchiladas,
  164–165
Root Vegetables and Potatoes
  au Gratin, 218–219
Salt-Brined Turkey Breast with
  Quinoa Stuffing, 201–202
Salt Potatoes, 211
Sheet Pan Baked Stuffed
  Shrimp, 151–152

Sheet Pan Chicken Fajitas,
  99–100
Sheet Pan Key Lime Pie Bars,
  235–236
Sheet Pan Paella, 153–154
Shellfish Newburg Casserole,
  203–204
Shrimp Bake, 149–150
Soft Pretzel Sticks with Beer
  Cheese Dip, 59–61
Soy and Maple Salmon with
  Carrots and Bok Choy,
  147–148
Soy-Braised Chicken Wings, 86
Spanakopita Star, 67–69
Succotash, 171
Thanksgiving Side Dishes,
  212–213
Toad in a Hole with Crispy
  Bacon, 26–27
Tropical Fruit Leather, 54
Tropical Mahi-Mahi and
  Vegetables, 144–145
Nuts
  Double Chocolate Chip Walnut
    Biscotti, 228–229
  Hazelnut and Pretzel
    Brownies, 239–240
  Kung Pao Chicken Totchos, 85
  Lemon-Blueberry Crunch
    Coffee Cake, 49–50
  Party Snack Mix, 181–182
  Salted Butter Pecan Cookies,
    226–227
  Sheet Pan Cookie Bars, Two
    Ways, 230–231
  Sheet Pan Pies, Two Ways,
    222–223
  Spiced Apple Sheet Pan
    Pancake, 40–41
  Sweet and Savory Breakfast
    Stratas, 32–34
  Sweet-and-Spicy Candied
    Nuts, 180
  Sweet Potato Casserole,
    214–215

O
Oats
  Chocolate, Nut Butter, and Oat
    Breakfast Bars, 42–43
  Mexican-Inspired Turkey Meat
    Loaf with Chili-Rubbed
    Street Corn, 110–111

Olives
  Mediterranean Veggie Platter,
    183–184
  Mustard-and-Herb-Crusted
    Rack of Lamb with Warm
    Potato Salad, 131–132
Onions
  French-Inspired Chicken Stew,
    106
  French Onion Ring Soup
    Fritters, 80–81
  Roasted Leg of Lamb with
    Vegetable Medley, 198–199
  Sheet Pan Chicken Fajitas,
    99–100
Orange and Rosemary Chicken
  with Sweet Potatoes, 90–91

P
Pantry staples, 16–18
Parmesan-Crusted Beef with
  Bacon Potatoes, 194–195
Parmesan-Crusted Tilapia and
  Garlic Asparagus, 143
Parsnips
  Root Vegetables and Potatoes
    au Gratin, 218–219
Party Snack Mix, 181–182
Pasta
  Baked Macaroni and Cheese,
    173–174
  Pesto Gnocchi with Roasted
    Vegetables, 177
Peanut Butter and Jelly Crumble
  Bars, 232–233
Pears
  Corn Bread, Sausage, and Pear
    Stuffing, 205–206
Peppers
  Bacon-Stuffed Clams, 156–157
  Carne Asada Street Tacos, 114
  Chorizo-Stuffed Poblano
    Peppers, 129–130
  Garlic-Crusted Flank Steak
    with Roasted Vegetables,
    115–116
  Heirloom Tomato Pie,
    209–210
  Jalapeño Corn Dip with
    Homemade Tortilla Chips,
    57–58
  Jalapeño Poppers, 79
  Kung Pao Chicken Totchos, 85

Peppers (*continued*)
    Mediterranean Veggie Platter,
        183–184
    Pesto Gnocchi with Roasted
        Vegetables, 177
    Philly Cheesesteak Egg Rolls,
        75
    Roasted Mushroom, Poblano,
        and Corn Enchiladas,
        164–165
    Sheet Pan Chicken Fajitas,
        99–100
    Sheet Pan Paella, 153–154
    Sweet and Savory Breakfast
        Stratas, 32–34
Pesto
    Pesto Gnocchi with Roasted
        Vegetables, 177
    Potato Crisps with Creamy
        Pesto Dip, 76
Philly Cheesesteak Egg Rolls, 75
Pineapple
    Tropical Fruit Leather, 54
Pizza dough
    Cheesy Sausage Bread, 62–63
    Margherita Pizza, 65–66
Pizza function, 5, 7
Pizzas
    Margherita Pizza, 65–66
Plantains
    Cuban-Style Pork Roast with
        "Fried" Sweet Plantains,
        124–125
Pork. *See also* Bacon; Ham;
    Prosciutto
    Cheesy Sausage Bread, 62–63
    Chorizo-Stuffed Poblano
        Peppers, 129–130
    Corn Bread, Sausage, and Pear
        Stuffing, 205–206
    Cuban-Style Pork Roast with
        "Fried" Sweet Plantains,
        124–125
    Honey-Garlic Glazed Pork
        Tenderloin with Roasted
        Vegetables, 119–120
    Meatball Parmesan al Forno,
        192–193
    Mojito Mojo Pulled Pork
        Sandwiches, 126–127
    Pork Wellington with Garlic
        Green Beans, 122–123
    Sheet Pan Paella, 153–154

Portabella Mushroom Parmesan
    and Spaghetti Squash,
    169–170
Potatoes. *See also* Sweet
    potatoes
    Barbecue Meat Loaf and
        Crispy Ranch Potatoes,
        117–118
    Fish and Chips, 136–137
    Honey-Garlic Glazed Pork
        Tenderloin with Roasted
        Vegetables, 119–120
    Honey Mustard Chicken with
        Pretzel Crust and Crispy
        Potato Wedges, 102–103
    Kung Pao Chicken Totchos, 85
    Loaded Air-Fried Potato
        Wedges, 77–78
    Mustard-and-Herb-Crusted
        Rack of Lamb with Warm
        Potato Salad, 131–132
    New England Hot Dish,
        196–197
    Parmesan-Crusted Beef with
        Bacon Potatoes, 194–195
    Potato Crisps with Creamy
        Pesto Dip, 76
    Root Vegetables and Potatoes
        au Gratin, 218–219
    Salt Potatoes, 211
    Thanksgiving Side Dishes,
        212–213
    Tropical Mahi-Mahi and
        Vegetables, 144–145
Pretzels
    Hazelnut and Pretzel
        Brownies, 239–240
    Honey Mustard Chicken with
        Pretzel Crust and Crispy
        Potato Wedges, 102–103
    Party Snack Mix, 181–182
    Soft Pretzel Sticks with Beer
        Cheese Dip, 59–61
Prosciutto
    Pork Wellington with Garlic
        Green Beans, 122–123
    Prosciutto, Chive, and
        Parmesan Scones, 47–48
Puff pastry
    Asparagus, Ham, and Cheese
        Puff Pastry Bundles, 70–71
    Pork Wellington with Garlic
        Green Beans, 122–123

Quiche, Two Ways, 30–31
Spanakopita Star, 67–69
Pumpkin-Spiced Latte Bread
    Pudding, 247

Q

Quiche, Two Ways, 30–31
Quinoa
    Salt-Brined Turkey Breast with
        Quinoa Stuffing, 201–202

R

Ratatouille, 160–161
Razzleberry Hand Pies, 244–245
Recipes
    about, 21–22
    converting conventional
        oven, 8
Refrigerator staples, 18–19
Reheat function, 6, 7
Rice
    Sheet Pan Paella, 153–154
Ricotta cheese
    Eggplant Parmesan "Lasagna,"
        162–163
    Italian Eggs in Purgatory with
        Garlic Bread, 28–29
    Sweet and Savory Breakfast
        Stratas, 32–34
Roasted Carrots with Honey and
    Dill Butter, 207
Roasted Leg of Lamb with
    Vegetable Medley, 198–199
Roasted Mushroom, Poblano,
    and Corn Enchiladas,
    164–165
Roasting trays, 14
Root Vegetables and Potatoes au
    Gratin, 218–219

S

Salmon
    Soy and Maple Salmon with
        Carrots and Bok Choy,
        147–148
Salt-Brined Turkey Breast with
    Quinoa Stuffing, 201–202
Salted Butter Pecan Cookies,
    226–227
Salt Potatoes, 211

Sausage
  Cheesy Sausage Bread, 62–63
  Chorizo-Stuffed Poblano
    Peppers, 129–130
  Corn Bread, Sausage, and Pear
    Stuffing, 205–206
  French-Inspired Chicken Stew,
    106
  Sheet Pan Paella, 153–154
Scallops
  Sheet Pan Baked Stuffed
    Shrimp, 151–152
  Shellfish Newburg Casserole,
    203–204
Sheet Pan Baked Stuffed Shrimp,
  151–152
Sheet Pan Chicken Fajitas,
  99–100
Sheet Pan Cookie Bars, Two
  Ways, 230–231
Sheet Pan Key Lime Pie Bars,
  235–236
Sheet pan meals, creating, 15
Sheet Pan Paella, 153–154
Sheet Pan Pies, Two Ways,
  222–223
Sheet pans, 14
Shellfish Newburg Casserole,
  203–204
Shrimp
  Sheet Pan Baked Stuffed
    Shrimp, 151–152
  Sheet Pan Paella,
    153–154
  Shellfish Newburg Casserole,
    203–204
  Shrimp Bake, 149–150
Smoke, 9
Soft Pretzel Sticks with Beer
  Cheese Dip, 59–61
Sour cream
  Bacon and Kale Ranch Dip,
    55–56
  Baked Chicken Tacos, 104–105
  Cheesy Spinach and Artichoke
    Pinwheels, 73–74
  Green Chicken Enchiladas,
    107–108
  Honey Mustard Chicken with
    Pretzel Crust and Crispy
    Potato Wedges, 102–103
  Loaded Air-Fried Potato
    Wedges, 77–78

Soy and Maple Salmon with
  Carrots and Bok Choy,
  147–148
Soy-Braised Chicken Wings, 86
Spanakopita Star, 67–69
Spiced Apple Sheet Pan Pancake,
  40–41
Spinach
  Cheesy Spinach and Artichoke
    Pinwheels, 73–74
  Creamy Spinach Chicken
    Cordon Bleu, 94–95
  Spanakopita Star, 67–69
Squash. See also Zucchini
  Portabella Mushroom
    Parmesan and Spaghetti
    Squash, 169–170
  Ratatouille, 160–161
Steam, 9
Succotash, 171
Sweet and Savory Breakfast
  Stratas, 32–34
Sweet-and-Spicy Candied
  Nuts, 180
Sweet potatoes
  Orange and Rosemary
    Chicken with Sweet
    Potatoes, 90–91
  Root Vegetables and Potatoes
    au Gratin, 218–219
  Salt-Brined Turkey Breast with
    Quinoa Stuffing, 201–202
  Sweet Potato Casserole,
    214–215
  Thanksgiving Side Dishes,
    212–213

T

Thanksgiving Side Dishes,
  212–213
30 minutes or less
  Air-Fried Fish Tacos, 138–139
  Cheesy Cranberry Pull-Apart
    Bread, 187–188
  Chocolate, Nut Butter, and Oat
    Breakfast Bars, 42–43
  Cocoa Breakfast Popovers,
    44–45
  Crab and Avocado Rangoon,
    82–83
  Crab BLT Dip and Crostini,
    185–186

Heirloom Tomato Pie, 209–210
Pesto Gnocchi with Roasted
  Vegetables, 177
Philly Cheesesteak Egg Rolls, 75
Roasted Carrots with Honey
  and Dill Butter, 207
Sheet Pan Chicken Fajitas,
  99–100
Sheet Pan Cookie Bars, Two
  Ways, 230–231
Shrimp Bake, 149–150
Spiced Apple Sheet Pan
  Pancake, 40–41
Sweet-and-Spicy Candied
  Nuts, 180
Toad in a Hole with Crispy
  Bacon, 26–27
Tilapia
  Air-Fried Fish Tacos, 138–139
  Parmesan-Crusted Tilapia and
    Garlic Asparagus, 143
Toad in a Hole with Crispy
  Bacon, 26–27
Toast function, 6, 7
Tofu
  Coconut Curried Tofu and
    Vegetables, 167–168
Tomatoes
  Baked Chicken Tacos, 104–105
  Crab BLT Dip and Crostini,
    185–186
  Heirloom Tomato Pie, 209–210
  Italian Eggs in Purgatory with
    Garlic Bread, 28–29
  Pesto Gnocchi with Roasted
    Vegetables, 177
  Ratatouille, 160–161
  Sheet Pan Paella, 153–154
  Succotash, 171
Tortillas
  Air-Fried Fish Tacos, 138–139
  Carne Asada Street Tacos, 114
  Green Chicken Enchiladas,
    107–108
  Jalapeño Corn Dip with
    Homemade Tortilla Chips,
    57–58
  Roasted Mushroom, Poblano,
    and Corn Enchiladas,
    164–165
Tropical Fruit Leather, 54
Tropical Mahi-Mahi and
  Vegetables, 144–145

Turkey
  Mexican-Inspired Turkey Meat
    Loaf with Chili-Rubbed
    Street Corn, 110–111
  Salt-Brined Turkey Breast with
    Quinoa Stuffing, 201–202

U

Utensils, 16

V

Vegan
  Coconut Curried Tofu and
    Vegetables, 167–168
  Ratatouille, 160–161
  Salt Potatoes, 211
  Sweet-and-Spicy Candied
    Nuts, 180
Vegetables. *See also specific*
  "Fish in a Bag," 141–142
  New England Hot Dish,
    196–197
Vegetarian. *See also* Vegan
  Baked Macaroni and Cheese,
    173–174
  Brown Sugar and Cinnamon
    French Toast Bake, 37–38
  Cauliflower Gratin, 216–217
  Cheesy Cranberry Pull-Apart
    Bread, 187–188
  Cheesy Spinach and Artichoke
    Pinwheels, 73–74
  Chocolate, Nut Butter, and Oat
    Breakfast Bars, 42–43
  Cocoa Breakfast Popovers,
    44–45

Cookie and Candy Layer Cake,
  242–243
Double Chocolate Chip Walnut
  Biscotti, 228–229
Eggplant Parmesan "Lasagna,"
  162–163
Hazelnut and Pretzel
  Brownies, 239–240
Heirloom Tomato Pie,
  209–210
Italian Eggs in Purgatory with
  Garlic Bread, 28–29
Jalapeño Corn Dip with
  Homemade Tortilla Chips,
  57–58
Johnny's Corn Bread, 175
Lemon-Blueberry Crunch
  Coffee Cake, 49–50
Liz's Spoon Bread, 220–221
Margherita Pizza, 65–66
Mediterranean Veggie Platter,
  183–184
Mushroom and Swiss Bagel
  Pudding, 35–36
Peanut Butter and Jelly
  Crumble Bars, 232–233
Portabella Mushroom
  Parmesan and Spaghetti
  Squash, 169–170
Potato Crisps with Creamy
  Pesto Dip, 76
Pumpkin-Spiced Latte Bread
  Pudding, 247
Razzleberry Hand Pies,
  244–245
Roasted Carrots with Honey
  and Dill Butter, 207

Roasted Mushroom, Poblano,
  and Corn Enchiladas,
  164–165
Root Vegetables and Potatoes
  au Gratin, 218–219
Salted Butter Pecan Cookies,
  226–227
Sheet Pan Cookie Bars, Two
  Ways, 230–231
Sheet Pan Key Lime Pie Bars,
  235–236
Sheet Pan Pies, Two Ways,
  222–223
Spanakopita Star, 67–69
Spiced Apple Sheet Pan
  Pancake, 40–41
Succotash, 171
Tropical Fruit Leather, 54

W

Water chestnuts
  Kung Pao Chicken Totchos, 85
Whole roast function, 2, 3, 4, 7, 8
Wonton wrappers
  Crab and Avocado Rangoon,
  82–83

Z

Zucchini
  Pesto Gnocchi with Roasted
    Vegetables, 177
  Ratatouille, 160–161

THE NINJA® TEST KITCHEN

The Ninja Test Kitchen is comprised of a team of diverse chefs, each with a unique background. They spend hours upon hours testing Ninja's appliance prototypes. Every decision regarding our products and our recipes is made with you in mind—how it will improve your life and your experience in the kitchen. The Ninja Test Kitchen's goal is to make all the mistakes so that you don't have to. We find joy in transforming the way you cook and developing recipes that will allow you to fall in love with our projects.

Meet the Ninja Test Kitchen team:

KENZIE SWANHART
Director, Global Culinary Innovation and Head of Ninja® Test Kitchen

Kenzie Swanhart is a home cook turned food blogger and cookbook author, providing her readers with inspiration both in and out of the kitchen. With more than 350,000 copies of her cookbooks in print, Kenzie never wavers in her mission: creating and sharing easy, flavorful recipes made with wholesome ingredients with her readers.

As the head of culinary innovation for Ninja®, a leading kitchen appliance company, Kenzie and her team provide a unique, food-first point of view for the development of new products and recipes to make consumers' lives easier and healthier. You'll also see her serving as the face of Ninja on the leading television home shopping network, where she shares tips, tricks, and recipes for the company's full line of products.

Kenzie lives in the Boston area with her husband, Julien, and their dogs, Charlie and Milo.

SAM FERGUSON
Manager, Culinary Product Innovation

Sam Ferguson is a culinary innovation and marketing manager at Ninja®, overseeing and leading the culinary product development of heated cooking appliances. After 10 fulfilling years in the restaurant industry, Sam was ready to step out of the grind of kitchen life and into something less stressful but equally rewarding. Enter Ninja®! As a leader on the product development team, Sam strives to create high-quality, innovative, and truly useful cooking tools for home chefs around the world.

Sam lives in Boston with his wife, Lily, and his beagle, Waylon.

MEG JORDAN
Manager, Recipe and Culinary Content Development

Meg is an advertising agency professional turned culinary specialist after making a career change in 2017. After spending most of a decade working in media with Fortune 500 clients, Meg decided to pursue her lifelong passion of working in the culinary industry. A graduate of the Boston University Culinary Arts Certificate program, Meg studied under high-profile chefs in the Boston culinary scene as well as with Chef Jacques Pépin. Meg joined the Ninja® Test Kitchen team in 2018 and, in her spare time, she enjoys learning about the art of charcuterie and whole-animal butchery.

KARA BLEDAY
Senior Culinary Developer, International

Kara's love of cooking took her from the lobbying halls of DC to the Culinary Institute of the Pacific in 2010. After culinary school, she interned with Chef Masaharu Morimoto in his Waikiki restaurant, immersing herself in Asian cuisine and cooking techniques. Soon after, while living in Guam, Kara traveled throughout Asia and the Pacific learning about new- and old-food trends, studying different markets, and understanding how the world of culinary is interwoven.

Kara then relocated to upstate New York. There, while working for a local restaurant group, she opened a restaurant as a private consultant. Then, after building a consulting business in San Diego, Kara and her husband relocated to Boston, where they live with their two sons.

CRAIG WHITE
Senior Research Chef

Craig's love for cooking can be traced back to when he was four years old and his mother caught him cooking hot dogs in the middle of the night. A Le Cordon Bleu graduate, he was given his first chance in a kitchen by Chef Jody Adams at Rialto in Boston. He has worked under James Beard Award–winning chefs Nancy Silverton of Mozza in Los Angeles and Frank McClelland of FRANK in Beverly, Massachusetts. He opened and owned Half Baked Cafe and Bakery in Beverly Farms. After two years as chef de cuisine at Ledger in Salem, he joined Ninja® as a consultant and is now research chef for Ninja Motorized. Through his cooking he has been "positively impacting people's lives every day," and he is excited to do it "in every home around the world" with Ninja®.

Craig lives in Salem, Massachusetts, with his girlfriend, Michelle. In his free time, he enjoys traveling, collecting cookbooks, fishing, and playing guitar.

CHELVEN RANDOLPH
Research Chef

Cooking with love is the only way Chef Chelven Randolph knows how to cook. Raised in the kitchen by his mother, Linda McCoy, who was also a chef, Chelven fell in love with the idea of creating unique dishes as therapy. His family life was firmly rooted in the concept that breaking bread with friends and loved ones was a time to nourish the soul as well as the body. Born in Boston, Chelven acquired his culinary skills in an array of award-winning kitchens like Castle Hill Inn in Newport, Rhode Island, and Fig & Olive in Beverly Hills, California. Most recently he was the sous chef at Coppa Enoteca in the

South End of Boston operated by James Beard Award–winning chefs Ken Oringer and Jamie Bissonnette. Chelven brings fresh and unique ideas from his vast experience in kitchens around the country.

Chelven lives in Bellingham, Massachusetts, with his partner, Amy, and their two children.

MELISSA CELLI
Research Chef

Melissa is a New Jersey native who came to Ninja® after a 15-year career in the food industry. Her love of food and cooking began in childhood while observing her mother cook many meals and desserts for her family. After graduating with a bachelor's degree in Food Service Management and Culinary Arts from Johnson & Wales University in 2009, Melissa has gone on to work for the likes of Wegmans Food Markets, Walt Disney World, Steritech, Compass Group, and Whole Foods Market in various cooking, food safety, and management roles. Melissa's love for being a part of a food research and development team is what drew her to Ninja® as well as the escape from the everyday grind of the restaurant lifestyle. She is one of the lead culinary developers on Ninja® Heated.

Melissa lives in Framingham, Massachusetts, with her husband, Alfredo, and their dog, Carmella.

KELLY GRAY
Research Chef

Kelly Gray is a food scientist and travel enthusiast whose cooking style is influenced by childhood nostalgia and other cultures. Her experience spans many aspects of the food industry, from restaurant work to baking mix formulation—even shellfish farming! As an alumna of California State Polytechnic University, Pomona, with a degree in Food Science and Technology and Culinology, Kelly's culinary approach is as analytical as it is creative—quite useful in her current role in the Ninja Test Kitchen. As a believer in the relationship between good food, community, and well-being, Kelly hopes to encourage people to come back to the kitchen with approachable recipes and state-of-the-art appliances that make cooking enjoyable and stress-free.

When not in the test kitchen or cooking for her friends and family, you can find Kelly enjoying the outdoors, salsa dancing, or daydreaming about a trip to someplace new.

CAROLINE SCHLIEP
Research Chef

Caroline Schliep is a Midwest native turned New Englander who has had a passion for cooking since a young age. Her love of travel has led her to work at many restaurants around the country, even studying abroad in Singapore and Thailand with At-Sunrice GlobalChef Academy. She is an alumna of Johnson & Wales University in Providence, Rhode Island, where she earned an associate's degree in Culinary Arts and a bachelor's degree in Culinary Nutrition and Food Science. Nowadays you can find her in the Ninja® Test Kitchen, where she takes on many roles, from product development and testing to recipe development and validation.

NOTES

NOTES

NOTES

NOTES

NOTES

NOTES

NOTES

NOTES

NOTES

NOTES